to: Bob
   To a very good
the korean war d
          Best wishes
          Col (R) Ben S Malcom

White Tigers

Property of:

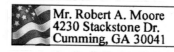
Mr. Robert A. Moore
4230 Stackstone Dr.
Cumming, GA 30041

Also by Ron Martz

*Disposable Patriot: Revelations of a Soldier in
America's Secret Wars* (1993) with Jack Terrell

Solitary Survivor: The First American POW in Southeast Asia (1995)
with Lawrence R. Bailey, Jr.

White Tigers

My Secret War in North Korea

Col. Ben S. Malcom, USA (RET.),

with Ron Martz

BRASSEY'S
Washington • London

Copyright © 1996 by Brassey's (US)

All rights reserved. No part of this book may be reproduced,
stored in a retrieval system, or transmitted in any form or by
any means—electronic, electrostatic, magnetic tape, mechanical,
photocopying, recording, or otherwise—without permission in
writing from the publisher.

Library of Congress Cataloging-in-Publication Data

Malcom, Ben S.
    White tigers: my secret war in North Korea/Ben S. Malcom, with
Ron Martz
        p.   cm.
    Includes bibliographical references and index.
    ISBN 1-57488-016-0
    1. Korean War, 1950-1953—Personal narratives, American.
    2. Korean War, 1950-1953—Military intelligence—United States.
    3. Guerrilla warfare.   4. Malcom. Ben S.   I. Martz, Ron.
    II. Title.
    DS921.6.M36   1995
    951.904'2—dc20   95-22095

10 9 8 7 6 5 4 3 2 1

Printed in Canada

To Mr. Pak Choll and his team of dedicated partisans
who fought for the freedom of their families
and their homeland in North Korea

An AUSA Book

The Association of the United States Army, or AUSA, was founded in 1950 as a not-for-profit organization dedicated to education concerning the role of the U.S. Army, to providing material for military professional development, and to the promotion of proper recognition and appreciation of the profession of arms. Its constituencies include those who serve in the Army today, including Army National Guard, Army Reserve, and Army civilians, and the retirees and veterans who have served in the past, and all their families. A large number of public-minded citizens and business leaders are also an important constituency. The Association seeks to educate the public, elected and appointed officials, and leaders of the defense industry on crucial issues involving the adequacy of our national defense, particularly those issues affecting land warfare.

In 1988 AUSA established within its existing organization a new entity known as the Institute of Land Warfare. Its purpose is to extend the educational work of AUSA by sponsoring scholarly publications, to include books, monographs, and essays on key defense issues, as well as workshops and symposia. Among the volumes chosen for designation as "An AUSA Institute of Land Warfare Book" are both texts and reprints of titles of enduring value that are no longer in print. Topics include history, policy issues, strategy, and tactics. Publication as an AUSA book does not indicate that the Association of the United States Army and the publisher agree with everything in the book, but does suggest that the AUSA and the publisher believe this book will stimulate the thinking of AUSA members and others concerned about important issues.

Contents

Foreword..xi

Acknowledgments xv

Glossary of Abbreviations xvii

1. THE TRIP TO CHANGSAN-GOT 1

2. THROUGH THE LOOKING GLASS 9

3. BEHIND THE LINES 30

4. LEOPARD BASE.......................................43

5. WAR OF THE DONKEYS...........................54

6. PARTISAN TRAINING 66

7. RAID ON THE MAINLAND 83

8. THE LOGISTICS NIGHTMARE....................109

9. THE INTELLIGENCE WAR........................121

10. THE MIDDLE GROUND: BAKER SECTION
    AND THE LINE CROSSERS.......................133

11. FLANKING MANEUVERS: KIRKLAND
    AND WOLFPACK 141

12. RECRUITING AGENTS 145

13. SPECIAL MISSIONS...............................161

14. ON LEAVING KOREA...............................174

15. DISBANDING THE PARTISANS 183

16. THE MISSING LINK 194

17. LESSONS NOT LEARNED 201

Epilogue..211

Appendix A 217

Appendix B 221

Endnotes 223

Bibliography 231

Index..235

Foreword

If the Korean War is the forgotten war in American history, the story of unconventional warfare operations in that conflict is the most unknown part of it. For more than forty years the operations involving North Korean partisans and a small group of brave and dedicated American advisers that took place deep in enemy territory remained highly classified.

Ben S. Malcom was a member of that small group of Americans handpicked to go far behind enemy lines to organize and lead North Korean partisans in their war against numerically superior Chinese and North Korean army forces. By the time the war ended, more than 22,000 partisans were operating behind the lines in a variety of covert activities.

Ben Malcom and I were assigned to Korea in January 1952 to work in unconventional warfare assignments. Although we had similar jobs, we were assigned to different commands and never came into contact with one another. I was a veteran of behind-the-lines activities during World War II, first in France with the Office of Strategic Services (OSS) and the famed Jedburghs, and later in China. In Korea I worked for the CIA as the deputy station chief. In this latter job I was responsible for training and deploying intelligence agents into North Korea and overseeing a network of covert bases on offshore islands from which these agents operated. Many of these islands were also used as headquarters for partisan groups operating under the Guerrilla Division of the 8240th Army Unit.

Ben Malcom, then a first lieutenant, was assigned to the Guerrilla Division of the 8240th Army Unit, a cover name for the top secret special forces operations in North Korea. The operation was so secret that few soldiers or civilians in Korea knew about it. Even after the war it remained unknown to even the most diligent scholars of the war because the unit's records were classified until 1990.

In early February 1952 Ben was assigned to Leopard Base on the island of Paengnyong-do, more than 125 miles behind the lines. Leopard Base was the headquarters for partisan operations for much of the west coast of Korea. He was the only American adviser assigned to what eventually became the 4th Battalion of the 1st Partisan Infantry Regiment, which was headquartered on Wollae-do, a small island just a few miles from the mainland of North Korea. He helped recruit fighters, trained them, and led them on raids onto the mainland in 1952. During Ben's time with the unit it grew from about three hundred fighters to more than eight hundred. For his efforts Ben was awarded the Silver Star, the Bronze Star, and the Combat Infantryman's Badge.

After more than a year of fighting in Korea, the Far East Command recognized the problems inherent in a situation where each of the military services and the CIA ran its own intelligence collection activities and covert operations. The result was the formation of a unit known as the Combined Command, Reconnaissance Activities, Korea (CCRAK). The 8240th Army Unit was a subordinate unit of CCRAK. While the CIA had a seat at the same table, it was not subordinate to those running the organization. We realized there was a lot of competition for personnel, funds, air support, and sea support, so we exercised our option and went outside the theater to bring in the support we needed for our operations.

I maintained extensive contact with the 8240th Army Unit and its operations through Mac Austin, who had served with me in France and China and was a staff officer in CCRAK. I knew the most successful partisan operations were in Hwanghae Province, the 4th Battalion's area of operations. The people of that province had begun resisting the Communists long before the war began in June 1950. After the war broke out, they actively fought back as partisans. By adding American advisers and shipping weapons and supplies to the partisans, albeit in a limited fashion, Far East Command was able to achieve some tactical successes in that area of North Korea.

There were numerous problems associated with Westerners operating behind enemy lines. They could never simply disappear into the civilian population as we had done in Europe. Secrecy and camouflage were paramount for those American advisers who went into North Korea. Those Americans operating in North Korean territory had to learn quickly to blend into the surrounding terrain and on occasion pass themselves off as Koreans or they would not be able to get the job done.

Unconventional warfare has never been popular with many of the senior leaders of our military services or with politicians. Although the OSS had been quite successful in Europe, China, and Burma during World War II, it was disbanded soon after the war and the qualified officers and NCOs who served in it were farmed out to other units or sent home. So, when more than ten thousand North Korean civilians and potential partisan fighters fled to the mountains and islands to escape the Communists in 1950, the United States military had no mechanism to aid them. There was a critical need for qualified special forces personnel that was not met for almost three years. The 8240th Army Unit was formed as an interim solution and proved to be the beginning of the army's Special Forces branch.

For the first time the story of how soldiers such as Ben Malcom served as the link between the OSS of World War II and the creation of the Special Forces in 1952 can be told. This book demonstrates how a few dedicated soldiers, despite a minimum of support from higher headquarters, still performed risky unconventional warfare operations in Korea and provided the framework for the establishment of the army's Special Forces.

During 1977 and 1978 I served as the chief of staff for Forces Command at Fort McPherson in Atlanta, Georgia. The post commander for Fort McPherson, nearby Fort Gillem, and Fort Buchanan, Puerto Rico, at that time was Ben Malcom. Although he briefed me weekly on matters relating to those bases for more than a year, we never knew of our similar backgrounds in Korea until recently because of the secrecy of our respective missions.

The story of the army's role in unconventional warfare in Korea has been in need of telling for some time. I can't think of a more knowledgeable person to tell that story than Ben Malcom.

Maj. Gen. John Singlaub, USA (Ret.)

Acknowledgments

The most difficult part of writing this book is acknowledging all the wonderful people who encouraged and assisted me over the years. It is impossible to name all those who aided my career and helped my co-author and me in molding the notes, records, and memories gathered over the last forty years into a readable and historically accurate manuscript. For that reason, my thanks will concentrate primarily on those people who provided direct assistance during the preparation of this book.

First and foremost I want to thank my wife, Joyce, for her support and understanding and for being an essential part of my twenty-nine-year military career. Not only did she adapt readily to military life, she typed numerous drafts of my notes and chapters over the last twenty years. Since the Department of the Army files on the 8240th Army Unit were classified until 1990, both of us had doubts we would ever see this book in print.

Next, I want to thank our son, Ben Thomas Malcom, for his support and adjustment to military life. He was with us during all our frequent moves, changing schools eleven times in twelve years and never complaining. He is still on the move as a project manager for Alcatel Inc., in Taipei, Taiwan.

Jim Mapp, a fellow lieutenant and partisan adviser at Leopard Base, now a retired brigadier general, provided a substantial volume of reference material on the 8240th Army Unit that was most helpful in our research. During his tour in Korea Jim worked with the northernmost partisan units on islands near the mouth of the Yalu River, one of the loneliest and most dangerous assignments in the entire Guerrilla Division.

Delvin Glenn, a good friend from Fort Knox, Kentucky, who served as adjutant of the 8240th Army Unit in 1953, furnished invaluable details and photographs of the final few months of the unit and its deactivation.

John deJarnette, a former classmate at North Georgia College, was extremely generous with his time and his memories about his duties as a tactical liaison officer (TLO) in charge of partisans who infiltrated North Korean lines from front-line positions.

My former boss, retired Maj. Gen. John Singlaub, was gracious enough to write the foreword for this book. He also provided names, telephone numbers, and other references that were helpful with our research efforts. When it comes to unconventional warfare and special operations, he is the most knowledgeable person I know, and his book *Hazardous Duty* confirms that.

I would also like to thank the staff at the U.S. Army Military History Institute at Carlisle, Pennsylvania, particularly Dr. Richard J. Sommers and his archivists, for providing advice on reference material on unconventional warfare and special operations and for making available the dozens of oral histories of veterans of Korea who were familiar with the partisan operations. A special thanks to Louise Arnold-Friend, reference historian at Carlisle, for so quickly and cheerfully filling requests for copies of documents.

Artist Dale Dodson spent many long hours working on the wonderful maps and illustrations that accompany the book and provide readers with a clear picture of the 8240th Army Unit's areas of operations.

A special thanks to my many other friends who provided references, photographs, and moral support, all of which contributed greatly to the final product.

Although this book is quite critical of the U.S. Army's understanding and support of unconventional warfare and special operations during the Korean conflict, I must say that I thoroughly enjoyed my twenty-nine years of military service. It was a great privilege for a country boy from Monroe, Georgia, to have the opportunity to work in the wide variety of command and staff jobs I held over the years. I never worked for a commander or staff supervisor I did not respect, and every one of my bosses helped me grow and learn more about myself, my job, and the U.S. Army. I was fortunate to command two companies, two battalions, an infantry brigade, and a U.S. Army garrison.

This book is not intended to be the definitive history of the 8240th Army Unit or its Guerrilla Division. Rather, it is one man's firsthand view of unconventional warfare and special operations in Korea. The opinions contained in these pages are mine. I accept responsibility for them and for any unintended errors.

It would be extremely difficult for anyone who was not there to write the true story of the Korean partisans and the Guerrilla Division of the 8240th Army Unit. The cold, sterile facts of history could never accurately portray the terrible frustrations of dealing with U.S. Army bureaucracy, the heartbreaking losses of individual partisans who were marvelous guerrilla fighters, and the triumphs of keeping North Korean troops off balance and on the run.

For that reason I would like to extend a heartfelt thanks to all the White Tigers who accepted me as a member of their team and taught me the fundamentals of unconventional warfare.

Glossary of Abbreviations

AFFE	Army Forces Far East
ARVN	Army of the Republic of Vietnam
CCF	Chinese Communist Forces
CCRAFE	Combined Command, Reconnaissance Activities, Far East
CCRAK	Combined Command, Reconnaissance Activities, Korea
EUSAK	Eighth U.S. Army, Korea
FEC	Far East Command
FEC/LD (K)	Far East Command/Liaison Detachment (Korea)
FEC/LG (K)	Far East Command/Liaison Group (Korea)
JACK	Joint Assistance Command, Korea
MACV	Military Assistance Command, Vietnam
NKPA	North Korean People's Army
OSS	Office of Strategic Services
ROK	Republic of Korea
ROKA	Republic of Korea Army
SOD	Special Operations Division
UNPFK	United Nations Partisan Forces, Korea
UNPIK	United Nations Partisan Infantry, Korea
VC	Viet Cong

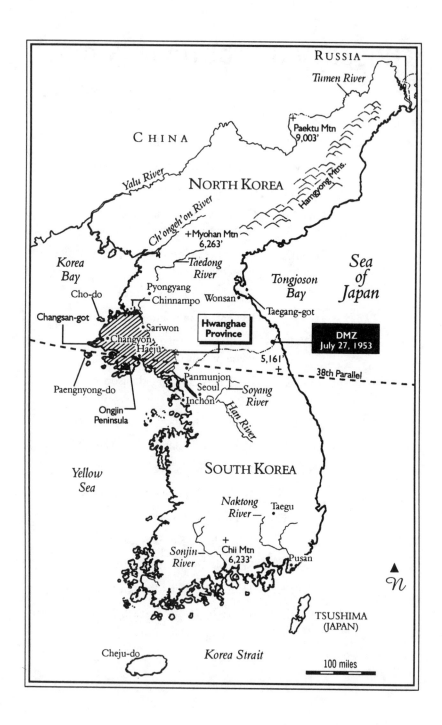

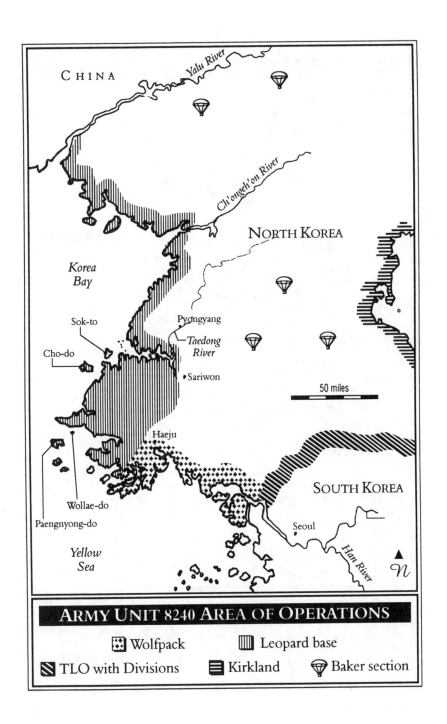

CHINA

Yalu River

Ch'ongeh'on River

NORTH KOREA

Korea Bay

Sok-to

Cho-do

Pyongyang

Taedong River

• Sariwon

50 miles

Haeju

Wollae-do

Paengnyong-do

SOUTH KOREA

Seoul

Yellow Sea

Han River

N

ARMY UNIT 8240 AREA OF OPERATIONS

Wolfpack

Leopard base

TLO with Divisions

Kirkland

Baker section

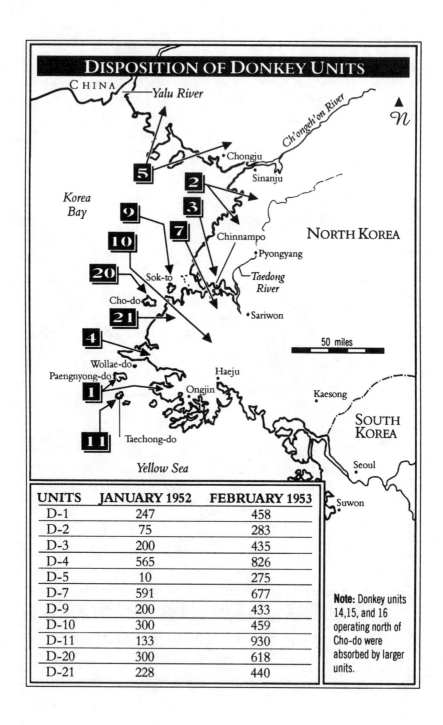

DISPOSITION OF DONKEY UNITS

CHINA — Yalu River

Ch'ongeh'on River

Chongju

Sinanju

NORTH KOREA

Korea Bay

Chinnampo

Pyongyang

Taedong River

Sok-to

Cho-do

Sariwon

50 miles

Wollae-do

Paengnyong-do

Haeju

Ongjin

Kaesong

SOUTH KOREA

Taechong-do

Seoul

Yellow Sea

Suwon

UNITS	JANUARY 1952	FEBRUARY 1953
D-1	247	458
D-2	75	283
D-3	200	435
D-4	565	826
D-5	10	275
D-7	591	677
D-9	200	433
D-10	300	459
D-11	133	930
D-20	300	618
D-21	228	440

Note: Donkey units 14, 15, and 16 operating north of Cho-do were absorbed by larger units.

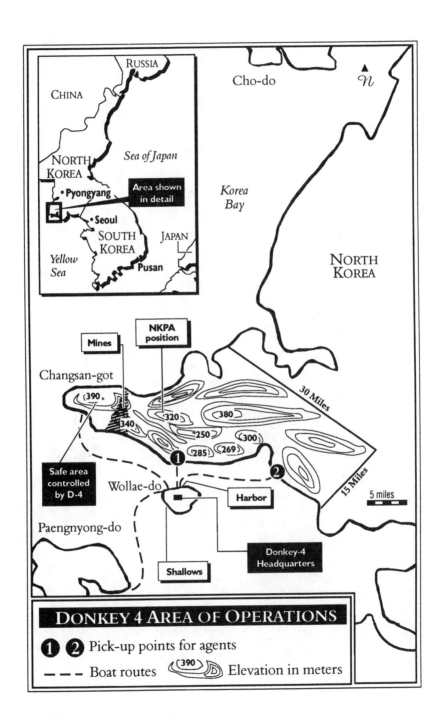

RUSSIA

CHINA

NORTH KOREA

Sea of Japan

• Pyongyang

Area shown in detail

• Seoul

SOUTH KOREA

JAPAN

Yellow Sea

Pusan

Cho-do

N

Korea Bay

NORTH KOREA

Mines

NKPA position

Changsan-got

(390)

340

320

380

250

300

285

269

30 Miles

Safe area controlled by D-4

1

Wollae-do

2

Harbor

15 Miles

5 miles

Paengnyong-do

Donkey-4 Headquarters

Shallows

DONKEY 4 AREA OF OPERATIONS

1 **2** Pick-up points for agents

- - - Boat routes   (390) Elevation in meters

White Tigers

1

The Trip to Changsan-got

Waves slapped against the hull of the old Chinese fishing junk, spraying us with icy seawater as the captain turned the boat into the cold March wind and headed northwest across an open stretch of the Yellow Sea. The boat's four-horsepower diesel motor, wrapped in rags and leaking fuel, fouled the air with fumes as it sputtered and gasped under the strain.

Little more than two miles off the boat's starboard rail the mainland of North Korea rose in an imposing jumble of mountains and centuries-old forests of pines, maples and birch trees. This was the southern coast of South Hwanghae Province where it thrusts westward from fertile farmlands to form a rocky spear of land jutting into the Yellow Sea known as Changsan-got (Changsan Peninsula).

Rocky cliff faces climbed straight out of the sea along the coast, offering no foothold for miles. In those few areas where patches of white sand dotted the coastline, rocky escarpments and thick forests blocked exits from the beach. This was forbidden and foreboding territory, wild, mountainous, and jealously guarded by the 23rd Brigade of the North Korean People's Army (NKPA).

I buttoned my fatigue jacket to my neck and folded my arms across my chest to ward off the wind's chill. The terrain here was easily defensible. Once won it could be held indefinitely by a few well-positioned, properly armed troops.

I sensed someone looking over my shoulder and turned to find Pak Choll standing behind me staring at the coastline. He had seen this part of North Korea hundreds of times before. He had worked these waters in his fishing boat before the war. This was his home. But now, nearly two years into the war, he could do little but look at it from a distance and long for the day he could go home again.

Pak Choll was a wanted man in his homeland. He was the leader of a group of about six hundred anti-Communist partisan fighters who were members of an American-backed unit known as Donkey-4 and who called themselves the "White Tigers." In March 1952 there were ten U.S.-sanctioned Donkey units with about 3,500 partisans operating from islands strung along the west coast of Korea from the Yalu River south to the Ongjin Peninsula. Headquarters was a top secret installation called Leopard Base on Paengnyong-do (Paengnyong Island), 125 miles behind enemy lines.

Thick layers of secrecy shrouded the existence of these units and of American efforts to conduct partisan operations and unconventional warfare in Korea. Only a handful of American soldiers were assigned to the operations, and few of the tens of thousands of troops serving in Korea knew of their existence. Although I was a twenty-three-year-old first lieutenant with no experience in unconventional warfare I had somehow been chosen to serve as an adviser to Mr. Pak's Donkey-4 unit.

My relationship with Mr. Pak was still in the formative stages that March morning. We had known each other just a few weeks and were trying to figure each other out.

Mr. Pak had taken over Donkey-4 following the assassination of the previous leader in January 1952, about a month before my arrival at Leopard Base. Mr. Pak's loyalties and motives were still in question. The previous head of the unit had been a good combat commander and was well liked by the Americans. No one was sure what role Mr. Pak had played in the assassination and whether he was truly anti-Communist or had been planted among the partisans by the NKPA and their Chinese masters. It was my job to find out.

Although Mr. Pak spoke relatively good English he preferred to speak to me in Korean through an interpreter when he had something important to say. The interpreter listened as Mr. Pak talked, nodding his head as he prepared to translate into English.

I understood little Korean but I heard "Lieutenant Malcom" and "Changsan-got" and saw my interpreter's eyes widen. The interpreter looked at Mr. Pak, seeking clarification for what he had just heard.

Mr. Pak smiled and nodded to the interpreter, indicating that he had heard correctly and should translate.

"Mr. Pak say: 'Now I want to show Lieutenant Malcom my safe area at Changsan-got,'" the interpreter repeated hesitantly.

Safe area? On the North Korean mainland?

I looked at the interpreter to make sure what I was hearing. He glanced at Mr. Pak and lowered his eyes. Mr. Pak was still smiling, rocking slightly from side to side as the boat plowed through the waves. I had heard correctly. Mr. Pak wanted to take me to North Korea.

I was too surprised to say anything. There were rumors at Leopard Base of a partisan safe area on the mainland in the vicinity of Changsan-got. But no Americans had dared venture out there. There supposedly were orders from U.S. Eighth Army headquarters in Seoul that Americans working with the partisans should not go onto the mainland for any reason, although I had never seen any such orders. But intercepts of NKPA radio traffic indicated there was a substantial price on the head of any American caught working with the partisans. I knew if I was caught behind the lines with the partisans my life expectancy would be rather short.

My concern must have showed in my face. Mr. Pak began trying to reassure me about his excursion. He told me he wanted me to see the area he controlled so I would better understand him, his men, and their operations. He felt it was important for the Americans in Korea to know the land and the people with whom they were fighting. It made sense, but I could feel the icy fingers of uncertainty clutching at my throat. Was this a trap? Was I to be taken ashore and handed over to the NKPA or the Chinese?

I was in a real dilemma. If this was a trap, my career as a partisan adviser would be short and rather ignominious. But if I refused to go, both Mr. Pak and I would lose face: he because I refused to trust him and me because I had shown fear in the face of the enemy. Whatever else I would do with him and his partisans over the next year would be colored by the decision I was about to make.

Mr. Pak had timed his surprise just right. He knew if he had mentioned Changsan-got while we were back on Leopard Base I would have sought permission from my superiors. Most likely any formal request to visit the mainland would have been turned down. His pretext for getting me off Leopard Base and out of radio communications was a tour of his home base on Wollae-do. I had agreed to it but now was trapped on a boat headed for the mainland of North Korea.

I was seriously undergunned for an assault on the mainland. I carried only my M1 carbine with two fifteen-round clips of ammunition and my .45-caliber pistol. Our attack force consisted of me; Mr. Pak; his chief of staff, Song Won Jae; and three bodyguards.

I wanted to ask Mr. Pak: "Could we do this some other time?" But that would have demonstrated a lack of confidence in his leadership and I did not want to do that so early in our relationship.

Mr. Pak smiled patiently as I argued with myself. I knew he had bested me and he probably knew it too. There was nothing I could do about it. I was at his mercy. I was on a boat 130 miles behind enemy lines that was chugging and sputtering slowly but steadily toward Changsan-got. No one at Leopard Base knew where I was.

I decided that if I was to assist Mr. Pak and his Donkey-4 partisans I would have to set examples. I could not show fear whatever the circumstances. To do that would be to blunt whatever effectiveness I might have as an adviser. I had to be as fearless as they, or at least pretend to be.

"Fine," I said finally. "Let's go."

I tried not to let any of my reservations creep into my voice as my heart shifted into a higher gear and I checked my carbine to make sure it was locked and loaded. I was nervous, but Mr. Pak seemed as relaxed as a tourist guide as he casually pointed out the scenic wonders of the North Korean mainland. He showed me several well-camouflaged NKPA gun positions along the coast and told me about the number of enemy troops in the area and their disposition. He also talked about how important it was for his partisans to control a portion of the mainland.

If the NKPA controlled the entire peninsula they would be able to install heavy artillery on the western tip that could harass the fleets of fishing junks the partisans used for their raids. That would force them far out to sea and create havoc with the timing of operations that already were at the mercy of the unpredictable boats. With the partisans in control of a few square miles of Changsan-got the boats could round the cape close to shore and not worry about the NKPA guns.

The partisans also harvested timber from Changsan-got. Wollae-do, the tiny island that served as Mr. Pak's Donkey-4 headquarters, was a rocky, barren piece of moonscape two miles from the mainland where the northwesterly sea breezes scoured the earth clean of any soil fertile enough for trees and rice. The wood from Changsan-got provided heavy timbers for bunkers on Wollae-do, lumber for boats, and firewood to ward off the numbing cold of the Korean winters.

"If we did not have this wood we would not be able to survive on the island," Mr. Pak said.

As we drew closer to the North Korean coast the boat turned north and headed for a small patch of white sand spread between two steep cliffs. I could see several men on the beach with weapons. I could not tell if they were Mr. Pak's men or an NKPA patrol, and tightened the grip on my carbine. Mr. Pak sensed my concern and in broken English said: "Okay. Okay. You are the first American to visit my safe area."

I relaxed a little, but not much.

Ten feet from shore the boat hit the sand and the engine wheezed to a stop. We slipped over the side to wade to shore in water that was still bone-chillingly cold from the Korean winter. I followed Mr. Pak, keeping my weapon and ammunition above my head and scanning the shoreline for any signs of NKPA patrols as we slogged through the two-foot waves. I still was not sure what I had gotten myself into and wanted to be ready in case this was a trap.

Ten of Mr. Pak's partisans emerged from the trees to greet us on the beach. I heard Mr. Pak say "Lieutenant Malcom" and "American" several times as he introduced me. There were handshakes and deep bows all around. The partisans seemed impressed and appreciative that an American had come to the mainland to visit their sanctuary.

Mr. Pak smiled broadly as he watched the partisans shake my hand. It was as important for his men to understand that he had brought this American onto the mainland as it was important for me to see their area.

The beach was only about fifty feet wide, blocked east and west by cliffs so steep they would have required climbing equipment to scale. To the north the mountains rose sharply, the huge pine trees on their slopes so tall they blocked the sunlight on the beach.

Mr. Pak told his men to load the boat with some timbers that had been cut and stacked to one side of the beach. Then he motioned for me to follow him.

Mr. Pak took off on a small, well-used trail that went north into the trees and then east. No sooner had we left the beach than we were immersed in a beautiful forest of richly scented evergreens more than one hundred feet tall. Lush green ferns grew in thick profusion along the slopes of the mountains.

The trail rose steeply from the beach and it was only a few minutes before I realized that my army-issue boots were going to be more of a problem than they were worth. The Koreans all wore tennis shoes that were light, comfortable, and dried quickly. My socks and boots were still wet from the dousing in the Yellow Sea. It would be hours before they dried, causing my feet much misery.

I made a mental note to wear tennis shoes the next time I did this—if I survived this trip.

We walked about a mile inland through the evergreens, Mr. Pak at the head of the column. He walked quickly and seemed unconcerned about the possibility of an NKPA ambush. I scanned the foliage on both sides of the trail, expecting trouble behind every tree. The partisans seemed relaxed and that only made me more vigilant. Mr. Pak paused at the top of a small hill and motioned me forward.

"Over the next hill is our outpost. Beyond that, across the valley, is a North Korean position," he said.

He dropped to his stomach and indicated I should do the same. Then we crawled up the hill to the outpost overlooking the valley.

The outpost was in a well-constructed bunker that started on the reverse slope of the hill and continued around the sides to the front, where a small peephole and two firing slots enabled the guards to watch the valley to the east. There were only two men in the outpost. One manned a .50-caliber machine gun, the other a .30-caliber machine gun. They also had a box of grenades and their personal weapons. But these were the only two men guarding the access to Changsan-got.

The two partisans greeted me with the usual smiles and handshakes and bows. They were also delighted that an American had come to visit them. I wondered if I could have been as courteous if I had spent the last few hours sitting on the edge of no-man's-land staring down the NKPA. Mr. Pak led me to the front of the bunker and explained the situation.

Shortly after the Donkey-4 partisans had claimed this end of the peninsula nine months earlier the NKPA counterattacked, reclaiming the area in heavy fighting but taking numerous casualties. Before the NKPA could reinforce with additional troops and heavy weapons the partisans took it back.

While the NKPA regrouped, the partisans set up an elaborate minefield in the valley below and brought their machine guns to this position. The partisans could not be outflanked from here because of the vertical cliffs on either side. The NKPA had to funnel through the valley to take the hill. They made one more attempt to drive the partisans out but were caught in the minefield and chewed up by the machine guns. Since then the NKPA had accepted a stalemate, leaving Changsan-got to the partisans except for a lone observation post to watch for infiltration.

Although manpower was not a problem for the Communists, the 23rd Brigade was not getting replacements for its losses at that time, so it had to be careful about how adventurous it was in its operations. Like their American counterparts, the NKPA focused their attention on the static front lines. Someone had decided it was not worth it to try to recapture Changsan-got.

"They are not prepared to pay the price to come back into this area. They don't need it that bad," Mr. Pak said.

But if they did, Mr. Pak said his partisans would take a toll of the attacking force before escaping by sea. He was in radio contact with the troops on Changsan-got and could quickly dispatch reinforcements or rescue boats.

In addition to providing timber and protection from NKPA coastal guns, these several square miles of liberated territory also had the potential to be used as a jumping-off point for additional operations in the enemy's rear areas if ever there was a push north again by the United Nations forces.

But as much military importance as this part of Changsan-got had, it had even more importance psychologically. It gave the partisans a morale boost just to know they controlled a piece of the homeland from which they refused to be driven.

We stayed in the bunker observing the terrain and the NKPA position across the valley for about fifteen minutes before wishing the two guards well. We crawled back down the hill to the trail and set out at a good pace for the beach.

I was impressed. Mr. Pak had confirmed the rumors about the safe area on Changsan-got. I could see where he had been harvesting timber for some time, an operation that appeared to go on daily without interference from the NKPA.

We returned to the beach and Mr. Pak took over supervision of loading the last few large timbers onto the boat for the trip back to Wollae-do. We would go there and off-load the timbers before the boat took me back to Leopard Base.

The return trip to Wollae-do was uneventful. We ran with the wind and tide, and the old boat moved along smoothly despite its load.

We pulled into the north harbor at Wollae-do to unload the logs. Just as the captain shut off the engine I saw a geyser of mud and water shoot up from the mudflats several hundred yards in front of us. Then a boom from the exploding artillery shell rocked the boat. The NKPA had seen us coming and opened fire with a 76mm gun hidden in a cave across the channel.

The captain quickly retrieved the anchor and tried to crank the engine. It would not start. Those old diesel engines refused to restart once they had been shut off after running for a while. It was a problem I would come to know well over the next year.

Mr. Pak's men clustered around the engine like shade tree mechanics, yelling at one another in Korean and trying to restart an engine that absolutely refused to start.

There was another boom, another geyser of mud and water. That round was fifty feet closer. Still the engine would not start. The third round was well short of the boat, landing in the water. The fourth round was long, landing on the beach.

Mr. Pak smiled, as he usually did in tense situations.

"Aim no good," he said cheerfully.

But I knew even the NKPA could get lucky if they fired enough rounds.

The rounds came in at a rate of about one a minute as the North Korean gunners adjusted their sights after every miss, trying to bracket us. The boat was drifting in the wind and bouncing on the choppy waters of the harbor, making it more difficult to zero in on us. The rounds were either long or short, left or right. Over the next fifteen minutes the NKPA fired maybe a dozen rounds, not one of which was close enough to even get us wet.

As I watched the Koreans labor with the engine, waiting for the next round to explode, I decided something had to be done about that gun.

Finally, after much pleading and shouting and waving of arms by Mr. Pak's men, the engine started and the boat slipped slowly out of gun range to the south side of the island to unload the timbers.

It was six P.M. by the time Mr. Pak's boat ferried me back to Paengnyong-do and Leopard Base. What I had thought would be a two-hour trip had stretched into more than eight hours. What I thought would be a routine excursion to Mr. Pak's base on Wollae-do had turned into a visit to the partisan sanctuary on the mainland.

I immediately sought out my commanding officer, Maj. Leo McKean, to tell him what had happened. McKean, because of his close relationship with the previous D-4 commander, had been quite suspicious of Mr. Pak.

"They really have a safe area there?" he asked when I told him where I had been.

McKean listened intently as I described in detail the visit to Changsan-got, including the defenses and disposition of troops. He seemed only a little surprised. He never admonished me, never told me I should not have gone or that I should not go again.

When I finished he nodded his head and said simply: "I'm glad to know that."

Over the next few days it became obvious that my trip with Mr. Pak had considerably lessened concern among Americans at Leopard Base about the loyalties of the new leader of Donkey-4. The old fears of possible Communist sympathies had been put to rest. He was now just one of the Donkey leaders, albeit one of the more successful and more innovative. It would be four months before another American in the Leopard Base area of operations would set foot on the North Korean–controlled mainland. And then it would be me again.

But this first trip to Changsan-got had served its purpose, both for me and for Mr. Pak. It created a bond between us that would last for the remainder of my tour in Korea. It had demonstrated to him that I was willing to take risks on behalf of his partisans. And it demonstrated to me that he was a man of his word and could be trusted. There would be no gamesmanship in our relationship, no American master teaching his Korean pupil. Instead, we would be equals, relating to one another as soldiers.

I would provide him with things he could not otherwise obtain because of his status as a North Korean partisan; he would provide me with competent, dedicated soldiers to train who were ready to die for me or for their primary mission—reclaiming their homes from the North Korean Communists.

2

Through the Looking Glass

In late January 1952 the U.S. Army replacement facility at Camp Drake on the outskirts of Tokyo was seething with the restless energy of hundreds of fresh-faced, eager young soldiers bound for Korea and their first exposure to combat. The camp was a brown, dusty place with row upon row of nondescript two-story wooden barracks whose hasty construction did little to keep out the winter winds or retain the heat from kerosene-fueled stoves.

Few of us felt the cold or worried about the heat, though. Our thoughts were almost exclusively on Korea and the prospect of getting shot at for the first time by an enemy about whom we knew virtually nothing and with whom we seemed to have little in common. What we knew about Korea and the progress of the war was what we could pick up from the newspapers, from friends returning from the front, or from barracks rumors that usually had little basis in fact but always managed to produce a few laughs or looks of concern.

We were segregated from those soldiers rotating home from Korea. They occupied one part of the base, we another. It was as if army officials did not want us contaminated by the reality of the situation that then existed at the front. We were young, excited, and eager to do for the country what our uncles and brothers had done in World War II. The army wanted to preserve that enthusiasm at least until we got to Korea and saw what life there was really like.

We seldom strayed far from a large bulletin board in our barracks on which were posted long lists of names and the units in Korea to which they were assigned. Those whose names appeared on the list rushed immediately to a large map of the peninsula to try to find where their

9

particular unit was located. We kept our duffel bags packed and were ready to go as soon as we received word that our flight to Pusan or Seoul was ready. Men moved out and men moved in to replace them in a continuous blur of olive drab uniforms and faceless names.

My name was on one of the lists posted on the bulletin board early the morning of January 31, 1952. I was assigned to the 3rd Infantry Division. I took a clean uniform shirt out of my duffel bag, shaved, closed the bag, and spent most of the rest of the morning studying the map, trying to figure out where the 3rd Division was. I was ready for duty with a front-line division.

It was about noon when the call came that changed all that.

At first I thought the call was to tell me my flight was ready. It was anything but. As soon as I lifted the receiver to my ear I stepped across that line separating the regular army from the clandestine army. I went from being another faceless name on an army roster to a handpicked player in a unique operation about which few Americans knew anything.

After the caller was reasonably assured that I indeed was 1st Lt. Ben S. Malcom he identified himself as a lieutenant colonel at Eighth Army Headquarters.

"We need to bring you downtown for an interview. You're being considered for another assignment," he said curtly.

"Yes, sir," was all I could think to say.

"Bring all your gear. There will be a car waiting outside."

"Yes, sir," I said again as I hung up the phone.

This seemed rather mysterious but the chance to do something different intrigued me, as long as it was not a staff job. I wanted to join a combat unit. I did not want to spend my tour in Korea behind a desk pushing papers or shepherding some general around the battlefield.

I made sure my bag was packed, then stepped outside to see if the promised car was there. An olive drab Chevrolet sedan sat idling in front of the barracks, its tailpipe spewing plumes of white exhaust into the cold midday air.

A Japanese driver stepped out and approached me.

"Lieutenant Malcom?" he said in broken English.

"Yes?"

"Get in and I will drive you downtown."

"Let me get my bag."

I retrieved my bag from the barracks, threw it into the back of the car, and left the regular army behind.

"Where are we going?" I asked.

"The Mitsubishi Building," he said, offering nothing more.

The driver spoke only when asked a direct question and did not seem interested in conversation. I sat back and watched the fragile, snow-covered Japanese landscape slide past the windows, wondering where I was going and why I had been singled out for this particular assignment, whatever it was.

About thirty minutes later the car stopped in front of a large, gray building in the middle of downtown Tokyo. I could tell it was a U.S. military installation by the scowling guards with spit-shined boots positioned on either side of the entrance. The driver indicated I should get out.

I hefted my duffel bag onto my shoulder and approached the guards. One had a clipboard with a list of names on it. He found my name and said simply: "Fourth floor."

I took the elevator to the fourth floor and entered the first office I found. A lieutenant colonel came in from another office, offered his hand, mumbled a name I did not catch, and indicated that I should follow him. He led me into his office and told me to have a seat. He settled in behind his desk, leaned back in his chair, and laced his fingers together on his chest.

He was probably in his late thirties or early forties but had one of those unremarkable faces whose features are quickly forgotten, the kind of face that is easily swallowed up in a crowd. His office was functional but had no distinguishing characteristics that would differentiate it from any of the thousands of other army offices in Tokyo. There was no nameplate on his desk, no name tag on his uniform, no photographs on the desk or walls. His desk was almost bare except for a telephone, an intercom, and a brown folder with my name on it that he kept referring to.

"Lieutenant Malcom," he said gravely, "I want to talk to you about a special assignment."

He looked at me as if waiting for approval.

"Yes, sir," I said expectantly.

"There are some interesting things going on in Korea and you've been selected as a potential candidate to join a special unit," he continued. "I'll give you a brief overview and if you're interested you'll get a more detailed briefing in Seoul. If you're not interested we'll send you back to Camp Drake and you'll pick up your orders to the 3rd Infantry Division."

He stared across the desk at me, his dark eyes unblinking as I tried to figure out what it was he was trying to say without really saying it.

"Sounds interesting," I offered. "What kind of assignment is it?"

"When the United Nations troops moved up to the Yalu River, we made some friends. When we moved back, some pockets of friendly resistance were left behind. These people are starting to organize. Americans are being assigned to operate those units behind the lines in North Korea and some of the islands off the west coast. Would you be interested in doing that?"

"I haven't seen anything in the papers about it," I said.

"We hope you won't see anything," he said. "That's the reason we're so careful about selecting the people who go into that unit. I can't give you any more details here, but we'll fly you to Seoul and they'll fill you in there. If at any point you want to decline you can and we'll send you to the 3rd Division."

I tried to elicit more information from him but was unsuccessful. The operation was such a closely held secret that it had been compartmentalized. This office was to recruit people. Information on the actual operations was controlled by the office in Seoul.

The lieutenant colonel asked a number of questions about my background, occasionally referring to the file on his desk. Unknown to me, army investigators had already talked to my family and friends as part of a background investigation for a top secret clearance. He had part of that file on his desk.

"Sounds interesting," I finally said. "When do I leave?"

"In the morning. We'll put you up tonight in a hotel across the street and fly you out first thing. A driver will pick you up at zero-six-thirty."

"What unit will I be assigned to?" I asked.

"It's called the 8240th Army Unit," he said.

That sounded like a rear area detachment. I had primed myself for combat. The disappointment must have showed in my face.

"Don't let the name confuse you," the officer continued. "We're using some unusual designations to cover what you guys are doing. They'll tell you more about it when you get to Seoul."

The lieutenant colonel called a sergeant into the room and instructed him to take me across the street and get me checked into the hotel.

"Good luck," the officer said, extending his hand. "Good to have you with us."

I still was not sure who or what I was with, but figured the mystery would be cleared up in Seoul.

That night I treated myself to a big steak and some wonderful tomatoes in the hotel dining room (only later did I learn that their rich redness was due to the fact that they had been grown in human fertilizer) as I tried to fathom why I had been singled out. I fell asleep still trying to make some sense of it.

A car and driver were waiting outside the hotel at six-thirty the next morning for the ride to the airport to catch the daily C-47 courier flight to Seoul. It arrived at K-16 airport, outside the South Korean capital, at about eleven A.M.

In February 1952 Seoul was still reeling from the two major battles that had been fought for control of it over the previous eighteen months. Hardly a building was left undamaged. Everywhere I looked walls had been pockmarked by bullets and gouged by shrapnel. Heaps of rubble that had once been buildings were on every block. Thousands of homeless Koreans huddled around cook fires beside the road, the smoke filling the air with a haze that dimmed the sun. Other Koreans had set up stands by the side of the road and were selling Cokes, beer, food, and bottles of Korean-brand whiskey, "OK" and "Lucky Strike."

"What kind of work do you do?" I asked the sergeant driving the jeep as we sped along the dusty streets.

"I work in supply, sir," he replied. "I take supplies up to the front for the line crossers."

"What's that?"

"Koreans we train to go across the line dressed as North Koreans to gather intelligence."

"I hadn't heard of that before."

He nodded and smiled and drove on, not offering any additional information.

Before long we came to a large compound with a high gate manned by guards carrying Thompson submachine guns.

"This is the 8240th," the sergeant said.

Behind the gate and up the hill was what appeared to be a dark and dreary Victorian mansion. It was all eaves and gables and large shuttered windows. It was strangely out of place in this setting; it looked like it belonged on the moors of England. I half expected to see bats flying out of the windows. Behind the mansion were three-story boxy brick buildings that served as offices and quarters. Before the war this had been a Methodist mission. Now it was headquarters for the 8240th Army Unit, one of the most closely guarded secrets in the Korean War.

The guards checked my military identification card against the names on their list, then opened the gates. The driver gunned the jeep up the shrub-lined gravel driveway and pulled around behind the headquarters building into the compound.

The sergeant led me into an office where Maj. William Patterson, the assistant commander of the Guerrilla Division of the 8240th Army Unit, introduced himself. He welcomed me aboard, then took me into another office to introduce me to the boss, Lt. Col. Jay Vanderpool.

Vanderpool was about five-foot-ten, tough and lean, with an angular face and high cheekbones that spoke of his Native American blood. His dark eyes, set deep in his face, would bore through you when he was listening, but would spark with enthusiasm when he spoke of his plans for the Guerrilla Division.

Vanderpool was a veteran of World War II, having fought on Guadalcanal before moving on to the Philippines to be an adviser to the guerrillas operating there. He had distinguished himself as a guerrilla commander and had become an expert in guerrilla tactics. But after the war the traditional army had little use for unconventional warfare experts such as Vanderpool and he drifted through a variety of jobs. In 1947 Vanderpool was assigned to be the army liaison to the Central Intelligence Group, the forerunner of the Central Intelligence Agency, as an adviser and self-professed "messenger" on the reorganization of national defense. When Congress authorized formation of the CIA later that year, the army loaned Vanderpool and his considerable experience to the fledgling civilian spy corps.

Vanderpool was chosen by the CIA to go to Korea in early 1950 to resolve a dispute over estimates of the number of North Korean troops. The British claimed the North Koreans had only 35,000 to 36,000 trained troops at their disposal. But Maj. Gen. Charles Willoughby, G-2 for the Far East Command (FEC) in Tokyo, was telling his boss, Gen. Douglas MacArthur, that the North Koreans had far in excess of that, about 136,000 troops.[1]

Those conflicting figures exasperated President Harry Truman. He wanted some definitive answers. The CIA dispatched Vanderpool, who spent several months in Korea and came up with a figure of 36,000 NKPA troops, although historians later agreed that Willoughby's estimate was much closer to what has become the generally accepted figure of 135,000.[2]

Nevertheless, Vanderpool sent back his report and was on his way home when the North Koreans attacked the South. Vanderpool thought he would be returned to Korea to work for the CIA or some other intelligence agency but instead was told to proceed to artillery school at Fort Sill, Oklahoma. Now he was back in Korea as the head of the Guerrilla Division of the 8240th Army Unit.

Vanderpool greeted me warmly and ushered me into his office. It was utilitarian, devoid of photographs or decorations except for a black curtain covering one wall.

"Good to have you with us," Vanderpool said. "Let me show you what we've got going on."

He walked to the black curtain and with a dramatic flourish pulled it aside, revealing a large map of Korea. The map showed the disposition of all forces in the theater. But highlighted in different colors were the operations of the 8240th Army Unit. There were a few arrows off the east coast and little parachutes in northern North Korea to indicate where partisans had been dropped. Off the west coast were a number of islands marked in blue, which indicated that they were in friendly hands. All of them had arrows pointing to the mainland to show where the guerrillas had hit.

For the next three days, with only short breaks for meals and sleep, Vanderpool kept me mesmerized as he recounted with great relish and in great detail the history of the 8240th Army Unit and its behind-the-lines operations in Korea. I was assaulted by a bewildering blizzard of acronyms and numerical designations for units involved in the guerrilla operations. It took weeks to sort them out. The command-and-control structure was a veritable Chinese puzzle, indecipherable to all but those few headquarters types who had designed it.

As early as July 1950, little more than a month after the North Korean invasion, the FEC began planning formation of unconventional warfare units to relieve some of the pressure on the forces being chased down the peninsula.

Colonel John McGee, a veteran of guerrilla operations in the Philippines, was dispatched to Tokyo and told to begin screening personnel for commando-type operations.[3]

McGee was well qualified for the job. During World War II he had been taken prisoner on Mindanao Island by the Japanese. He escaped after only a few months of confinement and joined the Filipino guerrillas. He spent the rest of the war with them. His brother, Col. George McGee, was also something of a guerrilla expert, commanding a battalion of Merrill's Marauders in Burma.

McGee was assigned to head FEC's G-3 (operations) Miscellaneous Division. In fact, McGee was the only member of the Miscellaneous Division, a one-man guerrilla unit.

His first duty was to prepare a staff study on the possibilities of conducting guerrilla operations against the North Koreans using some of the refugees from the north. But he was given two caveats: (1) he would receive no additional manpower from American ranks; and (2) no weapons were available for arming guerrillas.

Discouraged by these limitations, McGee nevertheless made a hurried trip to Korea to determine what he would have to work with. He went to the city of Taegu, northwest of Pusan. What he found there did little to encourage him.

He later wrote of this experience: "My visit to the thousands of Korean refugees choking the river bed, that winds through Taegu, revealed a dazed people without interest of return to their home areas as guerrillas. My organizational factors were an apparent cowed people and an enemy suppressive capability far exceeding that of the Japanese in World War II."[4]

McGee returned to Tokyo and put together a plan to utilize American troops, rather than Korean refugees, for the behind-the-lines operations. The result was the Eighth Army Ranger Company. The unit later became known as the 8213th Ranger Company and was attached to the 25th Infantry Division.

But before the 8213th could become fully operational the Inchon landing and subsequent breakout from the Pusan perimeter took place in September 1950. The United Nations forces began methodically pushing the NKPA northward, back across the 38th parallel, deep into North Korea. There now seemed to be no need for behind-the-lines operations.

As the United Nations forces advanced into North Korea, anti-Communists emerged from hiding to offer their services as police officials and government workers. Many had been driven underground by the Communist takeover in 1948 but now volunteered to provide a quasi-government infrastructure in the liberated villages. In some instances, they were in place before the U.N. troops arrived, having driven out the Communists on their own and taken control of government functions.

One resistance leader hiding in the remote reaches of Kuwol-san (Kuwol Mountain) in western Hwanghae Province heard of the approaching U.N. forces and came down to alert several villages. They rallied to him and attacked the local police station with clubs and rocks. Several days later they ambushed an NKPA truck convoy fleeing the city of Haeju.[5]

These volunteers were not so much enamored of South Korean president Syngman Rhee as they were opposed to the Communists. They had suffered through thirty-six years of Japanese domination and were not eager to be controlled by another foreign power, this time the Soviet Union. They saw the U.N. as their political salvation.

But the North Korean anti-Communists had little more than two months to celebrate their newfound freedom. By November, with the U.N. troops sitting on the Yalu and MacArthur urging his superiors in Washington to allow him to enter Manchuria, China plunged headlong into the war.

The massive assault by the Chinese Communist Forces (CCF) sent the U.N. troops reeling. With a seemingly inexhaustible supply of manpower at their disposal, the CCF sent wave after wave of soldiers into battle. Within days the U.N. forces were in full retreat back down the peninsula over which they had just advanced.

As the CCF pushed south the anti-Communists were forced once again to flee their villages. Some took what few weapons and little ammunition they possessed and went into the mountains to fight from there as partisans. Others formed resistance units and fought their way to the coast. Still others simply joined the hordes of refugees running south before the two armies, one fleeing, the other pursuing. Throughout December 1950 tens of thousands of refugees streamed across the 38th parallel or commandeered fishing junks and escaped to the islands.

At three-fifteen P.M. on January 8, 1951, four days after the Communists had retaken Seoul, Eighth Army Headquarters in Taegu received a rather cryptic radio message from the commander of Task

Group 95.7, a Republic of Korea (ROK) Navy operation to rescue some of the refugees fleeing the mainland. The message read:

> Incomplete info indicates majority reptd [reported] 10000 volunteers in Hwanghae Province West of Haeju and Sariwon are armed with Jap rifles model 99 and 38. Russian rifles type unknown and some US carbines. Contact has been ordered to ascertain apprs nmrs [approximate numbers] each types. Suitable dropping site for air drops. Additional info, related Subj, does EUSAK [Eighth U.S. Army, Korea] control any stocks Jap ammo. Believe many servicable [sic] rifles are available which might be used by volunteer groups if ammunition could be made available.[6]

The message generated only a small amount of interest at Eighth Army Headquarters. A query seeking clarification of the weapons possessed by the anti-Communist refugees was sent out on January 10.[7] A reply came back the same day that there were only about eleven hundred weapons among the refugees, seven hundred of Soviet manufacture, three hundred of differing types of Japanese rifles, and one hundred American M1 rifles and carbines.[8]

When news of this large group of refugees willing to fight reached the Miscellaneous Division, McGee quickly recognized the potential. Even bands of loosely organized, poorly armed partisans operating on the flanks or in the rear of the enemy could wreak havoc with his supply and communications lines. Similar units had caused the Japanese no end of problems in the Philippines. And those groups, in many cases, were not of a like mind politically or culturally. The only thing they shared was a common hatred of the Japanese.

These Koreans had much more in common. They were fervent anti-Communists united by the desire to free their homeland. If nothing else they were bodies in a war in which the U.N. forces found themselves badly outnumbered by the CCF. Any help, whatever the source, was welcomed.

The status of these refugees willing to fight was not clear at the time their potential was recognized. They were not guerrillas in the traditional sense of the word in that there was no definable organization among them. They were more like loosely organized bands of terrorists or partisans. It would be two more years before that status was clarified by the U.S. forces and Korean officials. But, for the sake of clarity, they will be referred to here as partisans.

There was throughout the ranks of the United Nations forces the belief that spring would bring a counteroffensive to repel the Chinese invaders. When that occurred the partisans would prove invaluable at harassment and interdiction of enemy forces. It was classic unconventional warfare strategy, using the partisans as an auxiliary to conventional forces on the attack, helping shape the battlefield.

By January 13 McGee had cobbled together a plan for attrition warfare, sent to Far East Command as a memorandum, to utilize this willing mass of refugees. His primary assumptions were first that the NKPA "is incapable of securing completely its rear area to include the coastline," and second that "pockets of friendly forces capable of organization into intelligence and guerrilla operations exist behind enemy lines."[9]

He cited successful employment of partisans and guerrillas in Europe, Burma, and the Philippines during World War II and made a convincing case that such operations could be successful in Korea.

But McGee knew that in order to make this work he would have to obtain the blessing of the FEC. He needed support from the air force and navy and made that clear in his plan. The Eighth Army had no such resources of its own and otherwise would be forced to go through FEC bureaucracy every time it sought air or naval assistance.

The Eighth Army was not quite sure what to do with this unexpected resource, but it clearly sought to keep the partisans under its wing for the time being. Realistically, the army was the only organization with any possibility of making such an operation work. While the Office of Strategic Services (OSS) was long gone, some of the organization's veterans of guerrilla operations in the Philippines and Burma and the partisan operations in France and Yugoslavia were still in the army.

The CIA did not yet have the expertise or personnel to run such a large covert operation. It also was hampered by MacArthur's dislike and mistrust of outside intelligence operations. He had not permitted the OSS in "his" theater during World War II and wanted nothing to do with the CIA in Korea. MacArthur wanted people in his chain of command, not some civilian agency over which he had no control, handling intelligence and operations.

And while the army's Special Forces were still largely a concept being bandied about the Pentagon, the army nevertheless had some of the resources necessary to make such a guerrilla operation a viable part of the combat package. What it did not have were the expertise and desire to make it work.

The Eighth Army had difficulty organizing the partisan units because it was not structured to provide training or the logistics to support such units. There was also something of a mind-set against the use of any covert, clandestine, or unconventional warfare operations.

There was no unit or organization within the army to do in Korea what the OSS had done during World War II and the Special Forces would do later in Vietnam. Korea was a vacuum for special operations and unconventional warfare. Few people wanted to do it. Fewer still knew how to do it.

Colonel John McGee was one of the few who could make it work.

Two days after McGee's initial request, FEC authorized formation of the Attrition Section within the Miscellaneous Division of G-3. While the nomenclature was somewhat baffling, McGee knew exactly what he was doing. Within a week Maj. William Burke, an armor officer by trade but assigned to FEC G-3, was scrounging for rice, ammunition, and radios for the partisan units.

Burke also began scouting for a west coast island from which the partisans could launch their forays into enemy territory. He found exactly what he was looking for on Paengnyong-do.

The island was about 125 miles behind enemy lines but just 15 miles from the mainland southwest of the Hwanghae Peninsula. It was large enough, about 64 square miles, to support substantial numbers of troops and had prominent hills where radar and radio antennas could be installed. Its harbor was on the southeast portion of the island, well protected from the prevailing northwesterly winds that swept down across the Yellow Sea from Manchuria with a frigid ferocity that cannot be described.

But Paengnyong-do's best feature was a lengthy beach of hard-packed sand running northeast to southwest from the harbor. Large aircraft up to the size of C-47s could land at low tide. Resupply would be no problem—as long as supplies were available.

On January 23 Burke submitted Plan ABLE, outlining the operational plans for the partisans, to McGee. That became Operational Plan One, the basic document under which early partisan operations were conducted.

The plan called for the establishment of bases on offshore islands where partisans could be trained in intelligence gathering, communications, demolitions, and basic infantry tactics. There would be "mobile units" sent back to the mainland and "base units" to conduct amphibious operations from the offshore islands. All units would be operational by the time U.N. forces began their anticipated counteroffensive.

Korea was perfect for such amphibious hit-and-run operations. The country's 5,400 miles of coastline are rough, irregular, and studded with thousands of inlets and coves easily accessible to a mobile amphibious force. The straight-line distance from Paengnyong-do to the Chinese mainland is roughly 110 miles, but the western side of the Korean peninsula offered at least three times that much coastline. Attacking it would be no problem. Defending it would. Military officials estimated that a partisan force of "25,000, well-led and properly trained, could be expected to divert from 375,000 to 500,000 regular troops from other duties necessary to a successful prosecution of the war."[10]

The plan anticipated withdrawal by CCF and NKPA troops to at least the 39th parallel in the initial stages of the counteroffensive. The west coast partisans, code-named Task Force William Able, were to seize the Hwanghae Peninsula and conduct operations to harass and disrupt the enemy as they retreated along the Sariwon-Kunchon Road. Another unit was to be air-dropped deep inside North Korea and begin operations there.[11]

The plan also had an extensive table of organization and equipment for the island base and the partisan operations. Command and control would be handled by the U.S. Eighth Army Headquarters in Taegu. McGee assumed that FEC would provide the necessary coordination with U.S. and ROK navies and air forces and other agencies he needed support from, although he also used his personal contacts within other services to get help for the partisans.

In addition to the west coast base, McGee sought permission to establish a mobile base in the mountains along the east coast (there are far fewer islands on the east side of the peninsula) and create an airborne unit to be trained to drop behind the lines by parachute. That airborne unit would be based near Pusan's K-1 airfield.[12]

The airborne operation began in mid-March and was known as the Baker Section of the Miscellaneous Division.

The east coast effort became operational on March 15 under the code name Kirkland. It was much smaller than the west coast operation and its missions were limited. They were unable to set up a mainland base because of North Korean security and instead ran the operation from the islands of Sol-som and Nan-do.

Paengnyong-do became the focal point of McGee's partisan operations. An advance party of Americans had been dispatched to the island in mid-January 1951 to begin preparing it for use as a partisan base. A contingent of ROK Navy provided security. McGee and the main body of troops and equipment departed Pusan the second week of February to establish what on the fifteenth of the month officially became known as William Able Base. Just a month later that was changed to Leopard Base, and it was known as that for the remainder of the war. McGee was met at Paengnyong-do by about forty guerrillas who had been assembled specifically to hear his plan for them.

"In my talk to them, I mentioned their outstanding example to fellow North Koreans as men determined to resist conquest and informed them that Eighth United States Army and its United Nation's [sic] members were now preparing another advance into North Korea which would liberate their people. I told them of the need for guerrilla help in the form of raids, ambushes, information, assistance to downed airmen and support of the final liberating advance," McGee later wrote of the experience.[13]

McGee urged them to be judicious in their raids and attacks. Just as he had advised the Filipino guerrillas nearly ten years earlier that they could not defeat the Japanese in a single day, so did he tell the Korean partisans that they would be most valuable when the counteroffensive began and they should bide their time until then.

The guerrillas were greatly cheered by the news that the U.N. troops would soon return. They were even happier when McGee's men began doling out weapons, ammunition, food, and clothing.

"The departure of the guerrilla leaders from Paengyong-do [sic] in their native boats was a picturesque, heartwarming one that boded success," McGee later wrote. "They were a colorful group ranging in age from youths to elderly men. Some wore ragged civilian clothing, others were dressed in North Korean Army uniforms, which included several formal officer uniforms with bright red piping. They shoved off for the dimly outlined coast of North Korea in the early evening. The small boats were nearly awash with their loads of ammunition, rice and standing guerrillas holding their new rifles. They shouted and waved back as they left Paengyong-do [sic] without apparent concern for swamping in the waves of the Yellow Sea or a possible Communist reception on going ashore."[14]

McGee and the partisan leaders firmly believed they were the vanguard of a new phase of the war, one that would include substantial use of unconventional warfare tactics in support of a major counteroffensive in the spring of 1951.

McGee estimated there were about twelve thousand potential partisans among the refugees. But he could not get enough weapons for all of them. Fewer than 10 percent of the partisans were armed, and many of their weapons dated from the previous war. Ammunition was not always readily available for them. By mid-July, when the cease-fire negotiations began, the partisans had about four thousand weapons at their disposal. The United States had contributed about half of them. The rest were what they had brought with them from the mainland or captured in subsequent raids.

McGee also had problems getting sufficient numbers of personnel to train the partisans, to provide maintenance for the weapons and radios, and to keep open the long supply lines stretching from Pusan to Paengnyong-do. By mid-February he had only thirty-two U.S. personnel working in the Miscellaneous Division, twenty officers and twelve enlisted. When Kirkland began operations it had only two American officers and two enlisted men.[15]

No one was quite sure where all of McGee's men came from. Some were Rangers. One was a British officer who later wrote a highly stylized account of his brief adventures with Baker Section. And others, apparently bored with desk work, seemed to have been collected from various offices throughout Korea. They were simply bodies to fill gaping holes in a unit that was not a high priority for the Eighth Army.

While Burke ran operations on Paengnyong-do, McGee scrambled from meeting to meeting throughout Korea and on ships off the coast trying to convince the navies and air forces of the two countries to contribute to his effort. FEC headquarters in Tokyo had saddled him with an awkward command-and-control arrangement that left him pleading for additional resources from his friends in the other services. He got only what they could spare, not what he needed. His operations were not a high priority to anyone but him.

McGee knew that such an operation needed air and naval support and thus could function only under a joint command. But FEC headquarters had rejected his plan for a combined staff (see figure 2-1).

Instead, the fledgling operation with so much potential remained under control of the Eighth Army's G-3 (operations) section. That permitted the Eighth Army to keep close operational control of the partisans, something that would be needed once the anticipated spring counteroffensive was launched. But it also kept the partisans from utilizing all the air and naval resources that would have been available to them under a joint command.

While partisan units began their first sporadic engagements with the NKPA on the Hwanghae Peninsula in late spring, McGee was finding himself more and more hamstrung by the command-and-control arrangements. Since the operations remained under the Eighth Army's G-3, McGee had no real command authority. He could only request and recommend. G-3 was a staff organization, not authorized to conduct combat operations. The Eighth Army only muddied the situation more when in early May it did away with the Attrition Section and renamed it Miscellaneous Group, 8086 Army Unit.[16]

McGee was doubly cursed by the fact that the Far East Command Liaison Group (FEC/LG), operating under theater headquarters G-2, had direct coordination with the Attrition Section. It continued that coordination after the cosmetic name change to the 8086th. That put McGee in a bind between the Eighth Army's G-3 and the FEC's G-2. It was a no-win situation. But, for the army, it was an effort to micromanage something many traditional officers did not understand and did not care for.

By early July the partisan effectives had grown to about seven thousand. There were fifteen partisan units under control of Leopard Base operating off islands strung along the western coast from Inchon to the Yalu River. The number of Americans assigned to the 8086th had doubled to twenty-one officers and forty-four enlisted. But few of these Americans had any formal guerrilla training or expertise in unconventional warfare, and they ended up occupying administrative or logistics positions.

FIGURE 2-1
Proposed Organization of Attrition Warfare Headquarters

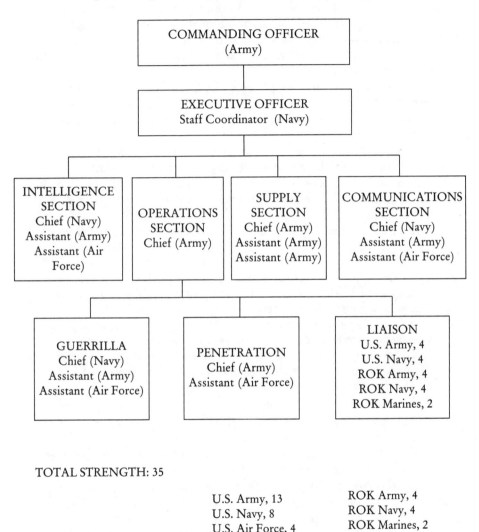

TOTAL STRENGTH: 35

U.S. Army, 13	ROK Army, 4
U.S. Navy, 8	ROK Navy, 4
U.S. Air Force, 4	ROK Marines, 2

Source: U.S. Army Forces, Far East, 8086th Army Unit (AFFE Military History Detachment), "UN Partisan Forces in the Korean Conflict, 1951–52: A Study of Their Characteristics and Operations," Project MHD-3, Tokyo, March 1954, page 74.

As the partisan numbers grew, so did the frequency of their raids, the number of weapons and Chinese fishing junks captured, and the number of casualties claimed. Since the amount of rice and supplies the partisans received depended on their combat performances, and since Americans did not accompany the partisans on their mainland raids to verify the actions, the system gave rise to what undoubtedly were terribly inflated body counts.

On July 10 the entire complexion of the partisan operations underwent a significant change. Peace talks opened in the village of Kaesong, north of Seoul. A wave of uncertainty swept through the ranks of the partisans.

No one felt the impending sense of abandonment more deeply than McGee. For months he had been seeking information about the counteroffensive. For months he had been snubbed by his own G-3. Finally, when he asked again when the advance would take place, he was told "Never."[17]

Writing about that betrayal more than thirty years later still pained McGee:

> The answer "never" to me immediately suggested the calamity of our Donkey Leaders, their unit members and probably family members had been forsaken by the United States, their Free World leader. A forsaking by a Cease Fire that was a sentence of them to death by a subsequent Communist methodically conducted extermination. A sentence that harked back to my now false promise of liberation at that joyous night of our meeting at the cove on [Paengnyong-do]. A sentence that I was never permitted to defend them.[18]

McGee left Korea in July. His replacement was the eager and energetic Lt. Col. Jay Vanderpool.

Vanderpool took over just as the unit was undergoing another metamorphosis. As the tempo of behind-the-lines operations increased through the spring and early summer, the partisans found themselves stumbling over agents from other services and agencies. The CIA had its own network of agents and behind-the-lines operations. The navy and air force were busily collecting intelligence for their own purposes, independent of everyone else. An effort was made to coordinate all covert activities in the theater into one headquarters.

The Far East Command Liaison Detachment, Korea, 8240th Army Unit [FEC/LD(K)] was formed under FEC/LG to coordinate intelligence activities. The partisans continued their operations under control of the Eighth Army. The result was only more confusion and the beginning of a blizzard of acronyms that would plague the operation for the remainder of its days in Korea.

Despite the sagging morale of the partisans and the rampant confusion over just who was doing what behind the lines, Vanderpool brought an insightful enthusiasm to the job that helped keep the Guerrilla Division revved up. That, in turn, helped assuage some of the partisans' fears of abandonment. As long as the partisans were actively engaged in operations, they believed they were working toward the liberation of their homeland.

Vanderpool's ideas were at times innovative, at times ingenious, at times downright diabolical. He sought to make the most of what resources were available to him in spite of the confusion over command and control. He was going to do what he could to make the operation a success.

One of Vanderpool's first efforts involved modification of some of the Chinese sail junks the partisans used to ferry men and weapons from the islands to the mainland. Thousands of these junks were used by Korean fishermen and it was not unusual to see fleets of them plying the coastal waters in search of red snapper, yellow corbina, mackerel, cuttlefish, and abalone. Partisan junks looked just like regular fishing junks, so the NKPA coastal observation posts had trouble distinguishing which were legitimate fishing craft and which were carrying raiding parties.

While that was something of a blessing, it was also something of a curse, as I found out much later. The junks, although quite seaworthy, were slow and ponderous, subject to the whims of wind and tide. The tidal surges were considerable in that part of Korea, in some places as much as thirty feet. If a junk was caught near the coast on an incoming tide there was nothing the skipper could do. For guerrilla units trying to escape the mainland after a raid, that could be particularly hazardous.

Some junk owners had installed small diesel engines in their craft, but often they were little better than sails.

Vanderpool developed plans to add guns, communications gear, and engines to some of the boats but to do so in such a way as to not compromise their appearance. What he developed were several well-camouflaged high-speed arsenals.

He began requisitioning Grey 225 marine engines and installing them in the junks. When those ran out he had his men get engines from General Motors trucks. Propellers and shafts were manufactured by Korean mechanics. Radio antennas were concealed in the masts of the boats. And 105mm recoilless rifles were installed behind collapsible walls.

Although each boat could hold barely a platoon of men, the partisans eventually accumulated enough boats to launch single raids of up to four thousand men.[19] As the boats were modified, many were put into service in operations just north of Inchon and the Han River estuary on the western flank of the NKPA and CCF front-line forces. By the end of the year the unit known as Wolfpack was developed to handle this area, allowing Leopard Base partisans to concentrate their efforts farther north along the coast.

Wolfpack took over the southern fourth of Leopard operations and was responsible for the coastline east and south of the Ongjin Peninsula. Leopard Base had everything west of the Ongjin Peninsula and north to the Yalu River.

Neither FEC nor the Eighth Army had any clear ideas of what to do with the partisans in the months following the first sessions of the peace talks. That was evident by the lack of directives from higher headquarters providing guidance for field commanders. The partisans continued to operate as instructed when formed earlier in 1951, as if the U.N. offensive were still in the works.

By early December the guerrillas had officially been operational for seven months as the 8086th Army Unit. They claimed to have conducted 710 operations in which they killed 9,095 of the enemy (a combination of NKPA, CCF, security police, and Communist officials), wounded 4,809, and captured 385.[20] They also claimed to have destroyed thirty-seven road bridges, twelve railway bridges, and twelve tunnels, and captured more than seven hundred weapons.

But when the Eighth Army plotted the actions on a map they found most had been in the Hwanghae Peninsula, far from any strategically important rail or communications lines. The closest was the Pyongyang-Sariwon-Kaesong corridor, east of the partisans' primary area of operations, through which moved many of the CCF and NKPA supplies and troops. There were two reasons for this.

The first was that the partisans had received little additional guidance from higher headquarters since they were formed. They were to conduct harassing operations on the enemy's flanks and in his rear in preparation of the offensive.

The second was that many of the operations took place in areas with which the partisans were familiar. Most partisans came from Hwanghae Peninsula. They knew the mountains, the villages, the towns, and the coastal areas. Many of their families were still in that part of the mainland. It was easier for them to operate there.

On December 10, 1951, the partisan operations underwent another thoroughly confusing command-and-control realignment. Responsibility for the partisans was shifted from the Eighth Army to a theater-level agency.

The Eighth Army's 8086th Army Unit (partisan operations) was absorbed by the 8240th Army Unit (intelligence) of the FEC/LD(K). The FEC/LD(K) was under operational control of the FEC/LG, which in turn answered to the assistant chief of staff for G-2 at FEC headquarters in Tokyo.[21]

To further confuse matters, at the same time another theater-level agency was set up, ostensibly to coordinate all behind-the-lines activities in Korea. It was known as the Combined Command, Reconnaissance Activities, Korea (CCRAK, pronounced "sea-crack") and as Army Unit 8242.

The primary problem with this arrangement is that instead of reporting to just one staff level, as they had before, field commanders working with the partisans now had to report to two such offices (see figure 2-2).

I have no doubts that G-3 was happy to turn over what was becoming a major headache to G-2. The partisans, however, did not realize the impact of this change because they knew nothing about the intricacies of the army's command-and-control structure.

But this was a clear signal to everyone involved in the operation that the partisans were no longer considered a viable operational resource. Their primary mission no longer was to prepare for a counteroffensive. It was to collect intelligence and do what they could to force the NKPA and the Chinese to hasten the peace process.

FIGURE 2-2
Organization of Guerrilla Section
Far East Command Liaison Detachment, Korea (FED/LD[K])
December 1951

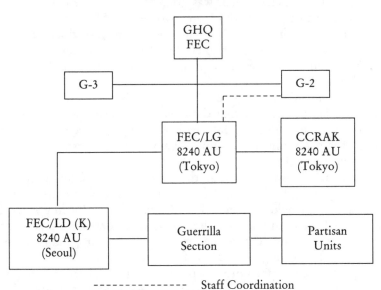

Staff Coordination

Source: Cleaver, Frederick, et al., "UN Partisan Warfare in Korea, 1951-1954," Study, Operations and Research Office, John Hopkins University, 1956, page 74.

When I arrived in Seoul to begin my tour with the clandestine unit, the members of the 8240th had accepted the fact that they were under G-2 and that they would have to make the best of it. I did not realize all the problems or the nuances of command and control at the time, but it became clear much later that this was not a normal way to run unconventional warfare operations.

Nevertheless, Vanderpool remained upbeat about what could be done with the various operations. By the time I arrived in late January 1952 there were five separate ongoing operations:

1. Baker Section: The airborne operation training partisans to jump behind the lines to collect intelligence and build internal guerrilla cells.

2. Kirkland: The east coast amphibious operation.

3. Tactical Liaison Officers (TLO): Assigned to individual front-line divisions, the TLO worked with Koreans who crossed the lines dressed as NKPA soldiers or refugees. Their mission was to gather intelligence and infiltrate back. They ran a high risk of getting shot by both sides and casualties among them were high.

4. Wolfpack: The west coast amphibious operation previously described.

5. Leopard Base: The largest and most active of all the operations.

Vanderpool knew exactly what was going on in each of the areas. I got the sense he wanted to be even more involved, that he wanted to get out of this office and into the field with the troops. No doubt he would have been happier commanding Leopard Base than sitting in this musty old mansion in Seoul. He was an artillery officer by training but a guerrilla at heart.

Despite the shortcomings of the command-and-control structure, I was impressed by the fact that there were about seven thousand partisans operating north of the 38th parallel. They appeared to be a viable combat force needing only some organization and training to make them even more effective.

My initial reservations about the 8240th Army Unit disappeared. Vanderpool's lengthy briefing left me enthusiastic about the operation and what role I would have in it. The idea that I might be in greater danger than if I were on the front lines in a static defensive position was never a consideration. This looked much more exciting and much more challenging than sitting in a foxhole for days on end.

It also was an opportunity to participate in something few people knew anything about. It was intriguing. Many of my fellow officers were concerned about getting into line units because they felt it was necessary to enhance their military careers. At the time I wasn't too concerned about what this would do for me because I had not committed to making the army a career. I wanted to do something that would contribute to the war effort and still be exciting.

"You'll be assigned to Leopard Base," Vanderpool said as he prepared to send me on my way. "That's where the action is."

As usual, he knew exactly what he was talking about.

3

Behind the Lines

The raw winter wind swirling down out of Manchuria and across the mountains of North Korea easily chewed through my heavy coat and boots as I waited at K-16 air base to board the C-46 for the flight to Leopard Base. The cold of Korea had an ominous bite that was frightening in its intensity. I had never felt cold as hard or as sharp or as penetrating as I felt in Korea. Nor would I ever feel it again.

My traveling companions that morning in early February 1952 were about twenty partisans who had been wounded and sent to Seoul for treatment. Now they were returning to their units. Many sported bandages and some walked with a limp. But they bore whatever pain they felt from their wounds and endured the cold with a hard-eyed stoicism that made me slightly envious, if not a bit unnerved. I was shivering under layers of clothing while they seemed impervious to the weather and their wounds.

The inside of the C-46 was as hospitable and as comfortable as a meat locker. The warm breath of the passengers created thick clouds of vapor as we strapped ourselves into our seats. I wiggled my toes inside my boots and my fingers inside my gloves, trying to stay warm. It was no use. The cold had set in and could not be driven off by any exertions on my part. Finally, the plane's engines reluctantly coughed to life and we took off, heading northwest out of Seoul.

I felt every inch the new guy, unsure where I was going or what I was to do. Lieutenant Colonel Jay Vanderpool, commander of the 8240th Army Unit's Guerrilla Division, had not gone into much detail about what life would be like on Leopard Base or what I would be doing with the partisans. He simply wished me good luck and told me to keep in touch.

I was still puzzled about why I had been chosen for this particular top secret behind-the-lines assignment. I did not feel I possessed any specific qualities that made me stand out in the crowd of thousands of young lieutenants headed for Korea in those days. Nor was there much in my background to suggest the reasons for my selection.

I did not come from a military family and had little interest in the military as a youngster growing up in the rolling green Georgia farmlands east of Atlanta. My father, Jamie Malcom, was a farmer, a part-time grocery store worker, and a power in local Democratic politics, which in the 1930s and 1940s was all politics in the little town of Monroe in Walton County.

I worked alongside my father in the fields, picking cotton, cutting hay, milking cows, and plowing the fields from the time I was old enough to walk. And as soon as my father felt I was responsible enough to own a gun he gave me a .410-gauge shotgun to hunt rabbits. We spent many afternoons stalking rabbits in the fields around our farm. On those hunts my father taught me to read the terrain, watching for folds and furrows in the earth and thickets where the rabbits would hide. Then he would show me how to get into position for a shot that might mean something extra in the stew pot that night.

In retrospect, my father was teaching me things about the land that would later prove invaluable to me as a guerrilla commander. Every dip or roll in the ground, every clump of brush, was a potential hiding place or escape route for rabbits. So too were they for a man who knew how to employ the terrain to his advantage. A rabbit would use his instincts, often taking the most difficult route to escape his predators. A man usually would take the easiest route, thus leaving himself vulnerable to his predators. I learned to be quick and to use my instincts, like the rabbit. But I also learned to outmaneuver the rabbits by thinking ahead and not relying solely on instincts.

I was at ease in the outdoors, spending long hours hunting rabbits or catching catfish by hand in nearby streams. The latter trick was taught me by an old black tenant farmer named Walter Hawk. The idea was to walk upstream, find a place where the water was three or four feet deep, then reach up under the creek bank, find the fish's head, put two fingers over his gills, and ease him out. If you grabbed a catfish wrong you'd get a nasty cut from his dorsal fin. And there were times I'd pull my hand out and find turtles or snakes attached to it. I learned to expect the unexpected.

My first exposure to the army came at North Georgia College, a state-supported military school tucked into the hollows of the heavily wooded slopes of the foothills of the Blue Ridge Mountains near the little town of Dahlonega, Georgia, a gold rush boomtown in the late 1800s.

I went to North Georgia College only because my uncle, Hugh Malcom, had attended it for two years and recommended I apply. It was my intention coming out of high school to be a teacher and a coach. The military held no allure, and I knew little about North Georgia College's military training program or what was in store for me when I began classes in the fall of 1946.

Graduates of the college's Reserve Officer Training Corps (ROTC) program, I learned later, are commissioned second lieutenants in the Army Reserves. The top 10 percent in the class, known as Distinguished Military Graduates, are commissioned into the regular army. My plans were to take my commission in the reserves and go on with my life.

But once immersed in the rigors of military training I found I adapted well. The discipline and hard work were not much different from what I had learned growing up on the farm in eastern Georgia. I gradually moved up through the ranks and by the end of my second year was a sergeant in the corps of cadets.

The turning point in my fledgling military career came that summer. The ROTC candidates about to enter their fourth year at North Georgia College are sent to a six-week summer camp at the sprawling infantry base at Fort Benning, Georgia, where they compete against ROTC units from other colleges and universities.

At summer camp we had the opportunity to serve as squad leaders, platoon leaders, company commanders, and in a variety of other jobs we would likely have later in army life. But it was during the third week of summer camp, when I was put in charge of the aggressor forces, that I came into my own.

The aggressors operated much like a guerrilla unit. My basic instructions were to be as unpredictable as possible. This was not a course designed to teach me guerrilla warfare. It was intended to give the other lieutenants-in-training a chance to learn how to deal with guerrillas. But it worked more to my advantage. I believe I learned more about how to conduct unconventional warfare than I learned about conventional army tactics.

I was fascinated by the concept of being able to strike when and where I liked, setting ambushes in the most unlikely spots, and never getting into pitched battles with the main force. I never had to put my force in a static position and could use the night, the weather, and the terrain however I saw fit.

I had two nine-man squads operating as the aggressors. Since we were numerically inferior in every engagement our only advantages were surprise and speed. We learned to get into an area without being observed by moving through the thickest undergrowth, where there would be fewer defenders and a less likely expectation of infiltration. We learned to hit sharply and run away quickly, inflicting maximum damage with a minimum of losses. We learned to avoid defending any position. Infantry officers are taught to defend ground. They learn to love defending ground. But it's death to a guerrilla force to try to defend ground.

We learned to attack or to try to penetrate a perimeter early in the morning, just before the guards changed. That way the man on duty, if not already asleep, would be thinking more about his bed than he would be about a possible attack or infiltration.

I continually analyzed the terrain the main force was defending and what would be the best way to get past the observation posts and through the perimeter without being detected.

On one occasion I was penetrating a perimeter of the main force at about three o'clock in the morning. There was no moon and the thick undergrowth blocked virtually all light. It was difficult to see anything more than a few inches in front of my face.

I knew there were at least two sentries somewhere to my front. But I was concerned about crawling up on one of them without realizing it. I took a stick and threw it out into the woods to see what kind of reaction I would get. Both sentries immediately hollered "Halt." I could tell from the sounds of their voices how far apart they were and crawled through the area between them.

Once inside the perimeter I set off a smoke grenade. Troops awoke with a start and began shouting at one another and shooting in all directions. In the confusion I was able to slip back out of the perimeter unseen.

The tactics of unconventional warfare afforded much more opportunity to be daring and creative than did being a platoon leader tied to traditional tactics and static defensive positions. Unconventional warfare tactics were simple and easy to grasp for someone who had grown up in the fields and forests, someone who was at ease in nature. The concepts seemed to come naturally to me. I found them much easier and much more enjoyable to employ.

With unconventional warfare I could do anything and everything that was counter to army doctrine. I could take that doctrine and stand it on its ear. As leader of the aggressor forces I was judged on my initiative and innovation, not on how well I adhered to doctrine, and I don't doubt the army captain grading me made note of my performance.

I learned a great deal about unconventional warfare tactics at Fort Benning that summer, although I learned it on the job. Neither I nor any of my classmates received any formal training in guerrilla tactics except for a few passing references in history lessons to the partisans in Burma, the Philippines, and Yugoslavia during World War II. In 1948 the U.S. Army had no doctrine for teaching or training troops in guerrilla operations.

What was learned from Tito's Yugoslavian partisans and from the American agents who worked for the Office of Strategic Services (OSS) in France and Burma was lost in the postwar drawdown. Traditional tacticians who dominated the army had no use for guerrilla operations or unconventional warfare. Guerrilla operations were dirty, nasty affairs the traditionalists believed had no role in the modern army.

After returning to North Georgia that fall I was put in charge of the aggressor force for military maneuvers we conducted as students in the mountains surrounding the campus. My detail of about forty cadets would set up ambushes and roadblocks, conduct raids, and employ all manner of unconventional tactics, usually against forces that outnumbered us more than ten to one.

I continued to hone my skills as a guerrilla leader without realizing it, even though nothing was being taught in the classroom about any of these tactics. My training was in the mountains, on the job. I was simply making things up as I went along, using the weather, the time of day, and the terrain to my best advantage.

My performance in summer camp, where I finished sixth among my North Georgia College classmates, and later as the leader of the aggressor force, raised my standing in ranks. By the start of my fourth year I was a first lieutenant in the corps of cadets and among the top 10 percent in my class. I did not realize it at the time but I had already been earmarked for selection as a Distinguished Military Graduate eligible for a commission in the regular army. On June 22, 1950, I received that commission. Three days later the North Koreans surged across the 38th parallel.

While many of my classmates were sent immediately to the Basic Infantry Officers Course at Fort Benning with the knowledge that they would soon be on their way to Korea, I was assigned to the 3rd Armored Division at Fort Knox, Kentucky, to be a training officer for new recruits.

I used that first year to learn about army life and what might be expected of me in Korea. A six-week survival and physical training course at Fort Bragg, North Carolina, in April 1951 was my only break in the routine of training new troops.

The Fort Bragg course was designed to overload us physically to see how much we could take. We would do twenty-five-mile marches with a full pack, then be sent out into the field overnight under all types of weather conditions.

Physically, the course was not that difficult because there was not much I had not already experienced as a training officer at Fort Knox. But the course gave me more confidence in my own training abilities and taught me a great deal about hand-to-hand combat, something to which I had had little prior exposure.

The survival training was only a small part of the course. For those sessions we were sent to the woods for several days with only a map, a compass, and a small amount of food. We had to find our way to specific checkpoints while avoiding the aggressor forces. There were two keys to this exercise. The first was being able to read a map. A lot of people in the course did not do well because they could not read a map and did not believe the compass. The second was being able to look at a piece of terrain and figure out where the aggressors might be hiding. If they caught us they took away our food. I was very successful in avoiding capture and keeping my food.

I felt very comfortable in that type of hostile environment. I went in with the attitude that the aggressors did not know any more than I did. Most of the time I could go into an area, quickly determine where they were, and bypass them.

I kept expecting them to do something unusual, like digging a spider hole and lying in wait for me. But I never got any surprises. I always expected the unexpected from the aggressors and was disappointed when I didn't find it. The aggressor forces acted more like conventional forces and were easy to outmaneuver.

When I returned to Fort Knox I found orders to attend the Basic Infantry Officers Course at Fort Benning waiting for me. It was the last stop in a lieutenant's training before Korea.

The six months of training at Fort Benning were a repeat of what every young lieutenant had learned since the end of World War II. Army doctrine is something like an old mule; once it's moving in a certain direction it is almost impossible to get it to move in another direction without a great deal of pulling and tugging and shouting.

What we were learning in the Basic Infantry Officers Course had relevance to the U.S. Army but very little relevance to what was going on in Korea. We were taught nothing about the tactics or the weapons of the NKPA or the CCF. Information was not being processed quickly enough by the army to teach those being sent to Korea how to fight that war.

Training in guerrilla tactics and unconventional warfare at Fort Benning lasted no more than thirty minutes. There were again some vague references to Burma and the Philippines and the OSS. But there was no mention of any guerrilla operations under way in Korea. And there was no indication that unconventional warfare as had been practiced for centuries was an acceptable—and, in some cases, the most effective—form of combat for certain situations. Yet the history of the United States military forces is filled with instances when unconventional warfare played critical roles.

Among early American settlers there was a tradition of fighting individually or in small groups, of living off the land, of striking when and where they liked. These were tactics learned primarily from the Indians, who were experts in unconventional warfare.

Francis Marion, the Swamp Fox, demonstrated during the Revolutionary War how a small, mobile guerrilla force could keep a larger force off balance through harassment and intimidation. John Mosby, the Confederate raider, did much the same thing for the South during the Civil War.

But when the military became more professional and officers were taught set-piece tactics on maps and sand tables at West Point, these freewheeling, innovative methods of combat seemed not at all in keeping with the chivalrous nature of warfare ingrained in young army officers. Unconventional warfare was equated to what in recent years has become known as the tactics of terrorism, tactics to which the honorable military officer should not stoop.

Yet the tactics of unconventional warfare were vital components of Allied strategy in Europe and the Pacific during World War II. While it is not my intention to revisit in great detail the partisan and guerrilla operations in those two theaters, it is necessary to discuss some aspects of them to demonstrate that there was a great deal of knowledge about unconventional warfare available. But that knowledge was discarded or ignored after the war, so we came to Korea with virtually no institutional foundation for conducting such operations.

The Korean partisan movement began much as the American Revolution and the uprising in Cuba against Fulgencio Batista in the 1950s. All were rebellions spawned by the dissatisfaction of a few people with the political system in power. All lacked outside support. All had limited popular support among their own countrymen.

There were several reasons the Korean partisans failed to advance their rebellion into a full-scale revolution as the American colonists and Cuban rebels were able to do.

First and foremost was that the Korean partisans lacked the necessary support from their countrymen in South Korea that would have made unification of the divided country a national priority. It was very much unlike the experience later in Vietnam, where the North made unification with the South its primary goal and used all means at its disposal to achieve that goal. In Korea many government officials in the South, including the Republic of Korea Army (ROKA), were skeptical of the North Korean partisans and their intentions. As a result, the partisans became wards of the U.S. Army, not instruments of South Korea's political and military unification strategy.

The second factor that kept the Korean partisan movement from becoming a full-fledged revolution was that it was an anti-Communist rebellion. Popular uprisings against Communist governments usually fail. The ruthlessness of the Communist security and counterinsurgency forces generally serves to limit popular support of anti-Communist rebellions.

So it was in Korea. The Communist regime in the North, aided by the Chinese, had such tight controls over the people and their movements that operating on the mainland was extremely difficult. Identification and pass cards were constantly being changed and checked by NKPA security forces. Strangers coming into an area were easily spotted and monitored. The partisans could go in and out of the coastal areas with some ease. But along the major supply lines and deep in North Korea there were tight security controls they could not avoid. Denying people their civil and individual rights to stamp out a fledgling insurgency is never a worry for Communist-controlled regimes.

In these situations concern for personal safety among the general population often outweighs the need for political change. Support of the people generally will go to whichever side offers them the greatest security and the opportunity to continue life as safely and as normally as possible, no matter what the restrictions. The great mass of politically neutral people will favor that side which affords it the greatest protection. In the case of the people of North Korea it was the Communist government.[1]

This type of oppressive security then makes it difficult for the partisans to develop bases deep within enemy territory from which they can operate. Those base areas provide safe areas for rest, medical care, training, and stockpiling weapons. They also are a sign to the people that the government's control of the countryside is tenuous.

T. E. Lawrence used the desert as his safe area during World War I, while the Turks against whom he fought seldom ventured far from the railroads and towns. The Russian partisans used the swamps and forests of the Ukraine to hide from the German counterinsurgency teams sent to hunt them down. Mao Tse-tung used the mountains of China. The jungles of Vietnam, the Philippines, and Burma were sanctuaries for guerrilla movements in those countries.

In Korea there were mountains. But the NKPA security forces were so prevalent throughout the North that the partisans were forced to operate in small teams and could never develop a large safe area. Only on remote Changsan-got were they able to carve out a piece of territory they could truly say they controlled. The partisans were forced to locate their safe havens on offshore islands, where they had the protection of the American, British, and Korean navies.

But the concept of operating with small units and not having a well-defined safe area had not hampered the Allied efforts in Burma. The Japanese controlled Thailand and much of Burma early in the war in their drive to India. But the Allies were able to utilize multinational groups made up of experts in weapons, communications, and medicines, known as the V-Force, and enlisted native Kachin tribesmen in northern Burma to keep the Japanese off balance and disrupt their supply and communications lines. Many of the Americans who survived their tour with V-Force later became a part of Detachment 101 of the OSS and carried over that knowledge and tactical expertise.[2]

Likewise in Europe the Germans controlled much of the continent with the same ruthlessness as would be displayed by the NKPA just a few years later. Despite this, guerrilla, partisan, and resistance efforts flourished in Albania, Denmark, France, Greece, Norway, Yugoslavia, and Russia, sometimes without large safe areas. The Germans defeated the regular armies of these countries but could never get a handle on the guerrilla problem. The French Maquis, the Yugoslavian Chetniks, and the Russian partisans all played major roles in preparing the battlefield for the conventional forces.

The common elements among the resistance forces in Southeast Asia and Europe were that all received massive infusions of outside aid, all were used in support of regular forces, and in most cases all earned the sympathies of the people in the areas in which they operated. The same could not be said of the North Korean partisans.

The North Korean partisans also lacked strong political underpinnings and a charismatic leader. The focus of the partisans was almost exclusively military, not political. They knew they wanted to return to a North Korea free of communism but they were unable to translate that into political action. They saw it almost exclusively as a military effort.

This lack of political focus prevented the rise among them of a single leader who could pull them together and provide some direction. There was no Mao Tse-tung, no Ho Chi Minh, no Tito, no Fidel Castro among them, and little chance for one to appear because of the manner in which the Eighth Army had scattered the units. The units and their operations were so compartmentalized that there generally was little overlap and no opportunity to develop a political framework.

Because of the ad hoc nature in which the partisans had been formed they had had little opportunity prior to combat of setting up a political structure vital to the development of all guerrilla movements. They had not had the opportunity to cache weapons, develop their political agenda, or acquire a leader. Their flight to offshore islands had been hurried. They were widely scattered. What organization they had had been thrust on them by Americans.

The fragmentation and compartmentalization also was encouraged by the ROK government, which had great reservations about the presence of thousands of armed North Koreans in the South. Better to keep them fragmented and loosely organized lest they present a serious threat.

During World War II the Soviets had the foresight to organize partisan groups prior to the German invasion of Russia. The Russian partisans not only were well organized, they had popular support, worked in conjunction with the regular forces, and were fighting on behalf of Mother Russia.

Guerrillas in the Philippines also had been organized into units prior to the Japanese takeover and thus were not an ad hoc creation, as were the Korean partisans.

Despite the fragmentation of the operations, the North Korean partisans had much more in common with one another than had the partisans and guerrillas who fought in the Philippines and Burma. The North Koreans had a common language, a common culture, and a common goal, all of which should have made it easy to sustain the movement. Ethnic, religious, and political differences among groups that had only one common goal—defeat the Japanese—made it difficult to keep guerrilla operations on track in the Philippines and Burma. Those who worked with the guerrillas in Burma and the Philippines had similar experiences in that regard.

Jay Vanderpool, my boss with the 8240th Army Unit in Korea, served as a guerrilla commander in the Philippines. But in his words he was not so much a commander as he was a "coordinator" trying to keep the coalition of anti-Japanese forces focused on their goal.

"There were ten or twelve different outfits which would as soon fight one another as they would the Japs," Vanderpool recalled.

"They were always bickering, so I decided I wanted to be a 'coordinator.' . . . As a coordinator I had no command and also, as such, I had no unit responsibilities. If someone committed a war crime, which they were doing whenever they felt like it; while they were doing it, I wasn't involved. Thus far, my job was not to go out and make a moral crusade or revolutionize that part of the world; it was just to get them ready to fight the Japanese when the time came."[3]

Roger Hilsman, who later served as an adviser on unconventional warfare and Southeast Asia to President John Kennedy, encountered many of the same problems while commanding a guerrilla unit in Burma that was part of Detachment 101 of the OSS.

"We maintained authority only to the extent that we continued to command the respect of the majority of each of the ethnic groups," Hilsman later wrote of his experiences. "If we violated the mores of any particular group, that group would turn on us. On the other hand, if we failed to exert the authority we claimed to have, they would obey only the orders they wanted to obey, and then only after debate and negotiation. Down that path lay military disaster for all."[4]

When the OSS was disbanded and the CIA attempted to assume responsibility for unconventional warfare operations, the Pentagon loudly voiced its objections. Hilsman was among those OSS veterans who tried without success to convince military planners of the importance of maintaining a capability for unconventional warfare and special operations. He advocated creation of a separate unit for such activities, if not within the military, at least within the CIA.[5]

"But the Joint Chiefs of Staff steadfastly refused to give a civilian agency responsibility for paramilitary activities or to accept the responsibility themselves," he wrote.[6]

Thus, the lessons learned about unconventional warfare were lost in the postwar bickering over reorganization of the military.

Had any of those valuable lessons learned in World War II been available to young officers assigned to the 8240th Army Unit, I don't doubt that the partisan operations in Korea would have been much more effective. Even a few hours of classroom instruction on what our predecessors learned would have been of great help to those of us sent to the field to work with the partisans.

But there was nothing. It was as if all records of unconventional warfare operations in World War II had been expunged. The traditional purists won out and purged the ranks of unconventional warfare experts in the years leading up to Korea. We were sent to conduct partisan operations with no knowledge of the history of these operations and no training in how best to implement them.

To a great extent the same thing would happen again in little more than ten years when Special Forces advisers went to Vietnam. Instead of learning from the lessons of Korea those advisers were forced to relearn the lessons two previous generations of soldiers had learned about unconventional warfare. The institutional knowledge we veterans of Korea had was ignored, just as the knowledge of World War II veterans was ignored.

It was not until the United States Army was well engaged in Korea and had already made some efforts to organize the partisans that an effort was undertaken to provide some formal doctrine for unconventional warfare. In October 1951 the Department of the Army issued Field Manual (FM) 31-21, "Organization and Conduct of Guerrilla Warfare," a classified 263-page publication that was given limited distribution.[7]

The decision in December 1951 to put guerrilla operations under control of Far East Command seemed in keeping with the guidelines of FM 31-21. The manual specifically called for guerrillas to be under control of a theater or unified command.

But at that point the reality of the situation in Korea deviated from theory. Field Manual 31-21 spelled out the problems of trying to conduct guerrilla operations as a staff function. It called for a "Theater Special Forces Commander" to be appointed to operate on an equal footing with the unified command's army, navy, and air force.[8] But in Korea guerrilla operations remained a staff function of the unified command's G-2.

Still, FM 31-21 was a much-needed addition to army doctrine. Unfortunately, it came far too late and received far too little attention for those of us who worked with the partisans in Korea. To my knowledge not a single copy of FM 31-21 ever filtered down to operational level even though many of the concepts of training, tactics, and logistics would have provided guidance for those of us thrown into the field and told to make this operation work.

Perhaps one of the reasons the manual did not receive wide distribution in Korea was because many of its guidelines had already been ignored or violated and there was little opportunity more than eighteen months into the war to suddenly start subscribing to this new doctrine. In addition, the idea of providing formal doctrine for unconventional warfare did not sit well with many more traditional officers who were running the war.

Because of the timing of the publication of FM 31-21 it was not surprising that many officers and enlisted who wound up in partisan operations in Korea never saw the manual during their training and never had any training based on it. It took some time after the introduction of the doctrine to put together a training package to support it.

So it was that I found myself in Korea with no real sense of what I was getting into. I was not alone, though. My predecessors and successors suffered through much the same confusion and frustration trying to deal with something for which many of us were not equipped. How well we dealt with the situation depended on how well we were able to adapt to unusual circumstances.

In that regard I was luckier than most. I had had some experience, however limited, operating as a guerrilla and was able to adapt my thinking more quickly. I did not feel tied to traditional army concepts and enjoyed the opportunity to improvise. Of course, little of this was of any concern to me as the C-46 droned on over the Yellow Sea toward Leopard Base and my new assignment. I was just trying to figure out where I would fit in.

We had been airborne only about thirty minutes when I felt the plane begin to descend. I looked out the window and saw a small island below.

"Leopard Base?" I asked an air force sergeant rigging a bundle of supplies for an airdrop.

"Wolfpack," he shouted over the din of the engines.

The plane dropped to about twelve hundred feet and made one pass over the island. The sergeant opened the cargo door and leaned out. A blast of frigid air swept through the plane. Below, someone tossed a red flare into an open field. The sergeant watched the drift of the smoke, then on the second pass he kicked the bundle out the door.

"Leopard's the next stop," he said, closing the door.

On the other side of the plane the North Korean partisans watched but said nothing. They neither smiled nor grimaced from the pain of their wounds, nor looked uncomfortable in the cold air that was swirling around the inside of the aircraft. They simply endured.

After the supply drop at Wolfpack the plane turned west, away from the mainland, and began gaining altitude. The Yellow Sea turned a deep, cobalt blue in the morning sun, its surface streaked with white foam flecks kicked up by the constant northwesterly wind.

After another thirty minutes of flying I could feel the plane begin to descend again, this time for Paengnyong-do and Leopard Base. To the north I could see the blue-green mountains of Changsan-got and the mainland of North Korea. To the west was Paengnyong-do, shaped something like a lobster's claw, its pincers creating a sheltered natural harbor facing southeast.

The plane dropped lower and the pilot made a pass over a long, sandy beach. "Buckle up!" he shouted back to the passengers. "It's going to be rough!"

I tightened my seat belt and looked out the window for the runway. Then it dawned on me—the pilot was going to land on the beach. This was the landing strip for Paengnyong-do, the guerrilla haven more than 125 miles behind enemy lines, the home of Leopard Base, my home for the next year.

4

Leopard Base

By air, Paengnyong-do was less than an hour northwest of Seoul in a C-46. By water, it was several hours in an LST, several days in a Chinese fishing junk. But by any other measure the island was a million miles from nowhere. It sat deep in enemy territory, a few miles south of the 38th parallel but 125 miles north of the front lines and a mere 15 miles from the mainland of North Korea.

Physically, philosophically, and strategically, Paengnyong-do was isolated from the main army effort in Korea, an island with its own top secret purpose. It was barren, rock-strewn, and wind-blasted. The northwest winds sweeping down out of Manchuria and across the Yellow Sea had wiped the landscape clean of virtually all vegetation. At times the wind was so vicious it ripped up tents and toppled hastily constructed buildings at a U.S. Air Force radar facility on the island's highest hill.

The island was selected as a base for west coast partisan operations because of its size, proximity to the mainland, protected harbor, and long beach with hard-packed sand that served as the landing strip for resupply planes. The beach also was used as a rescue strip for aircraft shot up over North Korea that were unable to limp back to their bases or aircraft carriers.

Originally known as William Able Base, the partisan operation on Paengnyong-do was now known as Leopard Base. Most of the eastern half of the island was taken up by the Leopard Base facilities. The west side had a few scattered fishing villages, some rice paddies, and stark, treeless mountains. There were probably no more than a thousand Koreans living on the island, not counting the partisan units that moved in and out. Most of the residents were refugees or fishermen.

There were about two hundred Americans on Paengnyong-do, only twenty-five (five officers and twenty enlisted) assigned to the 8240th

43

Army Unit. Most of the other Americans on the island supported the 8240th in some capacity. They included:

- A U.S. Marine Corps company of about a hundred and thirty men commanded by a captain that provided island security.
- A U.S. Air Force detachment of about thirty men, commanded by a major, that operated a radar station that could look deep into North Korea.
- An air-sea rescue unit with two officers, several NCOs, and a helicopter to assist the pilots of shot-up planes.
- A U.S. Navy medical detachment with a doctor and two corpsmen.
- A one-man CIA observation/listening post.

There also was an ROK marine unit of about fifty men that worked with the Marines on island security.

Except for the air-sea rescue team, which was housed in the 8240th Army Unit compound, each of the units had its own secured area. Our compound was about two miles inland and half a mile south of a Korean village. It was enclosed by barbed wire and guarded by ROK army personnel. It contained five large general purpose tents, each surrounded by sandbagged trenches. Two tents served as living quarters for the officers. Two others housed the enlisted men. The remaining two tents served as a supply center. Two small metal sheds were used as mess halls, one for ROK Army personnel and one for Americans.

We had separate mess facilities because of the great disparity in diets. The Americans lived on the usual army-issue meat-and-potatoes diet. The Koreans stuck to rice, fish, and kimchi, the latter a combination of fermented cabbage and peppers that is a staple of their diet. The rotten cabbage smell of kimchi is so overpowering it discourages most Americans from ever trying it. But the taste can be quite good once you get past the odor.

Our compound also contained a large communications van that was manned around the clock. Most of the American enlisted personnel assigned to Leopard Base were communications specialists. They stayed in constant contact with Seoul and monitored communications from the air force unit on top of the hill and the ships at sea. But their primary responsibility was sending and receiving dozens of messages each day, many of them intelligence from partisans operating on the mainland that had been received by Korean radio operators and translated for transmittal to Seoul.

Major Leo McKean was the officer in charge of Leopard Base at the time of my arrival. He was a tall, lanky, rawboned infantry officer nearing the end of his tour on the island. He was waiting in his jeep at the

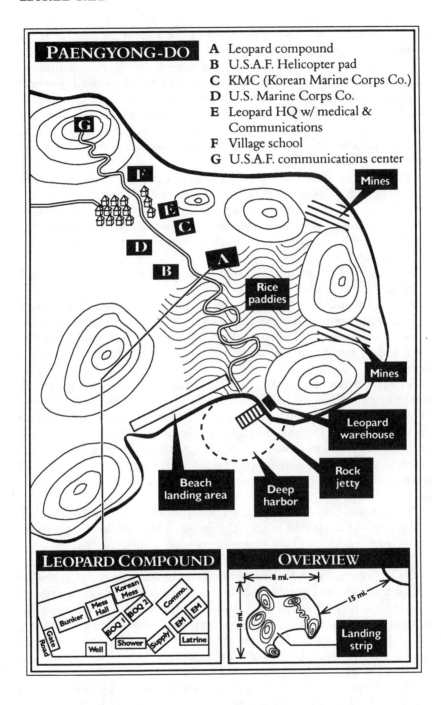

PAENGYONG-DO

A Leopard compound
B U.S.A.F. Helicopter pad
C KMC (Korean Marine Corps Co.)
D U.S. Marine Corps Co.
E Leopard HQ w/ medical &
   Communications
F Village school
G U.S.A.F. communications center

Mines

Mines

Rice paddies

Leopard warehouse

Rock jetty

Beach landing area

Deep harbor

LEOPARD COMPOUND

Bunker
Mess Hall
Korean Mess
BOQ 1
BOQ 2
Commo.
EM
EM
Gate Road
Well
Shower
Supply
Latrine

OVERVIEW

8 mi.

15 mi.

8 mi.

Landing strip

end of the landing strip when the C-46 carrying me from Seoul touched down on Paengnyong-do.

"Glad to have you with us. I can use some help," he said as I tossed my duffel bag into the back of the vehicle and we took off for his office.

McKean's headquarters office was in a large, one-room, mud-and-wood building that had been the island fish market prior to the war. On either end of the building were two smaller detached structures. One was the partisan radio shack; the other served as the dispensary for the navy doctor and his corpsmen.

"I'm going to start you off as headquarters commandant," he said as he outlined my duties. "I've got problems with inventory, problems with theft of rice from the port, and problems with security of the compound that I want you to attend to. I also want you to organize the guerrillas on the island into a company-size force to help evacuate if we're attacked.

"Later, after you get the feel of the place, you're going to be my S-2 and also work with D-4."

As S-2 I would be responsible for taking the translated intelligence reports from partisans on the mainland and deciding their disposition. Some would go to 8240th Army Unit Headquarters in Seoul, some to naval and air force units for targeting, and some would never leave the office.

Winter weather severely restricted amphibious raids on the mainland, and during this time we had to rely on deep penetration units for most of our intelligence. Some units and individual partisans holed up in mainland villages for the duration of the winter while others were dropped off for several weeks at a time, working their way from the beach to the mountains and reporting back via radio. (A more detailed account of the intelligence aspects of the Leopard Base operation is contained in Chapter 9.)

McKean was continually pressing the partisan leaders to do more, even in the worst of weather. But since the partisans had no direct supervision from American advisers they generally operated at their own pace.

The frustrations of dealing with the partisan operations were evident in the lines etched into McKean's thin face. Leopard Base was at the far end of the logistics pipeline, and the trickle of food and ammunition it received was barely enough to keep the partisans operating. McKean had to fight every day for the support necessary to sustain such a far-flung operation. His days usually were consumed by administrative matters dealing with logistics. Details of training and operations were left to the partisan leaders.

There were eleven partisan units operating out of Leopard Base in February 1952, down from fifteen two months earlier because of the creation of Wolfpack, with a total strength of about 3,500 men.

The partisan units used Leopard Base as a headquarters and supply center but actually housed their men and launched raids against NKPA targets from smaller islands closer to the mainland.

By February 1952 the area of operations for Leopard Base stretched from the Yalu River and the border with Manchuria in the north to the Ongjin Peninsula in the south, where it overlapped with Wolfpack.

The Yellow Sea in this region is relatively shallow with a large number of offshore islands. The tidal surges are extreme, in some places reaching up to thirty feet. At low tide, land bridges two or three miles long can form between the islands and the mainland, making some islands vulnerable to a land assault.

The most prominent terrain feature in our area of operations was the rugged Changsan-got. Leopard Base partisans operated on both sides of the cape but had to utilize different methods approaching each side of the mainland because of differences in coastline configuration.

The south side of the cape was far more rugged than the north. For a hundred miles the coastline was pocked with inlets, rocky headlands, and spits of land. Beaches were small and narrow, often cut off east and west by cliffs and to the north by steep coastal hills rising sharply from the beach. But it was relatively easy for amphibious raiders to steal ashore unnoticed on the south side of the cape because of the difficult terrain.

The north side of the cape, which ran northwesterly to the Taedong River, offered fewer hidden beaches. Numerous shoals and sandbars created shallow water over which surf as high as ten feet broke because of the exposure to the prevailing winds. Coming ashore on the north side of Changsan-got could be risky not only because of the high surf but because the terrain offered fewer hidden beaches and more chances of being spotted by NKPA patrols or observation posts.

Defending the entire western coast of North Korea was a physical impossibility for the NKPA. That made it easier for partisan commanders to find a spot to land and get their troops ashore, as long as they did so at night with the tides in their favor.

McKean seemed genuinely happy to see me because now he had someone who could work closely with the partisans. He said he wanted me to work with Donkey-4 because it had not been productive of late as a result of internal problems. The previous leader of the unit had been assassinated a month earlier and McKean had not yet sorted out the reasons behind it.

The new D-4 was Pak Choll, a man he did not know and did not yet trust. McKean had reduced Donkey-4's troop strength and its area of responsibility until he could figure out what had happened and whether Mr. Pak could be trusted.

"Let's move slow with this new D-4 and find out what the problems are, why this guy got assassinated," McKean said.

McKean was concerned that the Communists had infiltrated the unit and assassinated the old D-4, who had been one of his best combat leaders. We later learned that the previous leader had been putting family members into prominent leadership positions even though they were not qualified. He was also taking supplies and stockpiling a percentage of them for his own use while doling out only a small portion to the fighters.

The previous D-4 was approached several times and asked to change his ways. He refused. It was inevitable that his own men would get rid of him. One of them simply walked up behind him and put a bullet into his head. Mr. Pak, who had no part in the assassination, was elected to take his place.

But at the time I was assigned to work with the unit we knew none of this. The D-4 was a mystery. My assignment was to unravel the mystery and get the unit back into fighting trim.

As McKean and I sat in his office discussing my duties and his problem with D-4, I heard a plane coming in low over the island. I looked out the window, trying to figure out if it was one of ours or one of theirs.

"Don't worry," McKean reassured me. "It's just a Marine message drop. He comes through every day."

No sooner were the words out of his mouth than there was a tremendous explosion. The windows of the office blew in, half the roof collapsed on top of us, and McKean and I went diving for cover under the desk. We waited briefly for another explosion and when it did not come we jumped up and raced outside.

It took several hours to reconstruct what had happened. What we finally learned was that the pilot of the Marine Corsair making the message drop had approached the drop area as usual, no more than twenty feet off the ground. But as he leaned out the open cockpit and tossed out the message he accidentally hit the bomb release and unloaded a five-hundred-pounder less than one hundred feet from the headquarters building.

There were no casualties, but the headquarters building had suffered major damage and the Marines had one very embarrassed pilot on their hands when he got back to the carrier. The pilot later sent an apology, and some of the other pilots in his squadron told us he was quite shaken because the explosion had thrown the plane into the air and peppered the fuselage with shrapnel.

The message drop was quickly moved away from populated areas.

Since no one was injured the incident was actually more amusing than it was frightening. But it brought home to me the vulnerability of our position so far from friendly lines.

Although the North Koreans had no artillery that could reach the island, it was susceptible to raids by air and sea because of its isolation and proximity to the mainland. British and American aircraft carriers in the area provided air cover and protection from the occasional "Bed Check Charlie" who dropped in under radar to give us some nighttime fireworks. And a flotilla of Allied warships was on constant patrol around the island to defend against amphibious invasions.

The Marine and ROK Army security forces had roving patrols along the eastern beaches plus observation posts on the hills behind the beaches. The hills served as natural barriers to any invasion and forced troops through choke points that were mined and laced with barbed wire. Those choke points could be easily defended with some well-placed mortars and machine guns. Another impediment to any invasion attempt was the sticky, gooey, brown mud that emerged along the beaches at low tide.

The NKPA had a few motorized patrol boats, but they generally stayed far to the north, where they had some protection from their own coastal guns. The farther south and west the boats ranged the more likely they were to get into a fight with Allied warships that they had no chance of winning. We knew if the NKPA launched an amphibious assault it would have to be done in fishing junks and the invasion fleet would have to be so large as to give us plenty of time to prepare our defenses or flee the island.

Still, McKean wanted me to develop a quick reaction force to help us fight our way to the beach and get off the island should we be attacked. The contingency plan for an invasion called for us to get to a fishing village on the north coast and commandeer what boats were available.

Those partisan leaders who spent a great deal of time on the island agreed to furnish about twenty men each whenever possible for the quick reaction force. But when I began running alerts to see how many I could assemble in thirty minutes or less the results were disappointing. On some occasions I could muster no more than thirty-five troops. On other occasions I got as many as eighty. Seldom did I have the same person respond to alerts more than twice.

My little defense group had 57mm and 75mm recoilless rifles and some machine guns available to it. But it took a great deal of training to teach the troops to properly employ the weapons in defense of the island because of the high turnover in personnel. Despite the problems I was able to pull together some semblance of a reserve force after a few weeks of work.

Before I got that force fully assembled we had one major invasion scare that again demonstrated the vulnerability of Leopard Base and the tension we all felt at being so close to the North Korean mainland.

There were few ongoing operations because of the weather, and the donkey leaders had come to Leopard Base for their monthly supply allocation meeting. The leaders invited McKean and his staff, including me, to dinner at a local elementary school.

Dinner with the Korean partisans was never just dinner. It was dinner and numerous toasts and loud singing and drinking Korean whiskey until all hours of the night. These dinners were frequent occurrences, and to avoid accidents we usually left all our personal weapons under lock and key in our compound, as we did that night.

We had just finished eating and had launched into the first round of toasts when we heard naval gunfire coming from the area between Paengnyong-do and the mainland. We thought at first it was either the British or U.S. Navy firing on targets that we passed to them on a regular basis.

But the firing continued and it began to sound like a full-scale naval engagement. I asked McKean if I could take his jeep and drive back to the compound to contact the ships to find out what was going on. He agreed and as I departed the toasts resumed.

Driving through the Korean village I passed the Marine compound. The Marines were double-timing out the gate dressed in full combat gear and headed for their defensive positions on the beach.

When I reached our compound a few minutes later, Sfc. James Culp, the senior NCO, met me and quickly outlined the situation.

"The British report we are under attack by a fleet of North Korean boats," Culp said. "They sank eight to ten of the boats but the remainder have landed on the north shore of the island. They could be in our area within minutes."

I quickly rounded up fifteen weapons, loaded them in the jeep, and drove back to the elementary school. I gave McKean a brief rundown of the situation while the partisan leaders listened intently. The news of a possible invasion quickly broke up the dinner party. McKean ordered a full alert for the entire island. The partisan leaders went to retrieve their weapons and gather what troops they could while McKean and I and the remainder of the staff returned to our compound to check defenses and be close to the radio.

Once back in the compound McKean got on the radio and began talking with the commander of the British naval task force. He said they had spotted about twenty fishing junks headed for Paengnyong-do and ordered them to stop. They did not. Instead, they made a run for the north coast of the island. The British opened fire, sinking about half the boats.

Over the next few hours we continuously checked various observation posts around the island. Other than the British naval guns there had been no shots fired. There were no reported sightings of NKPA troops on the island. As the dark night wore on and the tension began to subside, it became more apparent that there was no invasion.

It was not until morning that the truth of what actually happened finally emerged.

It seems the "invasion fleet" was actually some local fishing boats that had been blown far out of their regular fishing areas by a storm. These boats usually were back in port before sunset. But this day they were returning to their village on the north coast of the island after dark by a route that made it appear they were coming from the mainland. The British did not recognize the boats and the captains of the small fishing vessels did not heed any of the warnings to stop. When the boats tried to make a run for the safety of their harbor the British blew them out of the water.

About fifteen fishermen and ten boats were missing, according to partisan leaders who made contact with fishermen in the village.

By dawn bodies and debris from the boats were washing up on the beaches along the north coast. For several days the Americans and partisans helped collect the bodies and transport them back to the village for identification. We met with the village leaders, expressed our apologies, and worked with the fishermen to come up with solutions that would prevent such tragic accidents from occurring in the future. Eventually we issued flares to the fishermen and told them to fire the flares if they were challenged by warships. That would be the signal they were friendly.

The deaths of the Korean fishermen were due primarily to a lack of communications, bad planning, and poor intelligence. Those problems seemed to plague many operations in Korea, and we were no exception. But on Paengnyong-do we were more vulnerable because of our proximity to the mainland; we could not afford to take chances that might result in us getting overrun by an NKPA invasion force. As a result, we were sometimes too quick on the trigger.

Another of the security issues McKean asked me to tackle involved securing the warehouse by the port where we kept all the rice designated for the partisans. The rice was kept there because it was more convenient for partisan leaders to anchor their boats next to the jetty, pick up their rice, and head back to their island bases. Rice was the linchpin to the entire partisan operation. It was the staple of the Koreans' diet. And it was the only means we had of paying them. The more a partisan leader and his men accomplished, the more generous their rice rations.

But we had a constant problem with theft of rice from the warehouse. The more rice we lost through theft, the less was available to pay the partisans. There was no problem with theft once the rice was distributed to the partisans. The Koreans did not steal from one another.

But while in the warehouse the rice was considered American property and fair game for the Korean "slicky boys," the most adept thieves I have ever seen. (A more detailed account of logistics problems and the artistry employed by the Koreans in their unauthorized requisitions of American property is in Chapter 8.)

During my inspection of the rice warehouse I discovered a two-by-ten-inch board loosely nailed to the back wall. Anyone wanting extra rice simply had to lift off the board, reach into the warehouse, cut a bag, and scoop out as much rice as he wanted. I went all around the warehouse noting the boards that had to be replaced or nailed more tightly.

The guards assigned to the warehouse were also a problem. They were not particularly alert. Nor were they overly concerned about the theft of rice from the Americans. Had it been their rice, it would have been a different story.

Still, they knew guarding the rice was a relatively easy job and if they fell out of favor with the Americans and lost the job they might have to do something else far more dangerous. So, when I showed up with my interpreter, the guards were usually awake and alert.

To keep them alert I started a series of surprise inspections. One night I'd go to the warehouse at midnight. The next night it might be two A.M. The next night I might not go at all. If I found the guards sleeping I'd rap them on the helmet with a stick.

After a while, the guards became more concerned about me than they were about the thieves. They weren't scared of the thieves. But they didn't want to see that American lieutenant with the stick coming their way, so they kept a watchful eye for anyone sneaking around the warehouse at odd hours. That helped discourage potential thieves.

I was given a myriad of other jobs to tend to my first few weeks on Leopard Base. I did a comprehensive inventory of all our gear and had our Korean laborers build shelves so we could keep better track of it. I also set up some recreation facilities for the troops that included exercise rings and ropes and a volleyball court.

I supervised construction of two Quonset huts inside the 8240th compound. One was used as the headquarters building. The other was cut in half and made into two smaller huts to be used as living quarters for the officers.

Everyone was pleased when the Quonset huts were ready for occupancy. McKean had a more secure headquarters building. The officers had warmer living quarters. And the Koreans got their fish market back.

Despite the numerous tasks given me as camp commandant the work went quickly. Within a few weeks I was able to turn my full attention to the more important assignments of S-2 for Leopard Base and adviser to D-4. I had no real concerns about handling the duties of the S-2. That was simply a matter of reading messages and judging their importance.

Working with the partisans was another matter. It was something for which I had not been trained, something for which the army had no doctrine or manuals I could consult, something I would have to feel my way through. I had no background, no preparation, no predecessor to give me pointers.

I was venturing into uncharted waters on this assignment, a lone American in the midst of hundreds of North Korean partisans whose loyalty at that moment was very much in question.

5

War of the Donkeys

Throughout February 1952 I devoted virtually all my attention to my duties as camp commandant and Leopard Base S-2 as I waited to meet Pak Choll, the leader of Donkey-4. I could not help but wonder what was in store for me in this assignment as an adviser to the partisans. Was Pak Choll a Communist? Was he a collaborator with the NKPA? Was I about to put my life in the hands of a man no one on Leopard Base trusted?

Compounding my concerns was my lack of knowledge of the language and culture of Korea. The army had provided no formal instruction in either prior to my arrival in Korea, and what little I knew had been learned from limited reading and from information provided during my indoctrination at the 8240th Army Unit in Seoul by Lieutenant Colonel Vanderpool. I had been thrown into this job and told to perform without any training beyond basic military necessities. It was my responsibility to learn everything else on the job.

Vanderpool had discussed in some detail the philosophy of the Korean people and the difficulties I might encounter working with the Donkey units. He had become something of a student of the region in the short time he had been there and provided some of the best—if not the only—advice I received from anyone in the military on how to deal with the Korean partisans.

Vanderpool said their first impressions of me would likely be lasting impressions. But even if the first impression was favorable it was my responsibility to create a climate of mutual trust. Without that trust the partisans would not work with me and I would be ineffective as an adviser.

By the same token, I would have to learn to trust the partisans if I was to be an effective adviser. That would take some work because of the unusual status of these units.

Although the partisans were operating as members of quasi-military units they were not military personnel in the truest sense of the word. Neither were they guerrillas by strict military definition. They were not citizens of the Republic of Korea. They were not members of the ROK army or of any other army. They had no serial numbers. They wore no standard uniform, as is required of guerrillas under the rules of land warfare. And, of course, they had no hope of being treated as prisoners of war if they were captured. There were many instances when wounded partisans committed suicide or were shot by their own men to prevent their capture by the NKPA, although in most instances every effort was made to bring out the dead and wounded.

The partisans had no legitimacy in anyone's army except that the United States provided them some logistical support and issued cards stating they were members of a partisan force and were not to be interfered with by civilian security forces or regular military personnel. Their existence among the Allies was truly tenuous, their war truly a war on the fringes.

About two hundred Americans had been assigned to work with the partisans during the year prior to my arrival, and most of these men occupied administrative positions. Only a few had actually served as advisers.

My arrival was a signal to Mr. Pak and his men that their role was still important despite the stalemate at the front. Although the possibility of using the partisans in support of a general U.N. offensive was distinctly remote by February 1952, the partisans still operated under the somewhat naive belief that they would be able to reclaim their homeland with our support.

The change to theater-level command in December 1951 had produced no official reassessment of the mission of the partisans. In lieu of clear directives from FEC/LD (K) as to how the partisan units should be employed, they continued to conduct the same types of activities as they had under the Eighth Army—small-scale actions that included harassment of enemy troops and interdiction of supply convoys, all intended to keep the NKPA off balance and relieve some of the pressure at the front.

The only specific missions given us by FEC/LD (K) were defense of the island bases, formation of units to operate within the interior of North Korea, finding and destroying enemy radar sites, and assisting downed airmen and escaped POWs.[1]

My primary assignment was to train and assist the partisans. At my level the strategic considerations were of little concern and there was not a lot of time to dwell on whether there would be another U.N. offensive. Dealing with day-to-day problems that included such mundane considerations as whether the partisans had enough rice or enough ammunition took precedence. But I must admit that once I started working with the partisans I wanted to believe that the offensive would take place, if for no other reason than I wanted them to have an opportunity to finish the fight.

The partisans had no other choice but to believe there would be a new offensive. To think otherwise would be to admit defeat and acknowledge that the years of fighting, some of which predated the June 1950 NKPA invasion of South Korea, had been fruitless.

They were a singularly focused group of people. Their own lives meant little to them. Most had abandoned homes and families to come to the islands to fight, realizing they might never be able to return.

Few of the partisans had any military training, although some had served with the Japanese during World War II. They learned unconventional warfare as they went. But they knew the land and they knew how to use it to their advantage and against the NKPA.

They became known as Donkey units—*Tang-na-gwi* in Korean—through circumstances that are as unclear today as they were then. There are several theories about the origin of the name, although it is generally accepted that it was adopted not long after Col. John McGee had his first meeting with the partisan leaders on Paengnyong-do in early 1951.

McGee believes the name came into use as a result of a speech he gave to that group. He cautioned them to be judicious in the use of their newly acquired weapons against the NKPA lest their units suffer so many casualties they would be of no use to the Eighth Army and U.N. forces.

"I pointed out that their behavior must be like the wise mule when entangled in wire, similar to their personal conquest, and not like the foolish horse," McGee later wrote. "The horse kicks until it destroys itself. The wise mule carefully waits out its entanglement. . . . My talk was through an interpreter who apparently changed unfamiliar 'mule' to familiar 'donkey.'"[2]

Another theory holds that donkeys traditionally were used by Korean officials and the privilege of riding one was reserved for men of importance within a community.

Others believed the name was an American corruption of the Korean words for "fighters of liberty," which includes the Korean word *dong-il* ("liberty").[3]

My own theory, and the one subscribed to by many others, is that the name derived from a particular radio used by the partisans, the AN/GRC-9, known as the "Angry Nine."

The AN/GRC-9 had a generator on a tripod that someone mounted and cranked with their feet to provide power. The man working the generator looked like he was riding a donkey. Whenever I saw the Koreans set up one of these radios there would be much laughing and braying to indicate that the "donkey" was being prepared for work.

Whatever the origin of the name, the Leopard Base partisan units were now known as Donkey units, each with a separate number. The unit itself was known by its full name, such as Donkey-1, Donkey-4, or Donkey-10. The leader of a particular unit was referred to only by letter and numerical designation. Thus, the leader of Donkey-1 was D-1, the leader of Donkey-4 was D-4, and so on.

The Donkey units generally were configured along geographical lines. That is, each Donkey leader recruited and led men from a particular region of North Korea with which he and they were familiar. They were then sent back into those areas to conduct operations. This enhanced unit integrity and cohesion and made it difficult for infiltrators and Communist agents to join the units.

An individual escaping the mainland who wished to join a partisan unit would be assigned to that unit which operated in the area he had come from. That way his credentials could be checked out. If he did not pass partisan muster he might find himself exiled to a refugee camp. Or, if it was determined that he was an infiltrator, he was simply shot and buried facedown so his soul would not go to heaven.

There were cases, though, when Donkey units captured NKPA personnel and quickly turned them. Once D-11 captured an NKPA squad leader and recruited him to become a partisan. When Leopard Base found out about it a month later D-11 was asked why the captured man had not been brought back to headquarters for questioning. He replied that the man was a good fighter, had already been on seven missions with the unit, and was an asset because of his NKPA uniform, which he continued to fight in.[4]

But many members of the Donkey units had been friends before the war. Although the units were organized along military lines and it was quite clear who the leaders were, they referred to their men as "friends," not as "soldiers" or "troops."

When asked how many men he had on the mainland, a partisan leader would usually reply: "I have fifty friends on the mainland."

The Donkey units usually operated independently of one another— and often of their American supervisors as well. They grudgingly accepted the fact that they needed American logistical support to survive, but for the most part, they selected their own targets, planned their own missions, and ran the operations as they saw fit.

The only support or reinforcements they could hope to receive if they ran into trouble would be from their own unit. Supporting fires simply were nonexistent. These were true small-unit actions with no backup anywhere along the line. In order to survive they had to perfect the tactic of never striking when there was a chance they might be fighting against superior numbers or be forced into a defensive posture. They would hit and run, strike and retreat, attack and then run away to live and fight another day.

The Donkey units were just as much political entities as they were military units. Leaders were chosen not so much for their military skills as for their leadership abilities. A leader retained his position only so long as he had the respect and confidence of his men. A Donkey leader might never go into combat but he had to make sure the fighters had proper leadership and enough food, weapons, and ammunition to continue the fight.

I never witnessed and never heard of any overt political indoctrination among the partisan fighters, although that is not to say that it never occurred. Depending on their leadership, some units were more military than others, some more political.

But there was within the units an intense and almost palpable peer pressure that kept the fighters pointed in the same direction.

Donkey-11, the unit comprised almost entirely of former students, had three major principles to which all its members were expected to adhere:

1. We will follow and we will justify the *wharang* spirit.

2. We will live in accordance with the pure racial spirit.

3. We will protect our beings as students and we will remain students.[5]

Wharang, as it was explained later to me, was an ancient Korean code of conduct not unlike the chivalric code of England and western Europe. It developed sometime during the seventh century, when the Korean peninsula and its culture were under attack from outside forces.

The code, which was used in the training of elite soldiers to guard the royal kingdom, involved benevolence, courage, fidelity, filial piety, and loyalty, of which the first two were considered the most important.

Donkey-15 had a more complex set of mottoes by which its members were expected to live.

1. We are guerrilla forces; we will fight for freedom until the last breath of life.

2. We are free fighters; we will continue fighting until the world's freedom is won.

3. We are pioneer patriots and we will continue fighting until the final minutes.

4. We will dedicate our lives to our country.

5. We will be living with guerrilla spirits and with the spirits of the foundation of our country.[6]

Donkey leaders were chosen by individual units, not by the Americans. We had virtually no say in who their leaders were or how they conducted their operations. Of course, if we did not like a particular leader or the manner in which his unit was operating we could make life difficult by withholding rice or other supplies.

The partisan leaders were those men who had been leaders in civilian life—schoolteachers, government officials, those with some formalized military training.

D-1, Chang Jae Hwa, was a former merchant from Choryong who had fled to Paengnyong-do in February 1951 and had been picked to lead his unit.

D-11, Lee Jung Hok, was a schoolteacher in a little town just north of the 38th parallel on the Ongjin Peninsula when the war broke out. He organized about eight hundred students into this partisan group, which was known as "the students." They continued their studies on the islands when they were not training or conducting operations.

D-13, Kim Chang Song, managed a fruit orchard in Sinchon before he became a partisan and fled into the mountains.

D-15, Kim Ung Soo, was a Manchurian-educated banker from Sinuiju who had served in the Japanese army during World War II and fought in China. His unit operated as far north as the Yalu River and was one of the few to have American advisers prior to my arrival.

Donkey-4, the unit to which I was assigned, had originally been formed in March 1951 by a man named Chang Sok Lin. Educated in Japan, Chang had served as a police official in South Korea, later joined the ROK navy intelligence corps, and was with the U.N. forces when they drove north in the fall of 1950. When the Chinese entered the war he went to Paengnyong-do, organized Donkey-4, and became the D-4.

D-4 and the twenty-five original partisans he commanded had among them ten Russian rifles, ten carbines of various makes, and one radio when they were sent back to the mainland shortly after the group was formed. They had little success gathering intelligence, recruiting other partisans, or finding food because of constant pressure from NKPA security forces. It was not long before the bulk of the unit fled for Cho-do, a large island on the north side of Changsan-got.

Ten men were left behind while D-4 and the rest of the partisans consulted with Major Burke at Leopard Base. Burke advised them to develop bases on small islands close to the mainland from which to stage their raids. Within a year they had four islands, including Cho-do and Wollae-do.

The ten members of Donkey-4 who had remained on the mainland began to have some success recruiting disenchanted youth to join them, and as the unit grew the members began staging some hit-and-run raids on police stations and government offices.

The early operations for many of the Donkey units were virtual suicide missions. They were given only two or three weeks of training, were equipped with weapons, explosives, and radios, and then were sent to the mainland in small groups.

One of the first actions was led by D-1, Chang Jae Hwa. In March 1951 he led a group of thirty-seven partisans to the mainland with orders to collect intelligence. When the group's radio began malfunctioning Chang was ordered to conduct operations. In late March the group hit a government headquarters, killing seven North Korean police and twenty government officials, according to his reports.

Chang continued to recruit partisans, and by April the unit had sixty members and had adopted a more aggressive posture. It hit an NKPA transportation center and discovered about seventeen hundred civilians imprisoned there. Chang freed the civilians but many were near starvation and were unable to keep up with the fast-moving partisans. The NKPA caught up with the column and killed what Chang estimated to be thirteen hundred of the civilians and fifty of his men.[7] Other Donkey leaders reported similar experiences.

In April 1951 D-11 and his "student" partisans staged a raid on the mainland in the vicinity of the Ongjin Peninsula but quickly found themselves outnumbered by NKPA troops and overwhelmed by refugees. The partisans loaded the refugees onto the nineteen fishing junks they had brought on the raid and allowed them to escape, but the fighters were trapped on the beach.

When D-11's men began running out of ammunition for their aging Japanese and Russian rifles they simply jumped into the Yellow Sea, where they were easily picked off by NKPA gunners.

"The ocean was colored by the blood of friendly partisans," said D-11, who estimates that twenty of his seventy-man attacking force were killed. He spent more than three hours in the water before he was rescued.[8]

Despite the hardships that included an irregular flow of supplies; a lack of weapons; no support from artillery, aircraft, or naval gunfire; increased pressure from NKPA defenses; and harsh weather conditions, the partisan units continued to sign up new recruits who were more than willing to fight.

By late summer 1951 Donkey-4 had absorbed a smaller unit, Donkey-3, which had taken refuge on Cho-do, and had grown to more than twelve hundred men. It had become the most aggressive and most successful of the partisan units. Donkey-4 members called themselves "The White Tigers," a name carefully chosen to represent the courage of the tiger and the immortality of white. They had also chosen to use the numeral 4 in their unit name, going against Korean tradition that the number is unlucky. It was the Korean equivalent of using the Nazi SS death's-head as a symbol.

From what Pak Choll later told me and other army officials, D-4's leadership abilities and combat efficiency began to erode when he realized in late 1951 that the peace talks were likely to bring an end to the war without liberation of the North. He began pushing aside the ten original members of the group and putting family members into key leadership positions.

D-4's younger brother was put in charge of Wollae-do. Another relative was put in charge of supplies the unit received from Leopard Base and those captured from the NKPA.

Mr. Pak said that D-4 became a "dictator." Two of the original members of Donkey-4 decided to assassinate the leader "to save the 1,200 people" in the unit. They did so on January 1, 1952.[9]

The unit was in turmoil for weeks after the assassination. It lost about half its men. A radio operator on the mainland, one of the original D-4's most loyal soldiers, disappeared with his radio, and it was feared he went over to the enemy. Following that incident most of Donkey-4's interior units were chased to the islands and NKPA coastal defense forces attacked the islands.

At that time Donkey-4's headquarters was on a small island known as Yuk-to. On February 2, 1952, the partisans on Yuk-to disregarded a signal from the mainland that an attack on the island was imminent and were not prepared when two hundred NKPA soldiers in motor launches descended on them. The defenders fled to a cave on one side of the island where their only choices were fighting to the death or jumping into the sea.

They fought until reinforcements arrived but lost a number of men in the process, including two leaders who were seriously wounded and, rather than surrender to the NKPA, thereby disgracing the unit, committed suicide with hand grenades.

Since then the unit had conducted relatively few missions. The unsettled conditions in Donkey-4 and the brutal winter weather had limited operations to a few small-scale ambushes of convoys or NKPA patrols, usually involving no more than six to ten men.

After becoming D-4, Mr. Pak was kept busy during the first two months of 1952. He had to move the unit headquarters to Wollae-do and prepare its defenses. He had to settle internal problems caused by the leadership change. He had to attempt to stanch the steady stream of defections from the unit. And he had to convince his American benefactors that he was neither a Communist infiltrator nor an NKPA sympathizer.

All these factors made it unclear just how Mr. Pak would accept me as his adviser, although Major McKean had let him know that he had to cooperate if he wanted to remain in the good graces of the U.S. government and the 8240th Army Unit. As a result, it was late February before

Mr. Pak came to Leopard Base for our first meeting. He saluted and bowed slightly when we met, as was the custom among partisan leaders.

Mr. Pak was short and wiry, no more than five-foot-six and 140 pounds, with a round, pleasant face dominated by a nose that was slightly too large, as if he had been a boxer at one time. He wore American fatigues but shunned boots in favor of dark gray tennis shoes, as did all the partisans. His eyes were shaded by the soft fatigue cap that he kept pulled low on his forehead, and it was impossible to read him by looking at his eyes. He could have been twenty-five years old or forty-five years old. It was difficult to tell his age and I never asked, although it was obvious he was my senior by a few years.

It was also clear by the deference with which his men treated him that he was older than they, commanded their respect, and was definitely the man in charge.

Mr. Pak and I talked through an interpreter for nearly thirty minutes in that first meeting about the training program I wanted to develop for his men. Despite my initial reservations about him he seemed pleasant, courteous, and eager to dispel the concerns McKean had about him.

He said he was happy to have an American working with Donkey-4 and seemed very pleased that I would be conducting the training for his people. Many of them had had little formal military training before joining the unit. I explained that I had been a training officer back in the United States for more than a year and could develop a thorough, rigorous program for his men that would make them more effective fighters. The more effective his unit, the more supplies it would receive.

Mr. Pak agreed to send fifty men to Leopard Base for training by mid-March and urged me to visit his base on Wollae-do so I could get a better sense of who his people were and how they lived.

He told me that of the roughly six hundred partisans under his command at that time, about fifty were on Leopard Base, two hundred were on the mainland acting as partisans or intelligence agents, one hundred were on Cho-do, and the remaining two hundred and fifty were at his main base on Wollae-do.

Over the next several weeks I continued my work as Leopard Base S-2 and began developing a training program for Donkey-4. Although I told McKean of Mr. Pak's enthusiasm and cooperation, he told me he still did not trust the man and urged me to be cautious in dealing with him.

On March 3, 1952, I was working at Leopard Base when I got a call that Mr. Pak was coming in and wanted to meet me. I grabbed my carbine, my .45, and an interpreter, and hurried down to the beach to meet his boat.

Mr. Pak had an old Chinese sail junk with a four-horsepower motor that provided just enough power to enable it to make headway against a stiff wind. It was also fortified with heavy timbers on the sides that were thick enough to stop small-arms rounds from NKPA coastal defense units that often fired on the boat during raids.

When Mr. Pak arrived he saluted and bowed and asked me to accompany him to Wollae-do. From Paengnyong-do, Wollae-do is a bluish smudge on the eastern horizon just south of the mountainous Changsan-got. But it was little more than an hour's trip by boat and I thought I could get to the island, do a quick tour, and be back in a few hours.

I did not realize that the trip to Wollae-do was actually Mr. Pak's ruse for getting me off Paengnyong-do and out of radio contact so he could induce me to visit his safe area on Changsan-got. Not realizing what he was up to, I quickly accepted his invitation.

On the trip to Wollae-do Mr. Pak pointed out features on the mainland while I surveyed them through my field glasses. As we got closer to Changsan-got I could see trees and spots of white sand on some of the beaches cut out of the cliffs. There was much more vegetation on the mainland than on any of the islands.

One of the features Mr. Pak pointed out to me was a mountain peak looming over Wollae-do where the NKPA had a field artillery piece that harassed the island almost daily. The 76mm gun was hidden in a cave dug deep into the mountain. The gun would be rolled out for firing, then rolled back inside the mountain and hidden behind camouflaged steel doors. Neither aerial bombardment nor naval gunfire nor several raids by the guerrillas had been able to knock out that gun.

Mr. Pak said he believed the NKPA was allocated an average of ten rounds a day to fire on the island. Some days they would fire three rounds. But if there was activity and boats moving around, the North Koreans might fire as many as fifteen rounds. His main deepwater harbor faced the mainland in full view of the gun crew and was well within range of the gun.

Wollae-do was little more than a speck in the Yellow Sea, roughly two square miles. It was no more than two miles from the mainland. The main harbor was on the north side of the island because the water on the south side was shallow and at low tide the mudflats extended more than five hundred yards from the beach. The island was barren, windswept, and treeless, like virtually all other islands off the west coast of Korea. Little grew there.

There were three prominent hill masses on the island that afforded Mr. Pak's partisans some protection from the NKPA gun. The only village on Wollae-do had about twenty mud-and-straw houses and was built on the reverse slope of a hill that faced the mainland. In the center of the island was a low spot protected by the hills where Mr. Pak had about sixty head of oxen that he had "liberated" from the mainland.

There were probably forty or fifty women and children living in the village. They were the families of some of the partisans. Most of the fighters had left their families on the mainland because they fully expected to liberate them with the help of U.N. forces.

Behind the village extensive fortifications were dug into the reverse slope of the hill. They were spacious enough to shelter all the people in the village when the gun started firing and were heavily reinforced. Large timbers from the forests in the safe area on Changsan-got had been used for the walls and ceilings, and then about four feet of dirt had been piled on top. A direct hit would not have damaged those bunkers.

The NKPA gunners were never noted for their accuracy and usually had to rely on luck to hit anything. But that is exactly how they had recently killed and wounded several of Mr. Pak's men. The partisans had been working in the open when the gun opened fire and were unable to scramble into the bunkers on time.

I spent about thirty minutes touring Wollae-do with Mr. Pak and meeting some of his fighters. They seemed tough, disciplined, and committed to their fight. And, despite their lack of formal military training, they had a military bearing about them that was evident in the way they took care of their weapons. They were literally under the gun here on Wollae-do and had to be prepared for an NKPA invasion at any time. Only a single squad with two machine guns in bunkers on hills overlooking the north harbor provided early warning and the first line of defense.

My visit to Wollae-do was as much for Mr. Pak's benefit as it was for mine. While it gave me a better indication of the hardships he and his men faced, it also told his men that from this day forward the Americans would work more closely with them. Whatever problems they might have had in the recent past with the change in leadership and whatever lingering distrust there might be about them on Leopard Base, the Americans had now taken a personal interest in their welfare.

I'm sure my visit to Wollae-do and my subsequent surprise visit to Changsan-got solidified Mr. Pak's political power base. He had brought an American to Wollae-do. He had brought an American to Changsan-got. And he had brought the promise of closer cooperation and more aid from the Americans. The previous D-4 had not been able to do that. My presence among them was a clear demonstration to the partisan fighters that Mr. Pak could do far more things for them than his predecessor or anyone thinking of succeeding Mr. Pak.

That excursion to Wollae-do and the trip to Changsan-got made allies of Mr. Pak and me. Our missions were now running along parallel lines. I had demonstrated trust in him and a willingness to work with him and learn from him and his fighters. He, in turn, knew he needed my backing to rebuild the support of Leopard Base leadership, which was then at a low ebb.

He would help me accomplish my mission; I would help him accomplish his. Our efforts would be mutually beneficial.

The first impressions apparently had been favorable for both sides. I had taken a large first step toward winning the trust of the partisans and their leaders by simply demonstrating my willingness to be among them and work with them. The next step would be to demonstrate my military prowess by making them more effective fighters through a rigorous training program.

In order to do that I had to make them something more than they already were. Many were seasoned combat veterans who had learned the tactics of unconventional warfare as they fought. My schooling at that point was more in the tactics of light infantry. I began to develop an idea to integrate some of those light infantry tactics into their experiences as partisans. In that way we might be able to develop a unit with some unique capabilities. Not only would they be able to conduct traditional partisan and guerrilla operations, but with the proper training they would also be proficient as a light infantry unit capable of using supporting fires in their operations. That would boost their firepower and their ability to hit larger targets.

But to do that effectively, I reasoned, there would have to be a goal on which to focus. And the most realistic goal at that moment seemed to be the NKPA's 76mm artillery piece that consumed Mr. Pak's thoughts and made life on Wollae-do doubly miserable for the partisans and their displaced families.

6

Partisan Training

One of Lt. Col. Jay Vanderpool's objectives when he took command of the Guerrilla Division of the 8240th Army Unit was to implement more formalized training for the partisan units. The North Koreans had adapted well to the concepts of partisan and guerrilla warfare but had virtually no knowledge of more conventional tactics

There was never any evidence that they had studied Mao Tse-tung's writings on guerrilla warfare, but they had become quite adept, as one partisan leader put it, of making a noise in the east and striking in the west.

A favorite tactic of the partisans was fake operational orders. On one occasion a partisan unit planted a number of mines on a hill, then printed up fake orders directing a certain NKPA unit to attack the hill. The commander of the unit accepted the orders, led the troops up the hill, and suffered eighty-two killed and twelve wounded.[1]

Guerrilla warfare seemed to come easily to the partisans. They knew the land they were fighting on and could quickly adapt to new situations and learn what they needed to survive. Although few of them had any formal military training, many could learn to fire, fieldstrip, and clean almost any weapon in a matter of minutes.

The partisans were in incredibly good physical condition. They could dogtrot for miles without tiring. They could endure extremes in temperature and weather conditions that would send most Americans scrambling for shelter. They could carry backbreaking loads up and down mountains for miles without slowing or complaining.

And they could move so stealthily they could surprise a sentry in the middle of an open field in broad daylight without being spotted. I thought it impossible for anyone to do that, but I saw them do it many times and became a firm believer in their abilities to move undetected through open country.

One midday attack on an NKPA command post in May 1952 is illustrative of the partisans' ability to move with that kind of stealth. The
officers in the command post were napping and the sentries were less
than alert. The partisans slipped into the command post without being
seen, placed an antitank mine in the kitchen stove, and slipped out
before the mine blew up. The resulting explosion and attack killed thirty-five NKPA and wounded sixteen more without any injuries to the
friendly forces.

The partisans seemed to have no fear of their own death. They rou-
tinely volunteered for what anyone else would consider suicide missions. In one such instance two partisans dressed in civilian clothes
boarded a sail junk loaded with NKPA and irregular troops. Once the
boat was out to sea the partisans dropped several hand grenades they
had concealed in their clothes, jumped overboard, and swam to shore.
They reported that the junk sank and sixteen of those on board died.[2]

On another occasion several members of one partisan group working
in an NKPA mess hall planted charges of TNT and C-3 under the floor
of the facility and in the barracks. They blew up the mess hall during the
evening meal and at about eleven P.M., when the troops had retired for
the night, they blew up the barracks. Casualty totals reported by the
partisans were ninety NKPA killed and five buildings destroyed with
one partisan killed and one wounded.[3]

But most partisans knew nothing about calling in artillery fire or air
support to a specific grid coordinate on a map. Even the idea of fire-
and-maneuver for platoon- or company-size units utilizing supporting
fires from machine guns was foreign to them. They depended primarily
on surprise, speed, and instantaneous violence in their raids. They would
hit quickly, hit hard, and be gone before the NKPA realized what had
happened.

Later studies of partisan operations indicated that the larger the
group in which they operated the higher the percentage of casualties
they suffered. If they used mines in their ambushes the casualty rates
would skyrocket. The optimum size of the attacking group was five partisans or fewer against selected small targets. Using groups larger than
that produced significantly higher friendly casualties, so there was reason to question how well they could adapt to the concept of fighting as
a light infantry unit.[4]

In his "Guerrilla Operations Outline, 1952," passed down in early
April, Vanderpool stressed that we should continue to press the guerrilla
tactics. "Initiative and aggressiveness tempered by calm judgment will be
encouraged," he wrote. "Avoid trying to win the war by yourself; pace
the attack in accordance with your advantage; when the advantage has
passed, get away to fight another day."[5] But he also wanted the partisans
trained to adjust naval gunfire, jump out of airplanes, use demolitions

more effectively, and become more proficient in regular infantry tactics.[6]

There were two problems with implementing that type of training. The first was that there were not enough Americans available to train all partisan units. As of April 1952 there were still only twenty-two officers and thirty-seven enlisted men working in partisan operations throughout Korea.[7] The second problem was that most of those Americans did not know how to set up the type of training Vanderpool wanted.

My arrival on Leopard Base gave my boss, Major Leo McKean, the opportunity to establish a training program for Donkey-4. Although I was working as camp commandant and S-2 for the entire partisan operation on the base, there was sufficient time in my daily schedule to allow me to oversee training of several dozen partisans. And my training background while serving with the 3rd Armored Division at Fort Knox, Kentucky, during my first year in the army gave me the knowledge necessary to implement such a program.

The question was how to go about doing that while keeping the attention and interest of the partisans. Virtually all of them had seen some form of combat so they knew what it was like to be shot at and to shoot at another human being. I knew, based on my past experiences with training, that in order to keep the attention of these veteran fighters I would have to have a goal-oriented training program. They would have to train to do something, not just train.

After mulling over the idea for a few days I finally hit on the concept of a training program that would include squad, platoon, and company tactics with a variety of weapons designed to knock out the battalion command post and the 76mm gun overlooking Wollae-do. The plan I envisioned would infiltrate about one hundred partisans ashore near the gun, then attack from the rear utilizing naval gunfire and air support. I would accompany the partisans to call in supporting fires.

When I had sketched out the plan I called Mr. Pak to Leopard Base to present it to him.

"We're going to destroy that gun position and blow up that gun," I told him.

His face registered only a hint of surprise but I could tell immediately that he liked the plan. Not only would destruction of the gun provide relief for the people on Wollae-do, it would also enhance Mr. Pak's stature as D-4.

"But how will you do this?" he said. "We have tried this three times and failed."

I quickly outlined the plan; the interpreter was barely able to keep up as I rattled off the details. When I told Mr. Pak about using naval gunfire and carrier-based aircraft to support the raiding party, he questioned how this would be done.

"I will be coming with you. I will control the naval gunfire and air support," I said.

He was stunned for a moment. Then he smiled, bowed slightly, and saluted, pleased that I thought so highly of him and his men.

"No American has ever gone on a raid on the mainland with us before. You will be the first," he said.

"But we have work to do before the raid," I continued. "I will need about two months to train your people and run some rehearsals."

I also told Mr. Pak he would have to get his agents on the mainland to provide detailed intelligence on the gun position and units supporting it so we could tailor the training appropriately. I told him we needed information on the positions and number of enemy troops in the area, locations and types of weapons, the communications setup, the number of reserve troops and how fast they could reinforce the main forces, and what the guard schedules were. In addition, I wanted a sketch of the inside of the mountain where the gun was hidden.

Mr. Pak agreed and said he could have fifty fighters at Leopard Base to start training by mid-April.

I set up the training in three phases. The first phase was basic training because some in the initial group were recent recruits and had no formal military training. Included in the first phase was instruction in the M1 rifle, carbine, .45-caliber pistol, and bayonet, plus map reading and familiarization with machine guns and recoilless rifles. The second phase was squad and platoon tactics to be used during raids, including communicating with arm and hand signals. The third and final phase was actual rehearsals for the raid on the 76mm gun, including how to deal with close air support and naval gunfire.

The training began on April 15, 1952. By that time the weather had turned for the better and had little effect on the schedule. While the mornings could be uncomfortably cool, the rest of the day usually was warm, though not oppressively hot, as it could be in the summer.

When I arrived at the training site that first morning I was surprised. Mr. Pak had fifty men in new uniforms standing at attention. He had gone through his ranks and carefully selected the men he wanted to receive the training.

I began by giving them a brief overview of the war and their roles in it. I stressed to the partisans that their primary role was to harass the NKPA, keep them off balance, and force them to allocate valuable resources to our area, which was far from the front lines. That would ease pressure along the front. Unspoken but implied in my words was that this training could be utilized to fight alongside United Nations forces if the new offensive ever came. I don't know whether that idea made it through the translation but that question was one neither I nor the partisans wanted to address at that moment.

I was thoroughly impressed with the men Mr. Pak had selected. As I spoke through the interpreter there was not a sound from any of them. They did not cough, shuffle their feet, or look at the ground. They stood perfectly still, watching and listening with rapt attention, a dream come true for any training officer. Obviously, Mr. Pak had told them what he expected of them and that anything less would disgrace not only him but their families.

When I had finished with my orientation speech I went through the ranks, asking each man his name, where he was from, why he had come to Wollae-do, and what he hoped to achieve as a member of Donkey-4.

Over the next two months we would train about two hundred partisans, but I used the same approach for each group, no matter how long they had served with Donkey-4. They seemed delighted to have someone interested in them as people, not just as soldiers.

We began training with the M1 rifle. Although it was relatively heavy at 9.5 pounds and long at 43.6 inches, not once did the Koreans complain. It was their weapon of choice because it had a longer range and hit harder than the carbine or the .45-caliber Thompson submachine gun.

Formal military training was a novel idea in that part of the world and created a few problems early on for those not used to it.

I set up a firing range on one end of the beach that also served as the landing strip for Paengnyong-do. One day the students were popping away at makeshift targets set up on the side of the mountain when I looked back to see a C-47 landing. The pilot apparently thought we were in a fight with the North Koreans because as soon as he hit the beach he slammed on the brakes, spun the plane around, and revved the engines to take off again. I called for a cease-fire, jumped into my jeep, and chased down the plane before it could get airborne. The next day we moved the firing range to a more remote beach.

The trainees quickly adapted to the M1. The .45 was another matter. They fired about twenty rounds for familiarization but few of the partisans liked the weapon. It was too heavy (more than 2.75 pounds loaded) and difficult to fire. Not many of them carried a .45.

We also did familiarization firing with the Browning automatic rifle (BAR), .30-caliber and .50-caliber machine guns, and 57mm and 75mm recoilless rifles.

The only problem I had with the trainees and the recoilless rifles was their tendency to fire without first checking to the rear. Twice trainees were burned by the backblast, though not seriously. On another occasion we nearly killed a civilian who wandered onto the range where we were firing the 75mm recoilless rifles.

I had placed a large piece of white cloth, about four feet by six feet, as a target on the side of a mountain about two thousand yards downrange. I returned to the firing line and began getting the men ready to shoot. We did not notice that an old Korean woman had come around the side of the mountain and was making her way up to that white cloth. Just as we fired the first round she picked up the target and started down the mountain.

Fortunately, the round was wide right and exploded far enough from her that she was not hurt. When she heard the explosion she simply looked up, dropped the white cloth, and scooted off through the bushes.

Hoping to avoid an incident with the local villagers, I grabbed my interpreter, hopped into the jeep, and went looking for her. We found her calmly washing clothes outside her house as if nothing had happened. She told us she thought somebody had dropped the cloth and she went and picked it up. Then when the round hit she decided that it must be somebody's cloth and they were upset that she had taken it.

The incident was a big hit with the partisans. Whenever we pulled out the recoilless rifles they would start laughing, point at the mountain, and talk about the old lady who stole their target.

In addition to weapons training we practiced a lot with dummy grenades. We wanted the partisans to be accurate from twenty-five to one hundred feet with grenades, and they worked hard at it.

We also did extensive training in setting and disarming mines. I set up minefields with mines that had training fuses that would pop out and smoke when they were tripped. If a trainee disarming a mine popped the fuse the others in his group would laugh and point their fingers at the offending party. But the guy who set off the mine never made that mistake again.

The only concept some of the guerrillas had difficulty grasping quickly was operating at squad and platoon level. They had fought individually and in groups of fewer than ten for so long that working in larger groups presented some conceptual problems. But they attacked this phase of training with as much enthusiasm as they did every other phase.

The partisans were quite serious about their training. They would do anything I asked of them. We would start training at eight A.M., and they were never late. They were always there before me. They always wanted to fire one more round or throw one more grenade. It was completely different from the training I had been a part of with the American draftees at Fort Knox. These Koreans had a mission. They wanted to learn to fight. They wanted to retake their homeland.

My approach to this training was somewhat different for the times and a complete contradiction of army doctrine. The doctrine on which the U.S. Army was based at that time was a throwback to World War II. It involved taking ground and holding it. Nowhere in my training with the partisans was there any mention or any consideration of taking or holding territory.

All I was doing was providing more capabilities to Mr. Pak's Donkey-4 partisans. I wanted to demonstrate that he could conduct larger raids if he had sufficient trained manpower backed by naval gunfire and air support. The heart of the partisan operations was still the small-scale raid. But I was helping Mr. Pak develop a unit that was similar to the Chindits of British Brig. Gen. Orde Wingate and later the American "Marauders" of Col. Frank Merrill, both of whom had fought in Burma in World War II.

Wingate had served in Palestine in the 1930s, assisting the Jews against the Arab rebellion. Later, in Ethiopia, he marshaled a small mobile force of Sudanese and Ethiopians to defeat the better-equipped Italians. Wingate brought to Burma an understanding of the tactics necessary to conduct behind-the-lines operations and utilized a variety of hardy, battle-tested troops that included Gurkhas from Nepal, the Burma Rifles, and the Royal West African Frontier Force. Although they suffered horrendous casualties, nearly 30 percent, primarily because of weather and disease, the Chindits were seen as a unique and innovative unit able to strike hard at a foe who was believed to possess superior jungle-fighting skills.

The Marauders were modeled after Wingate's Chindits as a light infantry unit that could be inserted deep behind enemy lines to gather intelligence, ambush convoys, and tear up communications. Although they functioned much like traditional guerrilla units, the Marauders and Chindits were still light infantry operating independently of the local populace.

But there was a general misunderstanding among the high command in the China-Burma-India theater about the proper use of these units. General Joseph Stilwell could not distinguish the differences between a lightly armed unit capable of deep penetration missions and a unit better suited to taking and holding ground. The Chindits and Marauders were ordered by Stilwell at times to hold ground or attack fortified positions without the proper equipment, something neither was designed or trained to do.[8]

My training program was simply an amplification of traditional guerrilla tactics using more men and more supporting fires. It evolved into a routine that enabled me to utilize some of the senior NCOs on the island as trainers so I could attend to my other duties as S-2. I generally would work in the S-2 office from shortly after dawn until about eight A.M., oversee the start of training, and then go back to the S-2 office. Depending on the volume of work, I would shuttle between the office and the training areas throughout the day to ensure that things were going as planned.

Mr. Pak visited once or twice a week and seemed pleased with the program and the progress his people were making. He was continuing to run small operations on the mainland while his agents gathered intelligence on the gun site. As each new piece of information came in we made appropriate changes in the plan of attack. Gradually, the mission took shape.

On June 2, 1952, Mr. Pak came to Leopard Base with another batch of intelligence and news that his first platoon, operating on the mainland, had overrun an NKPA outpost, killing eight and capturing some weapons and oxen. Before they could leave the area a truck convoy came through so they ambushed it, killing two NKPA and capturing two. The two POWs would be ready for pickup that night. I told Mr. Pak I wanted to accompany him to pick up the prisoners and he agreed. We piled into his boat and headed for Wollae-do.

The pickup was planned for twelve-thirty A.M. because that was when the tide changed. If we were not off the beach by then we ran the risk of trying to buck a four-knot tide with a motor that, if it worked at all, would push the boat along at only five knots.

At about eleven P.M. we loaded into three boats and headed across the strait from Wollae-do to the mainland. When we were within about a mile of the coast Mr. Pak signaled the captains to shut off their engines and raise the sails. But there was virtually no wind and paddles were broken out to assist our passage.

As we neared the coast a flashlight signal told us it was safe to land and we headed straight into the beach. There was just enough moonlight to distinguish someone moving about twenty-five feet away so we had no concerns about being spotted unless the NKPA patrol that made its rounds of this area every thirty minutes stumbled over us.

Eight of Mr. Pak's partisans were waiting on shore with the captured weapons, six oxen, some documents, and the two prisoners, who had been bound and gagged. We loaded everything into the boats, then led the oxen into the water, and tied them securely to the boats.

Although oxen generally are reluctant swimmers, the partisans had discovered that they would attempt it if their heads were kept out of the water. The partisans would tie the horns of the oxen to a ring on the side of the boat, then set sail for Wollae-do, dragging the reluctant beasts behind them. These six would add to Mr. Pak's already substantial herd on Wollae-do, which by then numbered about sixty.

British sailors who patrolled the coastal areas were often unnerved on still, moonless nights to be sailing along miles from land and hear oxen bellowing. When they turned on their searchlights they would discover fishing junks returning from a raid and towing as many as a dozen oxen behind them.

When we reached Wollae-do the two prisoners were hustled off the boat. By the time Mr. Pak and I waded ashore the two were surrounded by partisans, several of whom had pulled their .45s and had them pointed at the heads of the frightened young men. Three partisans had been killed on the raid and two others wounded, and their friends were intent on extracting immediate revenge with summary executions.

"No!" Mr. Pak said sharply before I could intervene. "I want to see how much they know about troop locations and plans. If they talk, we may let them live."

The prisoners were taken to Mr. Pak's bunker, where they talked all night and into the next morning until it was time to board the boat to Leopard Base. Once we got there I sent a message to Seoul informing them that we had two prisoners. A reply came back almost immediately that a special plane would be dispatched the next day to pick them up.

Vanderpool was continually encouraging the Donkey units to capture prisoners. He wanted specific types of prisoners, particularly intelligence officers, Chinese officers, and MiG pilots. Units would be rewarded with additional supplies for each prisoner.

But the requests for prisoners were often ignored. Prisoners were a burden to the fast-moving partisans. If they took prisoners they usually had to abort their mission. Still, we told them repeatedly not to kill or injure any prisoners. We didn't tell them how to interrogate them. We left that up to the partisans. And Mr. Pak said that the only way to get any information out of them was to convince them they were going to die, because they had been so indoctrinated and were such hard-core Communists that they would not otherwise talk.

I spent about six more hours interrogating the prisoners at Leopard Base, then turned them over to Mr. Pak for some final questions.

The next morning the plane came in from Seoul and landed on the beach at low tide, and we put the prisoners aboard. It was the last we saw or heard of them. They had been valuable sources of information about troop movements and gun positions, but once they got to Seoul they disappeared and we never got any additional information that might have been of use to us.

It was usually that way with prisoners. If we did not extract the information from them before we shipped them off to Seoul we never learned what they knew even though they had been captured in our area of operations. The information flow generally went one way—Leopard Base to Seoul. We got very little in return. We were never sure whether that was due to lack of interest or to the confusion that seemed so much a part of army life in Seoul. It was evident that there was a great deal of confusion when it came to dealing with the partisans, though. Higher headquarters had difficulty distinguishing them from the NKPA on some occasions.

One such instance involved two of Mr. Pak's partisans who had been wounded in January 1952, prior to my arrival. They were medically evacuated to Seoul but were mistaken for POWs from the front lines and were sent to the notorious prison camp at Koje-do. Mr. Pak tried repeatedly to get them out and Major McKean and his successor, Major Tom Dye, sent numerous messages to Seoul to try to liberate the two men. But we never saw them again.

As planning for the mission progressed we plotted gun positions, troop locations, and lines of communication on a large wall map. It was at about this time I learned that my name was regularly being mentioned on NKPA radio broadcasts as one of the Americans on Leopard Base who worked closely with the partisans. There was a price on my head, although I no longer remember the amount since it apparently was not too high and did not generate a lot of interest among would-be assassins. But the fact that information was being leaked to the NKPA by someone on Leopard Base bothered McKean. He wanted to know how the North Koreans got this information. Despite some diligent searching neither he nor I ever found the source of the leaks.

On June 17, 1952, Mr. Pak came to Leopard Base with the news that one of his men, disguised as a civilian, was now working as a laborer for the NKPA battalion that guarded the gun we had targeted. The man was sending out incredibly detailed maps showing troop locations and gun positions—many of the things we needed to fine-tune the plan.

"That artillery has really slowed down our movement on Wollae-do," he said. "They have fired on us ten of the last sixteen days."

I told Mr. Pak I would have a more precise attack plan ready for him the next morning. I worked most of the night, and by the time Mr. Pak and his staff arrived at the operations center at eight A.M. I was ready. The plan was sketched on overlay paper and pinned to the large map so I could run through the various phases of attack.

The plan called for 120 men from Donkey-4 and myself to slip ashore on the morning of July 14. That would give us more time for detailed rehearsals. We would move in behind the gun and be in position by four-thirty A.M. The naval bombardment would start at five A.M. It would target a reserve battalion camp about three miles north of the gun, a reserve company of about 250 NKPA four miles to the northwest, and the defenders dug in at the base of the mountain. The attack force would then advance on the gun site and several machine gun positions that, if not already knocked out by naval gunfire, could be hit by close air support.

The 76mm gun was on the tallest mountain in the area. There was a machine-gun position on top of the mountain and another just to the northeast. The gun itself was in a cave in the mountain with an opening facing Wollae-do. Steel doors covered the front of the cave and a camouflage net could be dropped over the entrance. The camouflage blended in so well it was impossible to spot the entrance to the cave when they pulled the gun in, closed the doors, and dropped the net. Built into the mountain was a bunker complex with room for about forty men, a mess hall, an ammunition dump, and several small entrances, all well-camou-flaged, that provided escape routes.

Our plan was simple but effective, relying on stealth, speed, and power to overwhelm a superior NKPA force and knock out the gun. But we would need a little luck and a lot of good shooting from our friends in the British navy and the U.S. Marine Corps, who would sup-ply air support.

The only thing we were lacking at that point was specific information about guard posts along the beach and roving patrols. Mr. Pak promised he would have his agent gather that information.

On June 23 Mr. Pak and I were sitting in the operations center going over the attack plan when he received a call that his agent had some of the information we needed. Mr. Pak instructed the agent to deliver it to the usual pickup point that night.

"We will pick up the information he has and send him back to work in the camp," Mr. Pak said. "He will continue to collect information and we will pull him out on the thirteenth before the attack on the fourteenth."

I asked Mr. Pak if I could accompany him on the pickup and he agreed. We left almost immediately for Wollae-do, where we would wait until eleven P.M. before heading for the mainland. The rendezvous with the agent was at five minutes after midnight.

We spent our time on Wollae-do drinking coffee and discussing the attack plan in Mr. Pak's underground bunker before setting sail pre-cisely at eleven P.M. The moon was almost half full in a cloudless sky, making our boat a wonderful target. We waited offshore for some clouds to develop but none did, so we pressed on. We figured we could cover half the distance without being seen but after that would be fair game for anybody looking out to sea. Still, we needed the information the agent had collected and had to risk the run in to the beach.

Halfway to the mainland the captain shut off the engine and ran up the sails. A tailwind and a flood tide pushed us along at a good clip. When we were about four hundred yards from the beach we began looking for a signal from the agent. Three short flashes of a yellow light meant everything was clear and we could proceed to the beach. Four short flashes of a red light meant danger.

There was no signal. We crept closer to the beach. At about three hundred yards I began to sense something was not right. I could not see anything moving on the beach but I could tell there was a problem. When we were two hundred yards from landing one of the men on the boat spotted a red signal light far to our left. The captain immediately threw the boat into a hard turn to the left.

No sooner did we start the turn than an NKPA squad on the beach opened up on us with burp guns and rifles. The muzzle flashes from their weapons lit up the beach and momentarily blinded us. One of our men was hit in the first volley and fell hard onto the deck. The rest of us dove for cover as the rounds thudded into the well-protected sides of the sail junk and snapped over our heads like angry insects.

The skipper was struggling to restart the engine as the volume of fire from the beach increased. The rounds were tearing large holes in the side of the boat near the waterline. Another man was hit. Then another. We could not fire back because it would have been suicidal to raise our heads above the gunwales. We had to lie there, defenseless, until the captain got the engine started.

By the time the engine coughed to life the boat was taking on water from numerous bullet holes. We worked furiously to plug the holes with rags and had some success until salt water got into the engine and it stopped. Water continued to seep into the bottom of the boat. When we tried to raise the sails we found that part of the mast had been damaged by gunfire. Slowly, we slipped out of gun range and into open water.

It took us nearly two hours to limp back to Wollae-do. We transferred the three wounded men to another boat and they were sent on to Leopard Base for treatment.

We had no sooner walked into Mr. Pak's bunker than a call came in from the agent on the mainland. He said he had been in position for the pickup when he spotted an NKPA patrol moving along the beach. The patrol saw the boat approaching and set up an ambush. He was not able to flash the red signal light until he was out of the ambush area and by then it was almost too late. He asked that we try to make contact with him that night at a different location. I decided to stay on Wollae-do overnight and go on the next run to the mainland because I needed that information to finalize the attack plan.

I had no real concern about compromising the mission with these frequent trips to the mainland. We had a continual series of boats going in and out of the coastal areas and it was not unusual for the craft to be shot at by roving NKPA patrols. But the North Korean soldiers usually thought we were coming to put somebody onshore and tried to run us off. I don't think they ever suspected we sometimes came in to pick up someone. If they had they would have waited until we were onshore and ambushed us there. Their intent was to keep us from landing.

What made it somewhat easier to put people ashore was the punctuality of NKPA patrols. The only time patrol members varied the time they would be at a particular spot on the beach was if they stopped and had a smoke somewhere along the way. If a new platoon was assigned to the patrol it might set up its own schedule. But in a matter of two or three days the patrol was in predictable routine.

That sort of behavior is so easy for a military unit to fall into. Americans do it all the time. The North Koreans obviously felt this was a relatively safe area and saw no need to vary the routes and times of their patrols. They assumed we just could not penetrate the area with large numbers of men because they had never been hit hard before.

We had good cloud cover for our trip to the mainland and the meeting with the agent. As we approached the beach we saw the agent's "safe" signal and continued on. Unfortunately, the bad light prevented us from seeing one of the numerous sandbars near shore. About thirty feet from the beach we ran aground.

The agent saw our predicament, waded out, and handed Mr. Pak several diagrams of the guard posts and information about the enemy patrols. He said a patrol was due in this area in about fifteen minutes and if we were not out by then we would be in big trouble.

The agent splashed back to the beach while all of us on the boat jumped into the water and began pushing or pulling to try to get free of the sandbar. We strained and sweated for several minutes, rocking the boat back and forth until it came free. The captain immediately cranked up the engine and we headed out to sea. We were just about to clear the area when the NKPA patrol spotted us and opened fire. About a dozen rounds splattered in the water around us but none was close enough to do any damage.

Once back at Wollae-do we examined the new information by the light of the kerosene lanterns in Mr. Pak's bunker. The agent's sketch maps and detailed notes confirmed many of the things we already knew about the bunker complex, the 76mm gun position, and the nearby reinforcements. What we had not known was that the machine-gun positions on top of the bunker complex had a 360-degree field of fire and could be reinforced through a trapdoor leading directly down into the mountain. Soldiers could get into the machine-gun positions without ever having to expose themselves to our fire.

In addition, we learned that there were four other defensive positions or listening posts about one thousand yards from the four corners of the bunker complex. Each was manned by two guards with telephones to communicate with the men in the bunker. The outposts were ringed with mines and trip flares, making them almost impossible to approach. But we could cut their telephone lines and neutralize them before we began the main attack.

There was a roving patrol, usually of four to eight men, that circled the area, including the beach. It took the patrol twenty-eight minutes to make its rounds but its times and routes were always the same.

The mountain in which the gun was hidden was steep and rocky with pine trees ten to twelve feet tall. Many of the trees had been cut for firewood or timbers to reinforce bunkers in the area, but there were still enough of them to give us some cover and concealment during the attack.

The NKPA had minefields and barbed wire at the base of the mountain. We would be able to bypass most of the minefields, but we would have to breach the barbed wire with explosive charges.

The nearest reinforcements for the bunker complex would come from a heavy machine-gun platoon of about thirty men. They were housed in a small village that we had not seen because it was concealed in a heavy growth of trees about one thousand yards northeast of the gun. Since the other guard posts and the main gun protected this platoon from attack from the coast, it had only two guard posts, each with one man in it.

I returned to Leopard Base the following day and checked on the three men wounded in the attack the night before. One had a shoulder wound, another a leg wound, the third arm and leg wounds. The men smiled when they saw me and indicated that they were eager to get back to Wollae-do to fight some more. Those wounds would have incapacitated most men. But not these partisans. They were the toughest people I have ever served with.

By June 28 I had completed the attack plan, and two days later we went into rehearsals with the three platoon leaders and twelve squad leaders Mr. Pak had personally handpicked for the mission. The hundred and five other men who would be the main force of the raid were also carefully selected by Mr. Pak.

I constructed a ten-foot-square sand table to show each of the men where they and their units would be and how they would attack. The partisans were incredibly attentive as I went over the plans with them. They had never seen this much detailed planning for an operation and were delighted to be a part of it.

We had no aerial photographs of the area, but that was not unusual. I never saw any aerial photographs the whole time I was in Korea. It would have been helpful, because there were usually large gaps in the maps we were using. We had to make do with what we could see and what our agents told us. That is why it was important to get such detailed information from agents on the ground.

On July 7 we moved into the final rehearsal phase in a secluded area of Paengnyong-do. For the next five days we walked through each phase of the attack until I felt the men knew exactly where they were supposed to be and what they should be doing every minute we were on the mainland. By this time the Koreans had adapted to the concept of light infantry fire-and-maneuver, something that had been totally foreign for them until just a few weeks earlier.

I had absolutely no reservations about accompanying this unit on the raid. The partisans had trained well and I knew they were good fighters who would not run even when faced with overwhelming numbers and heavy enemy fire. To do so would cause them to lose face with Mr. Pak, me, the other members of Donkey-4, and their families.

Mr. Pak told me he would have five of his best marksmen stay with me to protect me. I told him that would not be necessary. I wanted every man on the operation, including myself, concentrating on his mission. Having five of his best men doing nothing but watching out for me would reduce their effectiveness and could be somewhat cumbersome and dangerous for all of us.

On July 12 the British ship that would provide our naval gunfire and be the fire support center for the mission anchored off Paengnyong-do. A motor launch was sent to pick me up so I could meet with the ship's officers and go over final details of the plan with them and a representative of the U.S. Marine Corps pilots who would provide our air cap.

On the night of July 13 the ship would pick up Maj. Tom Dye, the Leopard Base commander who had replaced Major McKean, then would continue on its normal rounds of the islands. Dye would serve as the fire support coordinator for the raid. At three-thirty A.M. the ship would anchor in the channel between the mainland and Wollae-do. Radio silence would be maintained until four twenty-five A.M., at which time I would call the fire support center and provide last-minute target adjustments.

At four-thirty A.M. the ship would open fire on targets at specific grid coordinates. At five A.M. the naval gunfire would lift and air strikes by three carrier-based Marine Corps F-4U Corsairs would begin. Friendly troops would be identified by white marker panels. The aircraft would hit specific targets within a designated area but would be free to fire on anything that moved north and east of certain map grid lines. The aircraft would remain on station until we had withdrawn from the mainland.

The British gave me one of their radios to call the ship since the frequencies of our communications systems were not compatible. That meant I would be carrying two radios, one to communicate with the ship and one to communicate with Leopard Base. Internal communications with the men on the raid would be by arm and hand signals.

Mr. Pak also would carry a radio so he had contact with Wollae-do. A quick-reaction force of one hundred men would be ready to sail for the mainland if we got into big trouble.

I returned to Leopard Base at about three P.M. on July 12 and began my final preparations. I took my .45, my carbine with ten clips of ammunition, a soft cap, and a black Korean jacket to wear over my fatigue jacket. I would be going in as one of the raiders and had to look like them. There was no sense drawing too much attention to myself, even though being dressed in anything but a standard uniform most likely meant I would be shot as a spy if I was captured.

Mr. Pak's boat was waiting for me at the pier and ferried me through choppy seas to Wollae-do, where we landed on the south side of the island at about six P.M. The men who would be part of the raiding party were busily cleaning their weapons, loading their ammo pouches, or sharpening their bayonets. A few were test firing their weapons, something they normally did not do this close to the mainland. But the wind was so strong that it was carrying the sound out to sea and away from NKPA listening posts on the beach.

When the men saw me coming they snapped to attention, bowed, and saluted. I wandered from group to group, talking to the partisans in what little Korean I knew. They responded in a mixture of Korean and English. All seemed eager to be a part of the raid.

The men were working out in the open because the NKPA had fired twelve rounds from the 76mm gun shortly after two P.M. and it was thought the threat was over for the day. As darkness slowly settled over the island I made my way to the operations bunker, where Mr. Pak was continuing to receive updates by radio from his agents on the mainland. One, the laborer in the NKPA camp, was being brought out at that moment. Two others would meet us on the beach and lead us past the observation posts about two hundred yards inland. Everything seemed in place. There was not much more we could do now but wait until the next night.

"This is the night before our big operation and we always have a celebration before we fight," Mr. Pak said. "Let's go outside and join the men."

When we stepped out of the bunker I was stunned. Four huge bonfires were blazing away. One of Mr. Pak's precious oxen had been slaughtered and was roasting over one of the fires. Large tables were heavily laden with food and drink. The partisans had broken out their supply of Korean whiskey and were quickly emptying the bottles.

Mr. Pak must have seen the shocked look on my face as I surveyed the scene before me. This did not appear to be the appropriate way to prepare for a dangerous mission.

"These parties before a big operation are a very important part of Donkey-4," he explained. "Some of these men won't return from tomorrow's operation so they all celebrate as if this were their last party."

I shrugged my shoulders and smiled. If that was their custom, that was their custom, and I was not about to try to change it.

"Let's join the men," Mr. Pak said.

Just as we began moving toward one of the tables there was a blinding flash and a large explosion about one hundred yards in front of us.

I stopped, frozen in place for a few seconds, until I realized it had been an artillery round and not part of the celebration.

The next round hit about seventy-five yards behind us. I grabbed Mr. Pak and pulled him into the bunker because I figured the next round would be somewhere in the middle of those two. It was. It landed directly on top of the table Mr. Pak and I had been heading for, blowing it to bits and scattering food and glass shards all over the place.

Some of the partisans who had had too much to drink did not even bother to seek shelter. They simply sat and watched as the rounds continued to fall all around them.

After twelve rounds the firing stopped and Mr. Pak and I went out to survey the damage. Most of the rounds had fallen in the middle of the island and had done no damage. One had landed in the middle of our table, and two others hit in the housing area, knocking down a corner of one of the houses. Four partisans had suffered minor flesh wounds, but the damage was probably not as serious as what that Korean whiskey would do to them.

The wounded were quickly patched up, and within five minutes the party was back in full swing. Meat was sizzling over the open fires and the whiskey was being liberally dispensed. Some of the partisans celebrated as if they knew they would not survive the raid. And some would not. But I knew they would be ready to fight the next day and would fight even harder than they partied.

7

Raid on the Mainland

Any doubts that might have lingered among Mr. Pak's Donkey-4 partisans about the importance of destroying the North Korean artillery piece had been blown away by the barrage that landed in the middle of the preraid party the night of July 12. Resolve and determination were evident in the faces of the partisans as they made final preparation for the raid throughout the day on July 13.

Knocking out that gun was just as important to me, but for other reasons. Success would demonstrate to Mr. Pak that four months of intense training in light infantry tactics could produce a unit capable of engaging the NKPA in other than the traditional guerrilla actions that usually involved hit-and-run attacks on truck convoys or poorly defended supply points.

Success would also show the 8240th Army Unit's Guerrilla Division in Seoul that these were not just a bunch of ragtag partisans operating on the fringes of the war. These soldiers were as capable and as dedicated as those in any of the armies in Korea.

It was unusual for Americans to accompany the partisans on their raids, much less one this large and against such a well-fortified position. Orders from Seoul prohibiting Americans from going onto the mainland behind the lines supposedly were posted somewhere. But I never saw them and was never given a direct order not to go.

My boss, Maj. Tom Dye, had been in on the planning for this raid from the beginning and never voiced any objections about my intention to accompany the raiding party. I was eager to see if the intensive training I had put the partisans through was going to pay dividends.

More important, I would coordinate naval gunfire and air support for the partisans, something they were not used to having on their raids.

At about noon on July 13 Mr. Pak and I walked to the south harbor, where the four large Chinese sail junks that would carry us to the mainland were tied up. The mountains on Wollae-do shielded this anchorage from the NKPA observation posts across the channel so we were free to operate openly. The NKPA closely monitored activities on Wollae-do and would reinforce their coastal defenses and beef up the observation posts if they detected any unusual activities. We sent one small fishing boat into the north harbor during the day to make it appear that everything was normal. After spending so much time and energy planning this raid and coordinating with British naval gunfire and Marine Corps air support, we wanted to make sure we did nothing to arouse the NKPA before morning.

The attack force would be divided among four sail junks. Although these boats were balky and undependable, they were the safest means of getting close to the coast without arousing the suspicions of the NKPA since local fishermen also used them. The wooden side boards on the boats were six inches thick and would stop small-arms rounds, giving us some measure of protection if we were fired on before we reached the beach.

During the afternoon the partisan squads made their way to the south harbor to get their boat assignments and load their weapons. Two .30-caliber machine guns would provide some fire support when we attacked the NKPA machine-gun positions. But our weapons were an odd mixture of American, Chinese, and Russian rifles and submachine guns with a few old World War II Japanese rifles.

Each man carried one hundred to one hundred and twenty rounds of ammunition and at least four hand grenades. I carried ten fifteen-round clips for my M1 carbine taped together by twos for fast changing, two hand grenades, and a .45-caliber pistol.

Shortly after dark the sail junks were moved from the south harbor to the north harbor, and at about eight P.M. the men began loading. Each partisan rechecked his equipment once on board to make sure it was tied down, strapped down, or taped down. We would have to infiltrate past two NKPA observation posts to get into position behind the gun before dawn and any metallic clanking could be disastrous for the entire raiding party.

I went over my own uniform and equipment once again to ensure that I was not the loose cannon on the raid. I wore Korean tennis shoes, fatigue pants taped tightly around my ankles, and a black Korean coat over a short-sleeve fatigue shirt. I carried my .45 in a Korean holster and had the ammunition for my carbine stuffed into my coat pockets.

I also had my dog tags around my neck and my military identification card in my fatigue pocket, although I had no real hope that if captured I would be treated as a prisoner of war. NKPA radio had repeatedly warned that Americans caught behind the lines with partisans would be treated as spies, not as POWs. Even my own troops might have arrested

me for being out of uniform or mistaken me for a North Korean infiltrator. In the dark, with my face and hands blackened by charcoal, I was
virtually indistinguishable from my Korean companions.

When all the men were aboard, Mr. Pak and I shook hands and
climbed into our boat. At eight-thirty the boats weighed anchors and
set sail. Next stop: North Korea.

It was a good night for a raid. The light from the quarter moon was
obscured by cloud cover. We could barely make out the dim outlines of
the other boats, less than twenty-five feet away, as we moved out of the
harbor and into the channel.

Pushed by a five-knot wind and a three-knot tide, the boats soon
became separated. The boat with Mr. Pak and me and one other boat
remained close together. But a lighter boat with larger sails soon outdis-
tanced us. And the fourth boat, the oldest and heaviest, was lagging far
behind.

"We've got to keep these boats together," I told Mr. Pak, chastising
myself for failing to tie the boats together before we left. "If we don't
we could land as much as a mile apart and that will increase our chances
of being spotted."

Mr. Pak agreed and ordered our two boats to circle. We hoped the
slower boat would catch up and the faster one would drop back to find
us. We were little more than fifteen minutes out of the harbor and
already the mission was having problems. Were it not for my previous
experiences with these temperamental sail junks I might have considered aborting the mission right there. But these boats, while a continual
problem, were also our only transportation in these waters.

We circled for another fifteen minutes without spotting either of the
other two boats. I decided to push on to the mainland. We had sailed
only a few minutes before we overtook the older, slower junk.
Somehow it had passed us unnoticed in the dark. I gave the order for
the three boats to be tied together. As we got closer together the crews
of the two faster boats began chewing out the crew of the slower boat,
precipitating an argument that got louder by the second.

"No talking and no smoking for the rest of the trip!" I ordered.

Mr. Pak issued the order and there was immediate silence except for
the waves slapping against the hulls and the boats' rigging banging
against the masts. No sooner had we secured the boats together than
the hull of the fourth boat loomed out of the darkness less than twenty
feet away, heading straight for us.

"Turn! Turn!" the partisans shouted at one another in Korean.

The two boats turned in opposite directions but banged hard along
the rails. We did a quick inventory and found that the impact had damaged both boats, knocked the partisans off their feet, and tossed some
weapons into the sea. But no one was injured. We pulled extra weapons

from belowdecks, tied all four boats together, and set out for the mainland again.

As we approached the North Korean coast the dark mountains of the
peninsula loomed over us. Above us and off to the right was the mountain where the artillery piece was hidden. I could not see it in the dark
but I could sense it. So could Mr. Pak's partisans. The closer we got to
the beach the quieter they became. They clutched their weapons and
prepared to slide over the side into the chilly water. They had all been
through this before. Most had been on at least ten raids of squad or platoon size against the NKPA, so I had no doubts about their abilities
under fire.

We were three hundred yards from the beach when the white signal
lights from our two agents waiting there indicated that it was safe to
land. The cloud cover was holding and the boats had not been spotted
by the two NKPA observation posts five hundred yards inland. This was
a critical moment. Once we started for the beach there was no way we
could turn those old junks around if we were spotted. None had
engines.

We cut the tow ropes and the boats began drifting apart as the captains let the tide and wind carry them to the beach. The sound of waves
pounding on the sand grew louder. The surf was running higher than
normal, covering any noise from the boats or the men.

As soon as the big junk scraped bottom Mr. Pak and I and twenty
partisans slipped over the side into the water. We held our weapons and
ammunition above our heads as we waded through the pounding surf to
the beach. About thirty of the partisans had already assembled on the
beach and were moving inland behind one of the agents.

As Mr. Pak and I emerged from the water we saw about a dozen dark
forms coming down the beach toward us. My first thought was that this
was a beach patrol that had spotted our boats. We scrambled for cover
behind some rocks but held our fire.

First the boats, now this, I thought. This raid seemed doomed.

The men stopped about ten feet from us and began talking quietly
among themselves. Mr. Pak listened for a moment before realizing these
were our men. In our haste to get to the beach we had not noticed that
one of the junks drifted about a hundred yards north of the landing
area. Only the fire discipline of the partisans had prevented a mishap
that would have resulted in a number of friendly casualties and forced us
to abort the raid.

We assembled the remainder of the men and began moving inland.
The two NKPA observation posts were on small knolls about two hundred yards apart and five hundred yards inland.

We moved quickly in single file to a point about fifty yards from the
NKPA guards. The agent leading us motioned us to stop and indicated

that we would have to crawl through an open area past the guards for about one hundred yards until we reached a tree line. I slung my carbine across my back, tightened the strap, made sure nothing else was loose, and dropped to my stomach.

The infiltration route was rocky, with small bushes providing some cover. Several of the partisans moved on ahead of me. They were incredibly quiet as they moved across the rocky ground, reaching out with each hand to find obstructions and moving them aside before they continued on. They were like deer moving in the forest, so quiet they seemed a part of the landscape.

I was probably the noisiest of the 120 men on the raid, but the wind blowing in the pine trees and the surf pounding on the beach covered whatever noise I was making. As long as we didn't stand and present a profile we had a good chance of getting past the guards undetected.

I was about halfway across the open area when I stopped and looked up at one of the posts. A guard lit a cigarette, illuminating his face for an instant as the match flared. He was young and looked tired or bored. He obviously had no idea that 120 heavily armed partisans were crawling past him at that moment.

Mr. Pak tapped me on the foot and motioned me to move on. Just as I began to move the guard stood and walked toward me. I thought he had heard me. But the guard merely stretched his arms and continued to puff on his cigarette. I carefully moved on to the tree line.

One of the agents was waiting there and motioned for me to keep moving along a small trail. I checked my watch. It was one A.M. We still had three and a half hours to reach our positions north of the guns and call in the fire coordinates for the British navy and the Marine Corps aircraft.

We moved out in single file through the pine trees. The route was steep and rocky as we moved north around the side of a small mountain. But we were able to move quickly because there were no NKPA guard positions in this area. Once we got past the mountain we turned east and walked several hundred yards to our preraid positions about two thousand yards north of the target. A line of mountains blocked our view of the gun but also shielded us from the NKPA and would provide protection from the naval gunfire. When the British navy started firing, the attention of the NKPA would turn seaward and we would be able to infiltrate their positions from the rear.

The artillery piece was now between us and the Yellow Sea. We had succeeded in moving 120 men through enemy lines without detection. The only problem was that if we were discovered we would have to fight our way back to the beach through the NKPA positions.

We were organized into three teams for this raid, each with a specific mission that would determine whether we succeeded or failed. One team was to attack the NKPA machine-gun position to our left front. The second team was to attack the NKPA soldiers defending the artillery piece to our immediate front. The third team, which included Mr. Pak and me, would start out in reserve and pass through the second team after it had broken through the NKPA defenses guarding the artillery piece.

The third team was the key element in the attack. Our job was to overrun the gun position, destroy the underground bunkers and ammunition storage areas, and cover the withdrawal to the beach. This was to be the first test for the partisans as a light infantry unit assaulting a fortified position. It was an ambitious plan, but I was confident they could do it.

It was about two-thirty A.M. when I returned to the temporary command post set up behind the mountain. The clouds had lifted and the quarter moon gave us just enough light to enable us to distinguish a man from about fifty feet away. If the cloud cover had lifted while we were at sea we would never have been able to make the landing. The sail junks would easily have been spotted in that light.

The only sounds I could hear were crickets chirping and the wind blowing in the trees. Except for my interpreter, I could see none of the other men. They had melted into the landscape they knew so well. I took off my soft fatigue cap, hung it on a nearby limb, and leaned back against a pine tree.

The minutes ticked by with agonizing slowness. I shivered in the night air and looked at my watch again. It was three-forty A.M., less than an hour before I was to call in the naval gunfire.

Suddenly, one of the agents came running into the area, speaking rapidly to my interpreter in Korean.

"A patrol is coming; seven men," the interpreter said.

I relayed the message through the interpreter for the agent to alert the other men to hold their positions and not fire unless fired upon.

I grabbed my hat off the branch and slid into a ditch under a small bush about ten feet off the trail. I eased the barrel of my carbine over the lip of the ditch and slipped off the safety. From my vantage point I could see about fifty feet up the trail.

Just as I settled in, the patrol came meandering along. The seven NKPA soldiers were moving at a leisurely pace. I could tell from how they were moving that these were soldiers doing a job they thought was of little importance. They were carrying their weapons carelessly and were looking for a place to rest.

The place they found was right in front of me. One of the soldiers moved toward me and my finger tightened on the trigger. Then he leaned down and propped his weapon against a small tree. I could have reached out and grabbed him at that moment. But he walked back to the group and they all broke out cigarettes and lit up. I began breathing again and eased my finger off the trigger.

I understood just enough Korean to realize that the soldiers were talking about Wollae-do and the partisans. But it was obvious they thought we were still on the island. My interpreter later told me the soldiers complained about the futility of these patrols because there were no forces on the island that would dare attack their fortress. It was too strong and the beach guards were too vigilant.

The soldiers sat and smoked for no more than ten minutes, complaining all the while about their duty as only soldiers can complain. But it seemed more like ten hours. I could not move and barely dared breathe.

Finally, the NKPA soldiers shouldered their weapons, hitched up their gear, and walked down the trail. I waited about five minutes until I was sure they were clear of our positions before rolling out from under the bush. My right leg collapsed under me when I tried to stand. It had gone to sleep. I rubbed some circulation back into it and checked my watch again. It was four-fifteen A.M.

The first hint of sunrise was beginning to lighten the sky to the east. It would not be long before the NKPA guards on the beach would spot the British ship moving into position.

I motioned to Mr. Pak and we crawled to the top of the hill overlooking the artillery piece and the bunker complex. From there we could call in the naval gunfire and air support but would have protection against errant rounds.

We reached the top of the hill at four-twenty A.M., just as our agents were cutting the four telephone lines linking the bunker complex with the machine-gun position to the east, the reserve company to the north, and two guard posts south of the gun. This would divert the NKPA's attention but would not give them enough time to figure out what was wrong before we opened up.

The bunker complex housing the 76mm artillery piece was just as the agents had described it. The bunkers were built into the side of the mountain. On the south side, facing Wollae-do, was the cave housing the big gun with its steel doors closed against artillery and air attacks. There was a sheer cliff about ten feet high extending around the southwest side of the mountain. Firing positions for men in the bunker extended all around the mountain. From the top of the bunker the mountain sloped gradually up to the machine-gun position.

Two soldiers manned the wheeled 7.62mm heavy machine gun atop the bunker. One was holding the telephone to his ear and the other was looking over the side of the bunker in puzzlement. The lines had been cut.

I shifted my view to the base of the bunker and saw the trenches and stacks of barbed wire surrounding it. This would be a more difficult assault than I had thought.

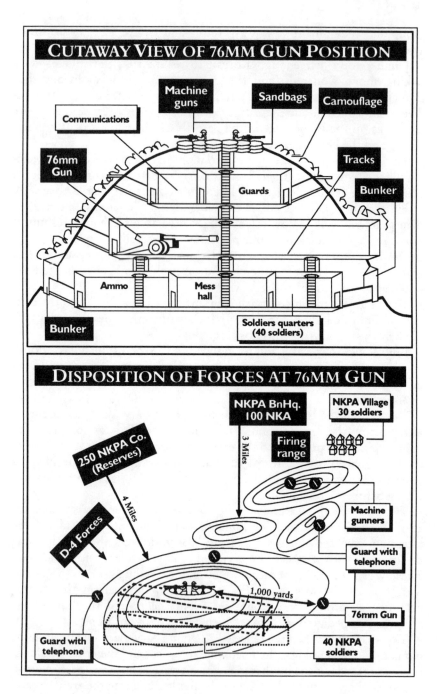

It was four twenty-five A.M. when I crawled away from the crest of the hill. I took the British radio from my radio man, hooked up the antenna, and propped it against a tree.

"Bulldog, this is Rebel. How do you read me? Over," I said into the transmitter.

Tom Dye's reassuring voice came crackling back immediately.

"Rebel, this is Bulldog. I read you loud and clear. Over."

"Bulldog, this is Rebel. We are in position and have not been observed. You will fire on targets one and two at oh-four-thirty hours. Shift fire to targets three and four at oh-four-forty-five hours. Lift your fire at oh-five-hundred hours and remain on call. Direct air strikes on primary air targets one and two at oh-five-hundred hours to oh-five-ten hours. Have air cap remain in area on call from Rebel."

I also told Dye that the aircraft were free to shoot at anything moving east and north of the "no-fire" lines I had established as perimeters for the mission.

"Good shooting," I offered. "Out."

Dye acknowledged my transmission and signed off.

I crawled back up the hill for another look at the gun position. There were soldiers everywhere now. A group of about thirty was exercising in a small open area beside the bunkers. The two manning the machine gun atop the bunker had stopped worrying about the communications problems to heckle the soldiers doing morning PT. In the waters off the coast the outline of the British ship was barely distinguishable. But neither the assault force nor the ship had been spotted yet.

I motioned the leaders of teams one and two to move into position behind two small hills that would protect them from the gunfire and keep them out of sight of the NKPA. If we could convince the NKPA guards that this was just another naval bombardment they were likely to button up in their bunkers.

Our agents told us that the last time this position had been hit by naval gunfire the NKPA had rolled the 76mm gun back into the cave, shut the steel doors, and holed up underground until it was over. If they did it again this time we would have time to break through the perimeter defenses. If not, we were in for a long day.

At exactly four-thirty A.M. the first round from the British ship's guns was fired. It was short. It hit about three hundred yards in front of the bunker without exploding, ricocheted over the top, and exploded about five hundred yards on the other side with a thunderous boom that split the morning wide open. The NKPA looked around, startled. They were caught out in the open as six of the ship's big guns opened up.

The first volley was right on target, knocking down six soldiers in geysers of smoke and dirt. The explosions rocked the ground under us. The other soldiers dived into the trenches. The guns had poured a continuous rain of fire and steel on the NKPA for five minutes before I saw that the bombardment was not having its desired effect. The troops were hunkered down in the trenches, cut off from the bunker. We needed them inside so they could not observe our movements.

I ordered the British to shift their fire to targets three and four to give the troops time to get inside. As soon as the fire shifted, heads popped out of the trenches to see what was going on. One by one the NKPA climbed out of the trenches and raced across an open field to the safety of the underground bunker. All but five left the trenches. For whatever reason, they elected to remain out in the open.

I shifted the fire back onto the NKPA trenches, hoping to take care of the holdouts before we began the assault. For the next twenty-five minutes the British guns worked over the artillery position, keeping the NKPA holed up deep in their bunkers.

At precisely five A.M. the British ceased firing. Even before the rumble from the last explosion had died away I could hear the deep growls of three U.S. Marine Corps Corsair aircraft approaching from the west. In single file they swooped low over the bunker, firing rockets and machine guns. With a half turn to the right they were back out over the Yellow Sea.

I picked up the radio and ordered the planes to make another pass over the bunker.

"Tell the pilots not to fire on the troops moving out of the woods north of the bunker and keep those rockets on the south side of the bunker," I said.

I motioned the two teams to move out. The partisans swarmed over the top of the hills through the pine trees. I knew where they were but could barely see them in the dim predawn light. I grabbed my carbine and the radio and crawled over the top of the hill and down the other side.

I was about fifteen hundred yards from the gun position when the Corsairs came through for their second run. Their rockets exploded on the south side of the bunker just as I had asked. Several of our men were already cutting lanes through the perimeter wire.

Just as Mr. Pak's point man got through the wire the five NKPA soldiers in the trench raised their heads to see if the planes were coming back for another run. They quickly spotted the forty partisans cutting through the wire. One of the NKPA soldiers raised his burp gun and fired a quick burst. Our point man crumpled. The partisans caught halfway through the wire reacted instantly. Machine-gun and rifle fire drove the defenders back into the trench. Partisans just entering the wire tossed grenades into the trench, killing two of the NKPA and keeping the others pinned down.

We actually had gotten farther than I thought we would before being discovered. I had hoped to reach the outside of the barbed wire without being seen. Once there I felt the partisans in the tree line with the .30-caliber machine guns and M1 carbines could provide a base of fire that would enable us to cut through the wire. We were already through the wire and had only three men to take care of before we got into their trenches.

The grazing fire from the tree line kept the NKPA pinned down in the trenches as the partisans finished cutting lanes through the wire. Four of our men got through and dashed for the trenches. We shifted our fire to keep it about three feet in front of them as they dashed forward. The four paired off, each team heading for one of the trenches. Back-to-back, they rolled into the trenches, firing their Chinese burp guns on full automatic as they dropped in. The remaining three NKPA soldiers were easily dispatched and the assault team swarmed into the trenches.

The NKPA holed up in the bunker had responded slowly to the ground assault. Not until our men were in the trenches did the defenders realize that this was something more than a run-of-the-mill naval and air bombardment. What they had considered to be an impregnable position was under ground attack—from the rear, no less.

I figured there were at least nineteen NKPA still in the bunker. There had been thirty outside before the naval bombardment began. Six died in the initial salvo and we had accounted for five in the trenches. Although the NKPA defenders were outnumbered more than four to one, they had the advantage of the bunker.

I had gotten about halfway through the barbed wire when a burst of machine-gun fire from the top of the bunker drove me to the ground. The NKPA were manning all the firing positions and had gotten men to the heavy machine gun. They had a clear field of fire from the top of the bunker.

A small sand dune gave me some protection, but it was being chewed up by the machine gun. I was one of about ten men caught out in the open. I tried to make myself as small as possible but it was not doing much good. The machine gun seemed to be looking for me. It had us stymied. If we did not knock out that gun the attack would falter right there and we would lose a lot of men.

Some of the partisans had reached the base of the bunker and were tossing grenades at the firing ports. But the grenades were having little effect. Several other partisans moved around to the base of the cliff on the southwest side of the mountain, where they were shielded from the machine gun.

One partisan tossed a grappling hook on top of the bunker. It hooked onto a wooden beam just below the crest of the cliff and held fast. He slung his Thompson submachine gun over his back and scrambled hand-over-hand up the cliff face. He avoided the firing positions in the bunker and reached a small plateau about five feet below the crest of the mountain and the machine-gun position.

The partisan slid the Thompson off his shoulder and popped up behind the gun. A quick burst cut the gunner in half. But before our man could turn and fire again, an NKPA ammo bearer opened up on him with his burp gun. The gallant partisan caught the burst full in his chest, and he was killed instantly.

The NKPA quickly reinforced the machine-gun position with four men. I knew we had to do something or we would get chewed up in a hurry. We were too close for naval gunfire, but I thought the Marine Corsairs might be able to help us out.

I rolled over to get the radio off my back and the NKPA let loose with at least two hundred rounds in my direction, reducing my little protective dune to a handful of sand.

"Bulldog, this is Rebel. Do you read me? Over," I said as calmly as the circumstances would allow, hoping none of the NKPA machine-gun rounds had damaged the radio.

"Rebel, this is Bulldog. We read you loud and clear. Over," came the reply.

I hastily outlined the situation and instructed the planes to make two firing passes, machine guns only, on the top of the bunker.

"On the second run come in low but fire high over the bunker," I instructed. "We plan to rush the position as the planes pass over and try to take them by surprise. Out."

I passed the word to the men through the interpreter that we were to rush the bunker as the planes made their second pass. I knew it was risky but it was our best chance. The NKPA held the high ground and the firepower advantage. If we were able to knock out that machine gun before their reinforcements arrived we could gain control of the bunker complex. I only hoped those Marine pilots would be accurate with their fire, because there were a lot of partisans lying out in the open.

Within minutes I could hear the planes coming in from the west. The partisans dived for the trenches as the Corsairs roared overhead, their machine guns chattering. The NKPA spotted the planes and dived for cover long before they were within firing range. It was just the reaction I had been hoping for.

The planes swept out to sea and turned for the second run. The NKPA resumed firing at us until they saw the planes heading their way again. As the defenders dived for cover the partisans surged out of the trenches toward the bunker. Three more grappling hooks hit the top of the bunker and men started scrambling up. I figured we had no more than twenty seconds to get to the top of the mountain and knock out the machine gun.

The first plane passed overhead, its machine guns firing over the top of the bunker. The second and third planes followed suit just as I had asked. By the time the third plane passed over we had at least twenty-five partisans on top of the bunker. The partisans climbing the ropes were throwing hand grenades in the windows and jumping inside after the blasts. I could hear Chinese burp guns and Thompsons chattering at one another and the dull thumps of exploding grenades inside the bunker as the partisans and the NKPA fought room-to-room.

I had cleared the barbed-wire fence and reached the base of the bunker as the first plane passed over. I climbed the rope behind the first wave of seven men and reached the plateau just below the machine-gun position as the partisans lobbed grenades into it. The grenades exploded almost simultaneously with a roar, spewing smoke and debris high into the air.

I clawed my way through the acrid smoke with the seven other partisans and found the four NKPA defenders sprawled lifeless around the upended gun. We now had control of the top of the mountain, although a fierce firefight was still raging inside the bunker.

Three of the partisans opened the trapdoor leading down into the bunker and I followed. I was only about waist-deep into the bunker when a burp-gun burst cut down the lead man and wounded another in the leg. I did a diving roll back onto the top of the bunker, the two remaining partisans right behind me. I called for a medic for the wounded man, then pulled a pin on a grenade, dropped it into the bunker, and shut the trapdoor. The explosion ripped off the trapdoor as smoke and dust boiled up out of the bunker.

As soon as the smoke cleared I went back down the ladder. The inside of the bunker was a shambles. Two NKPA soldiers were lying in a heap in a corner where the grenade had caught them. I pulled their ID cards from their pockets and moved into the next room.

I was met there by other partisans who indicated they had swept the bunker and it was now in our hands. The fight had been vicious but short. The NKPA defenders had been overwhelmed by the ferocity of the assault.

I examined the bunker, amazed by its construction. Neither the ship's guns nor the aircraft rockets had had the slightest effect on it.

The partisans were moving from room to room, examining the bodies and searching for intelligence documents. There were piles of paper everywhere. Our intelligence specialists were going through them, stuffing what appeared to be important into large bags to take back to Wollae-do. I pulled an NKPA flag from one wall, a Soviet flag off another wall, and a hand-painted canvas picture of Joseph Stalin off a third wall and stuffed them inside my coat.

Our demolitions men were placing C-3 plastic explosive charges to blow the bunker. Holes were cut in the corners of the concrete ceiling in each room, the charges stuffed inside and sealed with wet clay. The force of the blasts would be upward, ripping loose the ceilings on all three levels and sending them crashing onto the floors below.

I found Mr. Pak in the cave that housed the 76mm artillery piece. He was supervising the placing of the incendiary charges in the barrel of the gun. I could tell from the look on his face that the raid had been worth it. This gun had been harassing Wollae-do for more than a year, killing troops and oxen and destroying buildings and supplies.

"I would like to take this gun and ammunition back to Wollae-do, but we do not have the time to get it to the beach," Mr. Pak said. "Besides, it would not fit very well on our sail junk."

When the last charges were set Mr. Pak passed the word to clear the bunker. We moved to the south side of the mountain. From there I could see the British ship sitting offshore like a protective mother. I radioed that we had secured the bunker and were about to blow it.

I could still hear firing from the northeast, where our other team had attacked the machine gun position and supply bunker, and knew we had to move over there and help them before we began the movement to the beach.

The incendiary charges in the 76mm gun were set off first. They burned out the barrel and damaged the block, rendering the gun useless. Then the remainder of the charges went off in a deafening roar, throwing rocks and smoke more than fifty feet into the air. As the last echoes of the explosion drifted across the ridge lines we could hear a low rumble from inside the mountain as the bunker imploded. The top of the bunker collapsed and continued to fall until it came to rest about twenty feet lower than it had been. The mountain had been turned inside out. There was no more artillery piece and no more bunker.

But before we could congratulate ourselves on the victory one of the partisans from the other team came running up.

In rapid-fire Korean he told Mr. Pak that the team had run into a three-man patrol before it got to the machine gun position and the ensuing firefight had alerted the defenders. The partisans were caught outside the barbed wire and were pinned down and taking casualties.

A quick hand signal and a few yells got the remaining partisans moving at full speed in the direction of the machine gun position with Mr. Pak and me out front. We approached from the west using a small hill to conceal our movement.

Mr. Pak and I dropped to the ground as we neared the crest of the hill and crawled the remaining few yards to the top. Peering over, we could see that the machine gun was well protected with overhead cover and that barbed wire was strewn across a minefield around it.

I yelled for the demolitions squad to bring up some charges and Bangalore torpedoes to blow holes in the wire and set off the mines. The only problem was that there was no way to approach the wire without being exposed to the fire from the machine gun.

I called Bulldog and told him to bring the planes back for another firing run, this time on the machine gun position five hundred meters east of the main gun position we had just blown.

"I will mark the bunker with red smoke. Hit the bunker with machine-gun fire. All troops moving outside the barbed wire are friendly so concentrate on the bunker."

Bulldog acknowledged and signed off.

The demolitions team indicated it was ready, so I borrowed an M1 rifle from one of the men and fired a smoke grenade at the bunker. It bounced on top and began gushing red smoke. The partisans broke out white marker panels to indicate friendly positions just as we had practiced. Within two minutes the first plane was in sight.

It came in low, machine guns ripping up the earth around the bunker. The NKPA soldiers left their positions and dived for cover. The demolitions team raced out and placed the charges in the wire. It took them no more than fifteen seconds to set the charges and get back. The resulting explosion blew a large gap in the wire.

Without any further instructions Mr. Pak and I and the remainder of the partisans were up and running for the wire, firing as we went. The third plane swooped in for its firing run, and the rounds from its gun began bouncing all around us. We hit the ground until it passed and then were up and running again.

The NKPA machine gun opened up on us almost immediately. But there were so many targets the gunner could not move his gun rapidly enough. He tried to fire at all the attackers at once. The result was that he fired wildly, hitting almost no one.

The original team that had been pinned down began cutting through the wire from the north and the gun swung in that position. That gave two of our demolitions men an opportunity to dash through the wire with antitank mines rigged to explode on impact.

They were just a few feet from the machine gun when they tossed the mines. The top of the bunker blew off with a roar. The two partisans were blown backward by the explosion and killed instantly. But their sacrifice saved us a number of casualties.

As we approached the bunker, detonations continued to shake the ground. Ammunition in the underground bunkers was cooking off. Finally, there was one huge blast that shook the ground like an earthquake and created a large hole in the ground just to the east of the machine-gun position. We apparently had found the NKPA's main ammunition supply point.

The partisans moved into the bunker to mop up. But as they did so two NKPA soldiers popped out of spider holes behind us to the west and began spraying the area with their burp guns. My radio man was hit in the leg and went down. Bullets were tearing up the ground and ripping the bark off trees behind me.

I spun around, falling to the ground and opening up with my carbine. Four of the partisans also returned fire almost immediately, while two others tossed grenades at the spider holes. Within seconds the two NKPA soldiers fell back into their holes, dead.

A three-man NKPA patrol reporting back to the bunker stumbled into the area and we exchanged some sporadic fire with it before the soldiers disappeared into the trees to the north. We decided to let them go and concentrate on the bunker.

The partisans began passing undamaged weapons and ammunition out the top of the bunker to take back to Wollae-do. I got on the radio and informed Bulldog that we had secured this bunker and were about to start moving to the boats. When I asked if the air cap had spotted NKPA reinforcements moving in our direction I got exactly the answer I did not want.

"Rebel, this is Bulldog. Enemy reinforcements have been observed moving through the woods in your direction. They number about seventy-five or more and were last spotted about one half mile from your position. The air cap was unable to catch them in the open so be prepared for a counterattack."

No sooner had I informed Mr. Pak and the team leaders of our predicament when we were hit with a blast of automatic-weapons fire from the tree lines north and east of us. We jumped into the trenches and returned fire, but the NKPA had us outgunned. We could see NKPA soldiers filtering through the trees to the east and south, cutting off our route to the coast and the boats.

The boats were moving into position to pick us up, and I knew that if they continued on course they would come under NKPA fire in just a few minutes. I yelled across the trenches to Mr. Pak to radio the boats to circle in position until further notice. He nodded and picked up his radio. I could see the boats turn and slowly start to circle in place in the water to the south.

We would have no use for those boats if we could not find a way out of the mess we suddenly found ourselves in. We were taking heavy fire from three sides and were in danger of being surrounded.

I crawled down the trench to Mr. Pak to discuss our situation. He let me know that it was worse than I thought.

"We have to break out of here in the next fifteen minutes or else we will miss the high tide," he said. "We can't get those boats in or out without a high tide."

I had few options. We could stay there, miss the tide, and get chewed up piece by piece by the NKPA, who could reinforce at their leisure. Or we could attempt a breakout. Desperate situations sometimes call for desperate measures, and I decided this was one of those times.

"I'm going to bring air strikes in on top of our position," I told Mr. Pak.

He nodded in agreement, no emotion in his face, as if this were something he did every day.

I told him to have the men lay out their marking panels to identify their positions for the planes. The planes would make three firing runs. The last one would be just above our heads and would lead us right into and, I hoped, through the NKPA counterattacking force.

Mr. Pak nodded again and crawled down the trench to pass the word to his partisans.

I called Bulldog and told him our plans.

"Hit the position hard on the first two passes but raise your fire at least ten feet on your third pass," I informed him. "We plan to rush the enemy position during this high firing pass and attempt to break out of the trap."

Bulldog acknowledged and said that the planes would be on target in five minutes.

I spotted Mr. Pak across the trench and held up five fingers to indicate the time. His partisans were already laying out their marking panels. He nodded and went back to work.

The volume of fire was increasing. Any movement in the trenches drew a response from the NKPA. I lay flat in the trench and waited for what seemed like an hour, although it was only a few minutes.

Finally, the first Corsair came roaring toward us. I flattened myself against the trench wall facing the plane's approach just as the pilot fired his rockets and squeezed off the first rounds from his guns. The rounds rumbled across the top of my position, tossing dirt and bark and bits of pine tree on top of me.

By the time the three planes had completed their two firing runs I was covered with dirt and wood from the exploding rockets. I only hoped that the NKPA positions had been hit as hard as mine. If they had, we had a chance of breaking out.

I pushed the trash off me and peered over the lip of the trench. Smoke and dust hung in the air. Parts of shattered trees littered the ground and trenches were caved in all around me. A few NKPA bodies were lying on the hill about a hundred yards from my position, but I could not tell how effective the air strikes had been.

A burst of machine-gun fire stitched the ground in front of my face and drove me back into the trench. I decided to stay there until the planes made their next run. It did not take long. I tightened the grip on my carbine and shifted my weight to be ready to move. I just hoped I wasn't the only one left alive.

When the pilot of the first plane opened up with the machine guns I pushed myself out of the trench. All around me dusty, dirty partisans were swarming over the tops of the trenches. They looked to see if I was still with them. I held a finger to my lips to indicate that our move should be as noiseless as possible until we were discovered. Then I pumped my arm up and down twice, telling them to move out.

The partisans began to run toward the NKPA positions to our south, our most direct route to the boats and the last area the counterattackers had moved into.

The machine-gun rounds from the second plane began bouncing among the partisans and several of them hit the ground. I motioned for them to get up and continue moving.

We were about thirty feet from the NKPA positions when several of the soldiers looked up. I can still see the startled looks on their faces as they realized that about one hundred partisans were bearing down on them at full speed.

The NKPA hesitated only slightly before opening up on us with their machine guns. The first blast swept through our ranks when we were about ten feet from the trenches. Mr. Song, the Donkey-4 chief of staff, who was running next to me, took two bullets in the leg and went down. Two men in Mr. Pak's group were killed and several others were wounded.

We rushed on and piled into the trenches on top of the NKPA. In the next few seconds the air was filled with the screams of wounded men and the grunts and groans of men fighting one another with fists and feet and rifle butts. The fight lasted only a few seconds. Our speed, surprise, and numbers enabled us to easily overwhelm the defenders. We had broken out of the trap and now had a clear path to the beach, although it was about two thousand yards away over rough terrain.

Quickly we collected our casualties as Mr. Pak called the boats to the beach to pick us up. We had six dead and seven wounded, four of whom had to be carried. The partisans never left anyone behind on the battlefield, dead or wounded. The NKPA would do unspeakable things to the wounded. They buried the dead facedown, which the Koreans believed meant they would never get to heaven.

I grabbed the radio and called Bulldog again. I gave him our grid coordinates and told him we were going to start moving toward the beach but that we needed naval bombardment and air strikes to get there. We were taking small-arms fire from the NKPA positions to our north and west. I told Bulldog I wanted the rounds dropped just north of our positions, which we would mark with a red flare.

I told Mr. Pak to have two squads remain in this position while our main force pulled back. Two squads would drop off on a ridge line about eight hundred yards south to cover the withdrawal of the first two squads while the remainder of the men made a dash for the beach.

Mr. Pak gave the orders and twenty men took up firing positions. The remainder of the attack force began moving off the hill toward the beach. I glanced at my watch. It was seven-thirty, only three hours since the British ship had fired the first salvo. It seemed more like three days because we had been under fire that entire time.

We ran to the ridge line to the south. I could hear the air strikes hammering at the NKPA positions behind us. When we reached the ridge I dropped off with Mr. Pak and the two squads that would remain there while the other men continued on to the beach.

As soon as we were in position the first two squads broke contact and began running in our direction. The air strikes were keeping the NKPA pinned down and the partisans were only a few hundred yards from us when the first troops popped up on the hill we had just overrun. We provided covering fire for the withdrawal, then marked our position with a red flare.

The British opened up with the ship's big guns again, plastering the hillside north of us. We could see the NKPA scrambling for cover as the shells exploded. The first two squads passed through us and continued on to the beach. Mr. Pak and I left the two other squads behind and worked our way down a rocky ridge line to the beach.

The loading was going smoothly. Partisans had packed into two of the boats, which were pulling out of the harbor into the open sea. But there seemed to be more people on the beach than the remaining two boats could handle, and we still had about twenty men left on the ridge to evacuate.

While I was trying to figure out how our attacking force had suddenly grown, Mr. Pak immediately sized up the problem—refugees. About thirty local citizens had heard the firing in the hills and seen the boats in the harbor, and hastily packed up all their meager possessions, and headed for the beach. They wanted us to take them with us, no matter where we were going.

I was stunned by this unexpected development. Mr. Pak had never mentioned the possibility that we might have to deal with refugees. The area was relatively uninhabited. Most of the people in this group were used by the NKPA for laborers and had been permitted to stay in the area to farm what little arable land was available.

Many of the refugees had waded out into the water and were trying to climb onto the boats. The partisans on board were yelling at them and pushing them away, trying to keep the boats from being swamped. I could see the fear in the eyes of every one of the refugees. It was the same look I saw in the eyes of virtually every Korean we had encountered trying to escape the mainland and the hardships of life under the NKPA and the Chinese.

But there was no way we could take all of them with us. The first two boats were so loaded with partisans they were in danger of capsizing when they pulled out of the harbor. We barely had room on the last two boats for the remaining men.

Mr. Pak ordered the two remaining boats out into deeper water until the situation on the beach could be resolved. Their captains moved them just beyond the reach of the desperate refugees. Then Mr. Pak asked to speak to the leaders of the refugees. Three older men with wispy white beards stepped forward.

Mr. Pak patiently explained our problem to them. He said we could take ten of them with us now, but the remainder would have to wait until later. We did not have room on the boats. He would send his agents to contact the others in about five days, when the area had cooled off. But the decision of who would go and who would stay had to be made before the NKPA spotted them.

The three old men returned to the group and it seemed everyone started talking at once. After several minutes the ten who had been chosen to go with us stepped forward. The remainder reluctantly picked up their cooking pots and blankets and began walking back toward their homes. Mr. Pak ordered the two boats back to the beach and the loading resumed.

The two squads covering the withdrawal were starting to take heavy fire from the NKPA but still had a clear run to the beach. When all but a few men were aboard I waved my arms at the two squads to withdraw. They did not need to be told a second time. They jumped out of their positions and began a mad dash for the beach, scrambling over the ridge like men being chased by demons.

I waded out into the water and climbed onto one of the junks as the last of our partisans reached the beach. I called Bulldog again and asked for covering fire while we maneuvered the balky junks out of the harbor and into the open sea. The covering force was being hauled aboard one by one, out of breath, exhausted from their dash to safety. They collapsed on the decks of the two boats.

The boat I was on was the last to leave the beach. We had about forty men and several boxes of captured weapons on the junk and were dangerously overloaded. In addition, the wind had dropped, which meant we were not moving. The other three boats were well clear of the harbor and into open water while we were sitting just off the beach, a very inviting target for the NKPA.

The British ship continued to pound the ridges above the beach but we could see the NKPA soldiers dashing from hole to hole and ditch to ditch, working their way toward the beach. It looked as if we had poked a finger into a nest of wasps, and now that we had pulled the finger out the wasps were swarming after us.

Try as we might we could not will the wind to blow or that junk to move. The boat sat there in the harbor like a big fat slug. The raid had been even more successful than I had hoped, but now we faced the prospect of being trapped there and cut to pieces by the NKPA. Once again these rickety boats were putting our lives in danger.

It was only a few minutes before the first NKPA soldiers reached the beach. They dropped behind a small mound of dirt and began firing. As they found the range, bullets began knocking large chunks of wood out of the side boards and chewing up the sails bit by bit.

The boat was so heavily loaded that the tops of the railing were only about six inches above the waterline, and the seas were getting increasingly choppy. Water was splashing over the sides as partisans sprawled on top of one another on the deck, trying to find cover and return fire at the same time.

We had three men working oars, one in the back and one on each side, but we were so overloaded that the boat refused to move. To compound the problem, the tide was beginning to shift and we were slowly drifting back toward the beach.

The British poured fire onto the beach, taking a heavy toll on the NKPA. But their numbers were increasing and now they were beginning to bring up some heavier weapons, including a mortar. The mortar began dropping rounds all around us and I knew it was only a matter of time before the NKPA got lucky and hit us.

I grabbed the radio and told Bulldog to direct his fire on the mortar. The marksmanship was excellent and it took only a few rounds for the British to knock out the mortar. But the volume of small-arms fire increased. If we sat there any longer the NKPA could sink us simply by knocking enough little holes in the boat and sails.

I had just about given up hope of getting out of there alive when the wind freshened, the sails blossomed, and the overloaded junk began ponderously moving out to sea. We lay on the deck, looking up at those tattered sails, seeking divine intervention to get the wind to blow even harder.

Ever so slowly the junk eased out of the harbor and into open water. The sounds of the NKPA guns faded, the last bullets kicking up spouts of water behind us as we peered cautiously over the railing.

When we were finally out of range, the men got to their feet and began cheering and singing and slapping one another on the back. They had reason to be proud of themselves. This motley assortment of farmers and students and teachers with little formal military training had just conducted a major raid against a well-entrenched, heavily armed enemy force with as much precision, spirit, and aggressiveness as I have ever seen in any fighting unit. I was proud to have been a part of it.

As we headed for Wollae-do we passed in front of the British ship that had been so instrumental in our success by providing the naval gunfire and the communications coordination with the Marine Corsairs.

The crew of the British ship lined the rails as our procession of shot-up junks passed. The well-scrubbed sailors stared at us in disbelief. No doubt we looked more like bandits than part of any army. The partisans wore an assortment of uniforms and had bandoleers of ammunition strapped across their chests. The decks of the junks were piled high with clothing, cooking pots, and captured weapons and ammunition. Swimming behind one of the boats were six captured oxen.

"Lieutenant Malcom," one of the sailors shouted in a clipped British accent, "are those your prisoners swimming along behind the last boat?"

The crew erupted in laughter, leaving the Korean partisans puzzled but smiling.

"Malcom and his cattle thieves will sell you oxen steak for five dollars a pound," I shouted back, inducing more laughter among the crew.

"Drop off your captured weapons. We'll take care of them for you," another man shouted.

"I'll trade you a submachine gun for a case of good Scotch," I replied.

The captain of the ship looked over the side, congratulated us on our mission, and asked for a quick summary.

I told him we had destroyed the gun as planned, killed about sixty NKPA, and captured a number of documents and weapons. I thanked him for his support and the accuracy of the ship's gunfire and returned his radio. The crew of the ship waved good-bye and we eased away from the ship on our way to Wollae-do.

The trip back to the base was no less eventful than the trip out. The NKPA gunfire had done far more damage to our boat than I had thought, and we were taking on quite a bit of water. Our boat dropped behind the other three and although we had four men continuously bailing, we were in danger of sinking unless we got rid of some of our load. We finally transferred eight of the men to another junk and were able to limp back into the harbor at Wollae-do.

It didn't matter if we were coming or going, these boats faithfully lived up to their name—junks.

Our boat finally bottomed out just a few feet from the beach at Wollae-do and I slipped over the side and waded ashore into the middle of a wild celebration. The beach was alive with people congratulating the fighters with shouts and slaps on the back as they came ashore.

I had just started to dump the water out of my shoes when I was hoisted onto the shoulders of several of the partisans. They ran down the beach with me, singing and chanting in Korean. I looked back and saw that Mr. Pak and several of the team leaders had suffered the same fate. For the next fifteen minutes we were paraded up and down the beach on the shoulders of the fighters, a prelude to the main victory celebration to come later.

This had been a great victory for the partisans. Not only had they silenced the artillery piece that had been harassing the island for more than a year, they had destroyed the cave and bunker complex to such an extent that it would take months for the NKPA to repair it.

More important for me, the partisans had demonstrated their fighting ability and courage under fire when operating as a light infantry unit. They had worked well with naval gunfire and air support, something they were not used to doing.

Mr. Pak was particularly impressed by the amount of firepower available to us on the raid. Language problems and the reluctance of some Americans to deal with Korean partisans had kept naval gunfire and air support from being a regular part of Mr. Pak's arsenal.

Only if an American accompanied the partisans to serve as a spotter and a communications link was there a chance the additional resources would be employed. But Americans were prohibited from going onto the mainland with indigenous troops to carry out raids. Or so the orders said.

Mr. Pak and I spent the rest of the day debriefing the team leaders and examining the weapons and documents we had captured.

Among the weapons were several new Russian PPSh submachine guns. Although they were the same model on which the Communist Chinese had patterned their Type 50 submachine gun, commonly referred to as the "burp gun" because of the distinctive sound it made, these were definitely Russian and definitely new. Many had been manufactured in 1952 and still had packing grease in their grooves. If those new weapons were getting this far down the line this quickly, it meant the Russians were shipping vast quantities of weapons to Korea.

The documents we captured also proved to be a windfall. There were detailed reports on coastal defenses, troop movements, supply depots, and plans to supplement the troops garrisoned in various areas of Changsan-got. The documents would provide Mr. Pak's raiders, the air force, and the navy with plenty of targets for the next few weeks.

In addition to those documents, we uncovered a few items of interest to the psychological warfare specialists in Seoul.

We found thousands of "safe conduct" passes in boxes in the NKPA bunker complex. These were to be directed at the partisans and ROK

Army forces, urging them to join the North in the war. We destroyed all but about fifty copies.

We found Christmas cards, North Korean war bonds, and new one-hundred-won notes, all of which we sent back to Seoul. The money eventually was counterfeited and tens of thousands of the counterfeit one-hundred-won notes were sent back to us for use by our agents operating on the mainland.

It was nearly five P.M. when Mr. Pak and I finished debriefing the team leaders. Based on our best estimates, the ground combat combined with naval gunfire and air strikes had killed about 225 NKPA and wounded 27. We had destroyed the 76mm artillery piece, two heavy machine guns, the bunker complex, an ammunition depot, a battalion command post, hundreds of small arms, and thousands of rounds of ammunition.

We had lost six killed and seven wounded, three of them seriously, but the mission had been successful beyond our wildest hopes.

As we finished our debriefings I could feel exhaustion overtaking me. I had barely slept in the last three days. I was ready to get back to Leopard Base and crawl into my cot for a few days. But Mr. Pak would have none of that.

"You must stay for our victory celebration tonight," he said cheerfully. "You will be guest of honor and you will have to toast each of the leaders and their men."

I smiled, but inwardly I groaned. That meant another night of endless toasts with Korean whiskey. Every one of the partisans who had survived the raid would want to toast me before the night was over. That would be at least one hundred glasses of whiskey. There just wasn't enough of me to go around.

The only way out of this was to swim back to Leopard Base. Mr. Pak controlled the boats and was not about to let me leave until the raid had been successfully celebrated.

I had learned to survive these Korean parties without too much of a hangover. The trick was to spill about half of each glass of whiskey onto the floor as the toast was being given, then spill another fourth as I was bringing it to my lips. That meant I had to drink only a quarter of a glass, unless I was caught. Then I had to drink a full glass. The more toasts and the longer I lasted, the greater the Koreans thought the party.

It was about midnight when the combination of exhaustion and Korean whiskey overtook me. I slid under the table and into oblivion, although the party went on long after I disappeared.

I was still sleeping on the floor when Mr. Pak finally shook me awake at about seven A.M. the next day.

"Wake up," he said in his usual cheerful manner, "the boat is leaving in about thirty minutes."

I groaned and rolled out from under the table. The morning was bright and sunny. I splashed some cold water in my face to clear away the whiskey cobwebs, and shaved.

I pulled out my binoculars and looked across the strait to the mainland. The bunker complex was a heap of rubble. About ten NKPA soldiers and laborers were digging around it. I scanned the coast and saw no other movement. There would be no retaliatory raids, at least not this day.

The boat ride back to Leopard Base was uneventful and gave me time to reflect on what the raid had meant to Mr. Pak and his partisans.

Its primary purpose—destroying the artillery piece—had been accomplished. But there was far more meaning here.

Mr. Pak and Donkey-4 accomplished things they never could before because of the naval gunfire and air support. That raised Mr. Pak's status in the eyes of the other commanders and with those people on the North Korean mainland who would hear of his exploits. Because of that, he would be able to recruit much more easily.

The raid also eliminated any lingering doubts about Mr. Pak's loyalty. Because of the manner in which he had ascended to the leadership of Donkey-4, Mr. Pak was never quite trusted by the American commanders until after this raid. But from being the most distrusted of the Donkey leaders, he became the most trusted.

Mr. Pak and I became fast friends as a result of that raid. Here was a man I knew I could trust with my life. My mind raced with the possibilities of what we could do. I was prepared to go onto the mainland with Mr. Pak beyond naval gunfire range to hit whatever targets we agreed were essential.

The raid was of significance in one additional area. It sent a message to the NKPA that no longer were they secure in their rear areas. The partisans had demonstrated a capacity to strike fast and hard and in sizable numbers far behind the lines.

If given the opportunity, we could do exactly what partisan forces are expected to do in a traditional war—help shape the battlefield. Whether anyone at Eighth Army Headquarters or the 8240th Army Unit recognized this potential was another question.

Unfortunately, as I came to learn, the American army commanders in Korea looked at the war in a more traditional sense. They either failed, or refused, to grasp the significant role partisan operations could have.

A week after the raid Mr. Pak sent to the Guerrilla Division of the 8240th Army Unit a detailed three-page "Recommendation of Awarding Reward for Meritorious Service" for me (see appendix A).

I have no doubt that this glowing report played a major role in getting me a Silver Star, awarded the following December.

What is interesting about the Silver Star citation is that its writers struggled to come up with wording that could be released to the public yet not jeopardize the highly classified operations of the 8240th Army Unit or Leopard Base.

They finally decided to physically move the location of the raid to "a small island off the enemy mainland" because no one was permitted to know that American military personnel were operating on the mainland of North Korea, far behind enemy lines (see Appendix B).

8

The Logistics Nightmare

One of the most frustrating aspects of working with the partisans was dealing with the army logistics system on which they were dependent for virtually every aspect of their existence. The slipshod manner in which the partisans were fed, clothed, and armed was evident to those of us trying to help them. We were concerned that higher headquarters did not consider them a valuable asset. Despite what we saw as the inherent value of a partisan unit attacking the edges of the enemy stronghold and keeping them off balance, there never seemed to be any great concern about the welfare of the partisans. There was never enough rice, weapons, or clothing to keep the partisans properly prepared to fight. We were on the far end of the logistics pipeline in terms of distance and priorities. What we received was usually late and far less than requested. The orders simply were not filled or there was substantial pilferage along the way.

Lieutenant Colonel Jay Vanderpool was of the opinion that the partisans should be able to live off the land, as had the guerrillas in Burma and the Philippines during World War II.

"It is the principle of guerrilla warfare to live off the land and to resupply from captured arms and equipment to the maximum. Complete logistic support is unnecessary," Vanderpool wrote us in the spring of 1952.[1]

But there was no way the partisans could supply themselves entirely with food and weapons taken during raids on the mainland. The NKPA and the CCF were having their own problems keeping their troops fed and clothed. Food, particularly rice, was also in short supply throughout

Korea, North and South, in 1952. It was terribly unrealistic to expect the partisans to be able to supply themselves in that manner.

We were demanding great sacrifices of the partisans but were unwilling to properly supply them.

The shortages and the late delivery of supplies were little more than inconveniences to the Americans attached to Leopard Base. In addition to my other responsibilities I was put in charge of supplies for the mess hall within the restricted compound. We would get resupplied every seven to ten days by an aircraft from Seoul. The front-line units on the mainland could send their trucks back to resupply points whenever need demanded. We did not have that luxury because of our isolation. And, since we had no aircraft of our own, we were forced to wait for the resupply flight.

When the resupply plane arrived it usually had at least seven days' worth of food on it. Unfortunately, that meant seven days of what had been issued that particular day—ham, turkey, chicken, spaghetti, or whatever the food of the day was. It was not a mixture. It was seven days' worth of one item.

We usually had a good supply of Spam, rice, and potatoes on hand so we could mix those items in when we ran low on other things. The inconvenience came when the weather socked us in and the resupply flight could not make it to the island. Then we had to resort to C rations or Spam done every way imaginable. We had Spam fried, broiled, grilled, battered, in sandwiches, raw, diced, sliced, and ground into Spamburgers and served between two pieces of bread.

But our problems with the logistics system were minor compared to what the partisans faced. When they fled the mainland they left everything behind. Many of them brought out the clothes on their backs and nothing more. They looked to us for help in their struggle for survival. Sometimes we were able to help. Many times we were not.

When the partisans were mustered into fighting units there were not nearly enough weapons to go around. As few as 10 percent of the men in any of those initial units had weapons, and there was no large-scale effort by the Americans or South Koreans to furnish what they needed. Obtaining weapons became the responsibility of individual partisan leaders and members of their units.

Once operations got under way on the mainland the partisans were encouraged to capture as many weapons and as much ammunition as they could. They were allowed to keep what they captured. We provided them with weapons only to supplement what they captured, based on the number of operations they conducted and their successes. The result was a hodgepodge arsenal of old Japanese and Chinese weapons dating from before World War II, some Russian and Chinese weapons of more recent vintage (including PPSh machine guns), and American weapons captured by the NKPA or Chinese in the 1950–1951 winter offensive and recaptured later by the partisans.

Donkey-4's arsenal was typical of what I saw among the partisans. About 60 percent of its weapons had been captured in various raids. If we lined up twenty of Mr. Pak's men in formation they would have at least ten different types of weapons, most of which took different ammunition, presenting another supply problem.

But finding enough food to feed the partisans was our greatest concern. The islands to which the partisans fled at the outbreak of the war were barren and offered no fertile soil for growing rice, cabbage, or any of the other vegetables that are a vital part of the Korean diet. They became dependent on us for their food, except for those few fishermen who had access to boats and could take advantage of the ample supply of fish in the surrounding waters.

It had been determined that the average partisan could sustain himself on about six "hops" of rice per day. A single hop was generally the amount of rice an average man could hold in his hand. Some enterprising soul figured out that there were 288 hops per hundred-pound bag. Partisan fighters were issued nine hops per man per day, with the high command figuring the three excess hops could be traded for vegetables, fish, or kimchi.[2]

Despite our constant need for rice to sustain the partisan operations, our supply never seemed to be more than a trickle. Since we were so far from headquarters and so far down on the list of Eighth Army priorities, it was easy to forget, overlook, or ignore us. Both Leopard Base commanders under whom I served, Majors McKean and Dye, spent a great deal of their time just trying to make an unworkable logistics system function well enough to sustain the partisans on a month-to-month basis.

But part of the reason rice came to us in a trickle instead of a torrent was the great demand for it all over Korea. People were not growing it because of the war. Much of what was being consumed at that time had been imported from the United States. People were starving to death and would do anything for a handful of rice. As a result, the Koreans became incredibly ingenious at finding ways to obtain rice. They did not consider it wrong to steal from the Americans. As long as we controlled the rice it was fair game. Supply officers said the loss and pilferage rate of rice often was as high as 50 percent.[3]

One unique method of obtaining rice was stealing it from a moving train. Rice was usually transported in railcars whose bottoms were made of latticed wood. By lying on the train tracks a single Korean could hold up a long, sharp knife and slice into the rice bags as the train passed over him. Women and children hovered near the tracks until the train passed, then scrambled out to scoop up the rice that had poured out of the cut bags.

There was such a dearth of items of value among the Koreans that they became incredibly adept at "liberating" things from the Americans, especially items they could resell or barter for food or clothing for their families. Had I been put in the same situation I don't doubt for a moment that I would have done the same thing. But it is still amazing to me just how enterprising they were.

This was brought home to me just a few months after my arrival on Leopard Base. I was sitting in my tent one day writing letters. I had a Panasonic Trans-World shortwave radio sitting on a table behind me playing music. A Korean "Slicky Boy," as the thieves were known, crawled underneath the flap of the tent, took a small cheap radio, set it on the same channel at the same volume as mine, and stole my radio. I did not notice that my radio was gone until I reached back to change the channel some time later. In my shortwave's place was this cheap little radio. The Koreans called that "stealing your radio and leaving the music in the air."

The compound was tightly guarded, so I figured the thief had to be one of the ten to fifteen workers we brought in each day to help with various jobs. I immediately rounded up all the workers, took them to the gate, and said through an interpreter that someone had stolen my radio. I did not accuse any of them of stealing it. But I said: "No more work until my radio is returned. Bring the radio back, give it to the guard, and you come back to work tomorrow."

That night, the radio mysteriously reappeared at the guard post. The next morning the Koreans were back at work. No more questions were asked of them.

Since the army had not provided any training or briefings in the culture or the customs of Korea we had to improvise and do what we considered reasonable when faced with these situations.

That threat of group punishment in lieu of singling out an individual and causing him to lose face among his friends and family seemed to work well with the Koreans. That same sort of approach was used later at CCRAK headquarters in Seoul in an incident involving stolen jeeps.

Jeeps were disappearing from CCRAK headquarters faster than they could be replaced, even though they were kept in a locked and guarded compound. Although most Koreans had no formal mechanical training they could steal and strip a jeep far more quickly and far more efficiently than the best American car thief. They could take a jeep and within minutes it would be down to the frame.

The Koreans who worked in the compound were called together and told that if the jeeps were not returned within seventy-two hours there would be no more work for any of them. Before those three days were up CCRAK had its full complement of jeeps back.

They were not the original vehicles, though. An assortment of jeeps from units all over Korea had been turned in at the headquarters compound. The Koreans had simply gone out and stolen jeeps from other units to replace those stolen from CCRAK.[4]

The Slicky Boys were still at it when I returned to Korea twenty years later as commander of a brigade in the 2nd Infantry Division. One day we were having a field exercise near a small village not far from our base. The commanding general of the division sent a large van containing his uniforms and boots to the exercise area as part of a convoy. As the convoy was slowly moving through the village some Slicky Boys hopped on the back of the general's van, opened the door, and stole all the uniforms and boots. By the time the van reached the other end of the village it was cleaned out.

Fortunately, the general had a Korean lieutenant colonel working with him as an adviser. The adviser went to the chief of police in the village and told him that if everything was not returned that day the village would be placed off-limits to Americans. By the end of the day all the items had been returned intact.

At Leopard Base our most serious pilferage problem was with rice. The rice came to us usually once a month by freighter, roughly 4,500 bags in each shipment. We had to carefully watch the rice being transferred from the freighter to smaller sail junks for delivery to the pier, where it was stored in the ramshackle warehouse, or large portions of it would disappear. If the unloading was being done late at night or early in the morning the Korean laborers would think nothing of tossing a few bags overboard to be claimed later by them or their friends. Any rice that spilled out of the bags was quickly swept up and put into a separate pile to be distributed to the Korean workers in our compound. It was not doled out to the laborers for fear of encouraging them to slit open bags, thus increasing the loss rate.

Rice was so valuable it became a medium of exchange. If you had extra rice, you could barter it for almost anything. Rice was also the only way we had to pay the partisans. The more operations they conducted and the more success they reported the more rice they received. Of course, without any independent verification of their claims there was great suspicion that Donkey leaders frequently abused the system with wildly inflated claims of successful missions.

There is a story that made the rounds of Leopard Base of one Donkey leader who became so upset by the constant questioning from his American superior about the veracity of his operational reports that one day he tossed a bag of ears onto the officer's table and said: "Here are your casualties." We also heard a story about one Donkey leader who reportedly collected the heads of the enemy to display to his American adviser to prove the casualty figures.[5]

There may be some truth to these stories, but I tend to believe that both are largely apocryphal, part of battlefield legend carried from war to war. The story of the ears has been told repeatedly in only slightly different versions by Americans who served with native Kachin and Naga tribesmen in Burma during World War II and was told again by Americans working with Montagnards and other indigenous personnel in Vietnam. As for the story of the heads, while it does not seem unreasonable to believe such a thing might have happened on limited occasions, given the brutality sometimes displayed by both sides, I can say that none of the partisans I worked with displayed any such ghoulish tendencies, nor did any other units with which I had occasional contact.

That is not to say that atrocities were not committed by both sides. The NKPA were particularly brutal in their treatment of captured partisans, which is why many wounded partisans who could not be evacuated chose suicide over capture. If they could not do it themselves their friends dispatched them quickly with a single bullet to the head. On several occasions partisans sent to rescue captured comrades found them so horribly tortured they could not be saved. They were mercifully put out of their misery on the spot.

But using body parts to verify casualty figures happened, if at all, only on rare occasions in the partisan end of the war. A more reasonable means of gauging the true effectiveness of individual partisan units was simply counting the number of weapons, boats, and oxen and the amount of rice its members captured. A partisan commander with large stores of rice, a number of head of oxen, a fleet of fishing junks, and a number of Soviet and Chinese weapons was obviously an effective commander because there was no way to get these things other than to take them during raids on the mainland.

No matter how aggressive or successful a Donkey unit might be, it usually found its stores of rice and ammunition running low near the end of each month. The arrival of the rice freighter was the signal for the partisan leaders to come to Paengnyong-do to replenish their dwindling stocks and plead with the Leopard Base commander for more food, clothing, weapons, and ammunition.

Each partisan leader had to be dealt with individually. Each request had to be negotiated separately in the context of what that leader and his unit had accomplished the previous month. Had they done enough to merit more rice, more guns, more uniforms? It was often a very subjective judgment on the part of the Leopard Base commander, sometimes based on how effective a negotiator an individual partisan leader was on that day.

I witnessed several of these sessions, although they were generally the responsibility of the base commander and we American advisers were more than willing to leave the bargaining to him. Some of the sessions went on for hours as the partisan leaders requested all manner of supplies and munitions. The partisans thought that because we were

Americans we could obtain anything we wanted. They believed the flow of supplies from the United States to Seoul and on to Paengnyong-do was unrestricted. Such was not the case, although they never accepted that and could never understand why we could resupply them on only a limited basis.

In the fall of 1952 a group of military historians came to Leopard Base and recorded verbatim one of the sessions between the base commander and a Donkey leader. Although many of the Donkey leaders spoke English, they preferred to negotiate in Korean through an interpreter. Because of the multiple translations the sessions sometimes seemed endless.

The following exchange is only a small part of a session held on November 2, 1952, between Maj. Tom Dye, the Leopard Base commander, and D-16. The questions as recorded were asked by the interpreter on behalf of D-16.

INTERPRETER: He [D-16] wants a squad tent.

DYE: Where's he going to put it up at?

INTERPRETER: Naksong.

DYE: How many people does he have up there? Doesn't he have any tents?

INTERPRETER: He has about thirty people there this week. He says they are having a difficult time.

DYE: They aren't having a difficult time. I'm having a difficult time. And what did Sixteen do last month? Nothing. Why should I give you tents when you do nothing? I think I should give them to people who do something, don't you?

INTERPRETER: He says, yes. He says he'll do much better now that he has a boat.

DYE: He's had his boat two months. I have heard the same excuse before. If he doesn't operate this month, he's through. I won't feed them all winter and nothing done all summer.

INTERPRETER: This month he'll do something.

DYE: If he doesn't he needn't come in next month. He's through! Another party would love his territory.

INTERPRETER: He is confident; he will do many operations. He wants maps of the . . . area.

DYE: All right.

INTERPRETER: Some paper and pencils.

DYE: If I have them.

INTERPRETER: Do you have overcoats?

DYE: No, I don't have overcoats. I'm sorry.

INTERPRETER: One case of hand grenades? Fragmentation.

DYE: Okay. What else?

INTERPRETER: He needs medical supplies.

DYE: How many men did he have last month? How many wounded?

INTERPRETER: No wounded, sir. He used up his medical supplies for patients.

DYE: What patients? What ailed them?

INTERPRETER: Diarrhea, colds.

DYE: But you don't need triangular bandages for colds, or plasma either.

INTERPRETER: Yes, sir. Now he wants explosives, rice, and gasoline.

DYE: Hmm. (Consults records.) Say! How come you got five drums on eleven October, Donkey-Sixteen?

INTERPRETER: That was the first time he had his boat.

DYE: All right. Now, how many drums and empty rice sacks has he brought back?

INTERPRETER: None, sir. They are in the other boat right now.

DYE: (Grimacing, as if in pain.) When is he going to do what I ask him?

INTERPRETER: He never had any gasoline drums or rice bags before.

DYE: Baloney! Buhl-loh-nee! You expect your supplies once a month, don't you, Donkey-Sixteen? Okay, I expect you to bring the drums and bags back.

INTERPRETER: Next month he will.

DYE: He'd better, or he'd better not come back here asking for more. How many drums has he left?

INTERPRETER: Seven or eight of gasoline.

DYE: All right. Next.

INTERPRETER: Seven cases of grenades.

DYE: One is all I can give you.

INTERPRETER: Two cases of TNT.

DYE: What did he do with the last I gave him?

INTERPRETER: He didn't get any.[6]

The session went on like this for some time, covering requests for everything from antitank mines to barbed wire to flares to food. Many of the requests were rejected either because Dye had none of the specific items to give D-16 or he thought by withholding some things he could encourage him to become more active against the NKPA. It was a very subjective exercise and one that had to be handled with equal measures of skillful negotiating and blunt bargaining.

I was happy to leave that bargaining to Majors McKean and Dye. But it was terribly frustrating to try to explain to Mr. Pak and members of Donkey-4 why we were not given the assets necessary to make the most effective use of the partisan units. We had more than fourteen thousand partisans operating off the west coast of Korea by November 1952 and would have had a much more significant impact had we been given such minor things as better boats, aerial photographs of the coastline, or a few additional American NCOs to help with training. But what reached us came in a trickle, not the steady flow for which the partisans or those of us working with them kept waiting.

Years later army analysts went back to try to figure out from 8240th Army Unit records what the partisan operations cost the United States government. They could come up with no figure for 1951. Supplies had been allocated on such an ad hoc basis that there was no way they could even estimate the cost. For 1952 and 1953, respectively, they estimated the cost was $21 million and $71.5 million. Overall cost of partisan operations for three years was estimated at somewhere between $75 million and $125 million.[7]

Using an arbitrary figure of ten thousand partisans per month over a thirty-month period (although the number of partisans did not exceed ten thousand until well into November 1952), that worked out to somewhere between $250 and $400 per partisan per month.[8]

While the analysts considered that an exorbitant figure, based on the limited effect they thought the partisans had on the overall war effort, I don't believe that judgment was fair. We demanded a great deal of the partisans, most of whom had already given up homes and families. We demanded they fight for us and risk their lives in what had obviously become a no-win war. Yet we were unwilling to keep the partisans adequately supplied. To then coldly put a price tag on those sacrifices was typical of the regular army mentality that consistently restricted unconventional warfare operations in Korea.

There was no doubt that some partisans and their leaders abused the American supply system, building personal fiefdoms on some of the more remote islands, especially after it became clear the war would end with a negotiated settlement, not with victory for either side. It is also true that profiteers in the U.S. Army made a great deal of money siphoning off supplies destined for the partisans and other units and selling them on the black market.

But for those of us out in the field working with combat-tested and combat-ready units who were continually running raids on the mainland, harassing the enemy, and keeping him off balance, it was terribly frustrating. We saw how much was being done with such little support and knew how much more could be done if the partisans had been a higher priority at higher headquarters.

There were occasions when a surprise allocation of assets allowed us to demonstrate the types of things we could do with them.

On June 11, 1952, I was running a training exercise near the beach on Paengnyong-do when two Korean PT boats pulled into the harbor. I took an interpreter and went to investigate. The commander of one of the boats said they had been assigned to us for seven days to be used as we saw fit. The boats were assigned to the Wolfpack area of operations to our southeast but were being loaned to us on a limited basis.

I saw some immediate possibilities for their use, as did Mr. Pak. Our slow and unreliable sail junks left us vulnerable to NKPA beach patrols and guard posts. In addition, there were certain areas of the North Korean coast we could not approach because of the shallow water. The boats would run aground too far from the beach, making them and the raiding parties easy targets. These fast-moving, shallow-draft PT boats could operate in as little as six feet of water and were armed with rocket pods and machine guns. The pods each carried sixteen five-inch rockets, which could be fired individually or in a volley.

I sent out word to the partisan leaders to furnish suitable targets near the coast for the PT boats. Within twenty-four hours we had a list of about twenty-five possible targets ranging from a company headquarters complex to artillery gun positions.

The boat commanders were given one target the first night and the partisan leaders reporting back were greatly impressed by the results. The boats, their engine noise muffled, slipped in close to the coast under a cloud cover and hit a barracks area, killing at least ten NKPA.

The next night the two boats were assigned a target in Donkey-4's area of operations about fifteen miles southeast of Wollae-do. One boat would serve as the primary attacker while the other was the backup. I requested and was granted permission by the commander of the attacking craft to accompany him.

The target was a small Korean village about a thousand yards from the coast that had been taken over by a platoon of about thirty NKPA soldiers. They drove out the villagers, some of whom had become refugees under D-4's care, and took up residence in the mud-and-thatched-roof huts.

Two of Mr. Pak's agents had scouted the village sometime earlier and provided us with a detailed sketch map showing the headquarters building, troop billets, ammunition storage area, and the communications shack. The two agents infiltrated back into the area before the raid and set up flares north and south of the village. The plan called for them to light the flares thirty minutes after midnight so the PT boat commander could pinpoint the targets he wanted to hit. The agents would then escape into the mountains to the east through a series of drainage ditches.

Our boat was to be in position about one hundred yards off the coast at midnight. We would wait for the flares to be lit, then saturate the village with five-inch rockets.

It was a perfect night for a raid. There was enough cloud cover to obscure almost all the light from the moon and we could barely see the shoreline. But we could hear the waves slapping against the rocks not far from where the boat rolled over the gentle swells.

We were supposed to receive a signal light from one of the agents at fifteen minutes after midnight that would give us an indication whether we were in the best position for firing on the village. The agent was using a regular flashlight with a disk blocking all but about a quarter of an inch of the lens. When the agent shielded the light with his body and pointed it out to sea, no one else could see it.

The signal came right on time but indicated that we were about a hundred yards too far south. The skipper and I discussed whether we should take a chance, pull the anchor, start the motor, and move to a better position to the north. Or we could shoot from here.

"With the waves hitting those rocks on the beach and with the ventilator covers over the mufflers I am sure we can make the move without being heard," the skipper whispered to me.

He was the boss so I merely nodded in agreement.

The engines grumbled to life, the anchor was weighed, and the boat began creeping slowly north along the shoreline. It took us ten minutes to move a hundred yards, still leaving us five minutes before the flares were scheduled to be lit. But no sooner had we dropped the anchor and settled in than the flare on the south side was popped, providing some illumination but not nearly enough to hit the targets with any accuracy. For about thirty seconds everyone froze, not sure whether to shoot or stand there and watch.

Finally, the second flare went off, lighting up the area. The skipper fired one marking round to measure his distance, adjusted the pods, and began firing at his targets. The rockets zipped out of the tubes in a blinding flash of orange-and-yellow flame. The fifth rocket hit the building in which the ammunition was stored, setting off a series of huge explosions.

The skipper continued to touch off the rockets, blasting the buildings apart and setting the thatched roofs on fire. NKPA soldiers scrambled out of the buildings in a daze, firing blindly in all directions, not sure where the attack was coming from. After the thirty-two rockets had been fired the crew of the PT boat opened up with a .50-caliber machine gun. The surviving NKPA soldiers began to recover, saw they were being fired on from the sea, and returned fire with rifles and burp guns.

We were out of range of small arms but not recoilless weapons, so the skipper decided to end the raid at that point. He cranked up the engines, turned the boat out to sea, and within a few minutes we were well offshore. We sat off the coast and watched the fires burn for about thirty minutes before turning for home. The air force communications and radar people on the highest peak on Paengnyong-do later told us they had seen the giant fireballs from our attack.

The two agents who had set the flares went into the mountains that night, stayed in hiding, then returned to Wollae-do the following night. We learned from them that the first flare had been accidentally tripped by an NKPA guard who apparently heard the boat moving into its new position and went to investigate. The second agent hesitated about thirty seconds before setting off his flare.

We never learned the full extent of the damage from that raid, but it was obvious we had obliterated most of the village, including the communications equipment and ammunition.

The PT boats stayed in the Leopard Base area of operations for a full week. Their last four days were spent on the north side of Changsan-got, hitting targets between Cho-do and the Yalu River. All the reports we received indicated that they were quite successful.

This was another clear indication to me and partisan leaders what could be done with just a few more assets. The old Chinese junks we were forced to use were too slow, too cumbersome, and could not be armed like a PT boat. A squadron or two of fast-moving, heavily armed PT boats crewed by Korean naval personnel, based at Paengnyong-do, and allowed to operate in conjunction with partisan units on the ground would have created incredible havoc with the NKPA coastal defenses.

After that week-long experiment the partisan leaders requested the PT boats every time they came to Paengnyong-do to meet with Leopard Base commander. They wanted rice, rifles, ammunition, clothing, and the PT boats. But we had had our shot with the PT boats. We never saw them again.

The headquarters of the 8240th Army Unit in Seoul. The building's architectural style was as different from that of other Korean buildings as the 8240th was different from other Korean War units. *D. Glenn*

1st Lt. Ben Malcom at the top-secret Leopard Base on Paengnyong-do (Paengnyong Island), 125 miles behind enemy lines. The building behind him shows the scars of an accidental bombing by a Marine Corps F4U Corsair.

Malcom and his guerrillas frequently visited the villages on Paengnyong-do to talk to guerrilla leaders who stayed in them on trips to the island.

Facing southeast from the Leopard Base compound toward the Yellow Sea and a likely avenue of approach for the North Koreans, this bunker was one of several whose machine guns provided interlocking fields of fire.

Pak Choll and the author. Pak was the leader of a donkey unit, one of the
U.S.-backed partisan groups operating along the western coast of Korea from the
Yalu River to the Ongjin Peninsula. Malcom worked closely with Pak's group,
Donkey-4, which comprised about six hundred guerrillas.

Donkey unit leaders and their chiefs of staff at Leopard Base.

Malcom with a platoon of Donkey-4 trainees in their graduation-day finest.

Republic of Korea Army 1st Lt. Cho Byung Chan, Leopard Base's interpreter and the heart of its intelligence operations.

Leopard Base adviser 1st Lt. Robert D. McBride at Paengnyong-do's harbor, with partisan sailing junks at anchor and a dilapidated rice warehouse at the left.

A partisan fishing junk sails past the headlands of Changson-got on the North Korean mainland.

Partisans captured these two artillery pieces from the North Koreans and brought them back to Paengnyong-do on rickety junks.

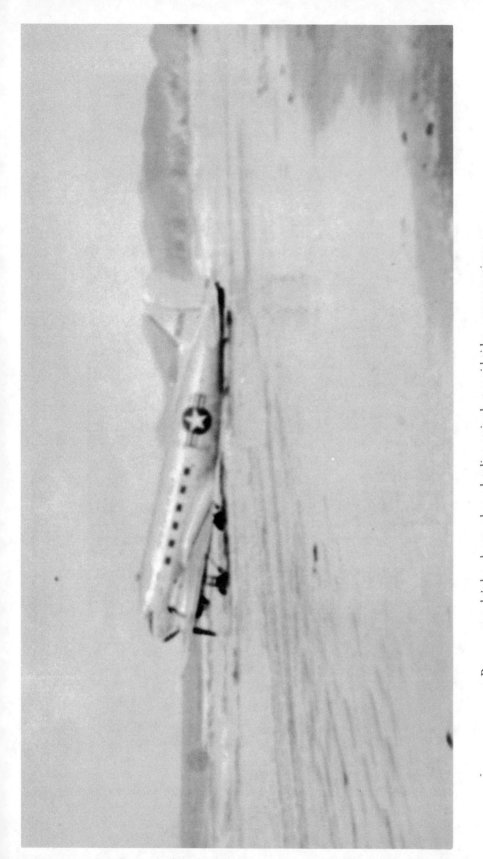

Paengnyong-do's beach served as a landing strip, but rapid tides were sometimes a problem. This Air Force C-47 had to be pulled from the water.

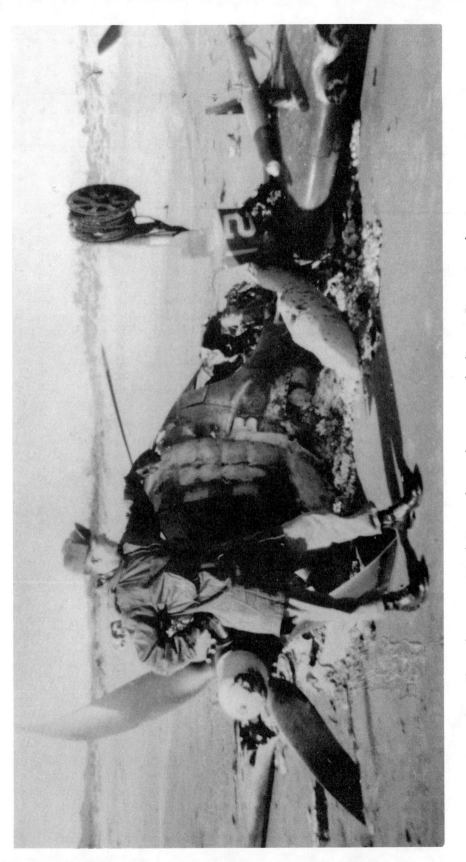

Planes shot up over North Korea often made emergency landings on Paengnyong-do. This Corsair was so badly damaged that Malcom was ordered to destroy it.

The author frequently flew in an Air Force helicopter to rescue pilots downed around Paengnyong-do. He later became an Army helicopter pilot.

1st Lt. Arnold R. Keller, a Leopard Base adviser, after a jump with Korean para-troopers. By late 1952, the guerrillas were developing airborne capabilities.

American advisers to the Leopard Base partisans *(from left)*: Capt. Don Seibert, 1st Lt. Jim Mapp, and Malcom.

The patch of the United Nations Partisan Infantry, Korea, designed by the Guerrilla Division of the 8240th Army Unit. The Army bureaucracy never officially approved it.

On March 3, 1953, Malcom received the Silver Star for bravery in combat, but he lacked a Combat Infantryman's Badge. Deeming special operations combat not real combat, the Army had not authorized the members of the 8240th Army Unit to wear it.

Malcom's final official Army photo. It took him nearly twelve years to convince the Army his special operations experience during the Korean War qualified him for the Combat Infantrymen's Badge. *Department of Defense*

9

The Intelligence War

The Leopard Base mission was an unusual hybrid of combat operations and intelligence gathering. We operated under G-2 of the Far East Command (FEC), but our primary mission was to conduct combat operations on the mainland. Intelligence collection was a secondary mission, even though our agents were among the few in the theater who could penetrate deep into North Korea and provide human intelligence for the 8240th Army Unit and FEC.

The FEC's intelligence was gathered from a variety of sources that included refugees, defectors, and line crossers. But there were few deep penetration capabilities within FEC outside of the Leopard Base operations. The CIA had its own intelligence operation at the time but information its agents gathered was shared on a very limited basis. And the line crossers and airborne intelligence forays designed for deep penetration and run by the 8240th, the latter known as Baker Section, had very little success, as will be seen in later chapters. The problems with trying to get reliable agents deep into North Korea were twofold, no matter which agency attempted it.

The first was that Caucasians obviously could not move around freely among the population of North Korea. The OSS agents in Europe during World War II could easily blend in with the local population simply by donning civilian clothes, but Caucasian infiltrators in Korea were Caucasians, no matter what disguises they employed. They were easily spotted and made wonderful targets.

The second consideration was the tight hold the North Korean security apparatus had on its own people. Even North Korean defectors sent back as agents had great difficulty fitting in after being gone only a few months. By 1952, after the front lines had stabilized, the North Koreans imposed strict controls over the movement of everyone and everything between the front lines and the Yalu River. The simple act of moving from one village to another required a number of different documents that were changed on an irregular basis. Sometimes the documents were color coded. Later in the war the North Korean security police went to an ingenious system of pinholes in the documents. The security personnel would have a key and would compare an individual's documents to that key by holding them up to the light. If the pinholes were not in the right configuration the individual carrying the documents was subject to arrest, torture, and death.

Despite the problems and dangers inherent in behind-the-lines intelligence gathering, there were occasions when FEC determined that the only way to get what was needed was to send in American eyes. Two missions in particular, both limited in scope and duration and done for specific intelligence-gathering purposes, demonstrate the need for such missions and the dangers involved.

The first and perhaps most famous of those missions preceded the Inchon landing in September 1950. Navy Lt. Eugene F. Clark, a veteran of nearly two decades in the Orient and well schooled in the difficulties of amphibious warfare, was recruited from a special planning group working on the invasion to lead a reconnaissance team ashore at the landing site to check tides, mudflats, seawalls, and beach defenses.

Code-named Operation Trudy Jackson, the reconnaissance team included Clark, four U.S. Army personnel, and two Korean interpreters. The team was put ashore on September 1, 1950, on Yonghung-do, fourteen miles south of Inchon. The island overlooked Flying Fish Channel, through which the invasion force would have to squeeze on D day.

A ROKA unit had preceded Clark's team by two weeks and found the island undefended by NKPA troops. When Clark arrived he organized the Korean civilians on the island into what he called the Young Men's Association. This group manned observation posts and ran intelligence-gathering missions on neighboring islands and the mainland. Clark also used a motorized sampan mounted with a .50-caliber machine gun to raid some of the nearby islands and harass NKPA sailing vessels in the surrounding waters.

Clark sent back nightly reports to his headquarters, where planners discovered that their tide charts were wrong. According to Clark's reports, an old Japanese tide chart was far more reliable and the invasion plans were adjusted accordingly.

As the invasion neared, Clark's team pushed on to Palmi-do, which featured an abandoned lighthouse atop a 219-foot peak commanding the approach to Inchon Harbor. Clark lit the beacon the night before the invasion force arrived and escaped safely with his team. He was later awarded the Navy Cross.[1]

Later, in the spring of 1951, another little-known behind-the-lines foray involving an American took place on the east coast. This one was to gather information about a disease ravaging NKPA and CCF troops and civilians. The disease was called "black death" by the Koreans who saw those who died from it, and there was concern among FEC officials that it might be bubonic plague, typhus, or smallpox.

If it was bubonic plague, tens of thousands of United Nations troops and millions of South Koreans would have to be inoculated to prevent the spread of the disease. Typhus and smallpox did not present as much of a threat. Most of the troops had received the serums necessary to prevent those diseases.

In order to gather firsthand information about the disease, Dr. Crawford Sams, an army brigadier general serving as the chief of public health welfare in Tokyo, volunteered to lead a raiding party ashore. He wanted to bring back a black death corpse—or, at the least, a blood sample from a victim.

The team was to go ashore on the east coast, near Wonsan, in March 1951. But nine recon teams sent in ahead of the main party to prepare the way were never heard from again. It soon became clear to Sams and his party, waiting in a boat offshore for nearly two weeks, that some team members had been captured and tortured into revealing the nature of the mission. The NKPA radio broadcasts cited Sams by name and provided numerous details of the operation.

Even though the NKPA knew Sams was coming, he managed to get ashore briefly. And while he was not able to return with a body or a blood sample, he saw enough victims of the disease to determine that they were suffering from smallpox, not the more dangerous bubonic plague. The harrowing mission completed, Sams returned to Tokyo, where he was awarded the Distinguished Service Cross.[2]

My own forays onto the mainland were operations oriented. Intelligence gathering was largely left to the North Korean agents who had some knowledge of the area where they were working and could blend in with the local population. But there was one occasion in May 1952 when I went deep into North Korea by air to assess defenses along the western coast.

I had just returned from five days of rest and relaxation in Tokyo and was on my way back to Leopard Base when Vanderpool intercepted me in Seoul. Vanderpool had asked me to come see him whenever I was in Seoul to discuss Leopard Base operations. Whenever I did he peppered me for hours with questions about the details of what we were doing. He said he would have preferred to be out in the field with the troops rather than sit in a sterile office. But as head of the Guerrilla Division he was resigned to his fate and had to get assessments through me and the few other officers working directly with the partisans.

Vanderpool said since I was the S-2 for Leopard Base, handling more than 90 percent of the intelligence reports that came from our agents in the North, and because we were planning some operations along the North Korean coast, he wanted me to see the area from the air before we actually went in. This personal reconnaissance would take the place of the aerial photographs we were never able to get from the air force.

Vanderpool specifically wanted me to look at the NKPA gun positions on the mainland that were firing on Cho-do to see if we could pinpoint them any better, and check out some of the other defensive positions along the coast. We would be flying to the west of the North Korean capital of Pyongyang, he said, but the pilots had been instructed to stay out of MiG alley, to the north. A B-26 was standing by at K-16 airfield for the trip.

Less than an hour after my meeting with Vanderpool I was aboard a lone B-26 heading for North Korea. We had no armed escorts. I was sitting in the middle of the aircraft looking out a small window and making notes as we proceeded up the west coast when the crew chief came back and said I would have a better view from up front. I grabbed my binoculars, map, and notepad as he motioned me into the crawl space that led to the nose of the plane.

I got to the end of the crawl space and stopped dead. Below me was nothing but green mountains and deep blue water. Ahead and above me was nothing but sky. The crew chief wanted me to sit out in the nose gunner's position. The Plexiglas shell looked as if it would break if I stepped on it.

"Crawl on out into the shell," the crew chief said confidently. "It's hard as a rock."

Gingerly, I stepped into the nose. It did not break, but I was not nearly as confident as the crew chief that it would hold my weight. Slowly and carefully I sat down. Riding out there in a plastic bubble five thousand feet above ground did not seem natural. It was like floating in the air without any visible means of support.

Despite my misgivings I unfolded my map and began comparing it to what I was seeing below me. I could see the area on Changsan-got where Mr. Pak had taken me in March and the area around the 76mm gun position across from Wollae-do we would hit in June.

The farther north we went the more difficult the terrain along the coast. Mountains crowded up to the Yellow Sea, leaving little area for beach landings. I saw a number of fishing boats offshore and oxcarts moving along the roads through the mountains, but no military vehicles.

We had been in the air for some time and were approaching Pyongyang when I looked up from my notepad and saw a series of large red objects floating up toward us in a line. I stared at them for a few seconds in fascination before realizing they were tracers. We were being fired at by NKPA antiaircraft artillery.

The pilot wheeled the aircraft hard to the left toward the Yellow Sea, began some evasive maneuvers, and called for assistance. I felt the plane bump a few times as we were hit. In no time the air around us was red with tracers as other antiaircraft units spotted us and opened fire.

I felt helpless sitting out there. Not only was this Plexiglas nose particularly vulnerable to antiaircraft fire, I had not brought my parachute with me. I gathered up my map, notepad, and binoculars and scooted back through the crawl space to the relative safety of the middle of the aircraft and my parachute.

Before long we were far out over the Yellow Sea. The west coast of North Korea was a vague, blurry blue line of mountains. We flew toward Paengnyong-do in case we had to make an emergency landing on the beach but the plane was still in relatively good shape and we continued on to Seoul.

When we arrived at K-16 the crew inspected the plane and found nine holes in the wings and fuselage from what appeared to be machine-gun rounds. Anything larger would have caused structural damage and probably brought the plane down. If we had been able to get out of the aircraft before it crashed we would likely have become guests of the NKPA.

The crew was relieved to be finished with that mission, but no more relieved than I. Nevertheless, the aerial reconnaissance was invaluable. It provided me with a much better picture of what the partisans would encounter when trying to land in certain areas of North Korea. The next day I returned to Leopard Base via C-47 and went back to training the partisans and writing intelligence summaries.

The Leopard Base intelligence operation had three basic components: the partisans on the mainland, a radio shack on Paengnyong-do manned by Koreans where messages from agents on the mainland were received and translated, and the American communications van inside the secured compound where the translated messages were sent on to Seoul. It was my job to take the messages that had been translated by our Korean interpreter and decide which were sent to Seoul, which were sent to the air force and navy as targets, which were filed away for possible future reference, and which were discarded.

Partisan units sent to the mainland usually took two types of radios. One was the SCR-300, a small, battery-operated unit easily carried by troops on the move. The other was the larger AN/GRC-9, the "Angry Nine," which was carried in deep and set up in remote areas to serve as a relay station between units or individual agents and Leopard Base.

The Leopard Base partisans realized the value of their radios and guarded them with their lives. The radios were their most prized possessions and were treated as such. They would do almost anything to get one of their radios back if they lost it. They considered loss of a radio more serious than loss of a man. Although the interior units were continually on the move, they were careful to protect their radios.

We lost very few radios and I don't recall a single case where we had a problem with false transmission from a captured radio. The airborne operation of the 8240th Army Unit and CIA behind-the-lines operations had frequent problems with captured radios and false radio transmissions. But our partisans never had that problem.

The messages we received from units and agents on the mainland were by voice, usually relayed through one or two AN/GRC-9 operators inside North Korea, then relayed again through our partisan base on Cho-do on the north side of Changsan-got.

The messages were received in the radio shack on Paengnyong-do. The shack, on the south side of the fish market building that once had served as Leopard Base Headquarters, was no more than twenty feet long and eight feet wide. Made of mud with a tin roof and false ceiling, the building had been constructed specifically to house the radios. Running the length of the back wall was a wooden table that held ten AN/GRC-9 receivers hooked to a common generator outside. Depending on the pace of operations, at least three of the radios were monitored at all times. On busy days all ten were monitored. At those times the inside of the shack was alive with radio static and rapid-fire Korean.

Although we had several interpreters, one man was primarily responsible for translating the messages from Korean into English before they were passed on to me. This translation was perhaps the most important step in the process of determining what was sent on to Seoul and what was not.

Cho Byung Chan was a ROK army lieutenant assigned to Leopard Base as an interpreter. Lieutenant Cho was well-educated, well-spoken, and incredibly hardworking, and his command of English and Korean was excellent. It was he, more than any other single person, who kept the Leopard Base intelligence operation functioning efficiently. Even on the busiest days he remained calm and professional. I never saw him get rattled or angry. I never heard him complain. I'm not sure what we would have done without him.

Lieutenant Cho was in great demand by all the Americans to serve as an interpreter, but we tried to restrict him to translating messages because of their importance. I found some Korean laborers who knew a good bit of English to serve on other occasions as interpreters, a job for which I paid them with extra rice. We actually had a number of Koreans who spoke some English. Several of the partisan leaders had taught English in schools before the war, but they never spoke English in our meetings. They didn't want anyone to know they understood or spoke the language because they felt it gave them an edge on us.

Before Leopard Base Headquarters was moved into the secured compound, Lieutenant Cho had a desk in the fish market building where he would translate the stack of radio messages into English before sending them to my desk. When the headquarters moved, Lieutenant Cho came with us. A series of runners brought messages to him that he in turn would translate and send on to me.

The messages generally contained information about operations of individual Donkey units and the intelligence they gathered. Major McKean found that information particularly useful in keeping tabs on which unit was doing what so at the end of the month he had a running total for each Donkey unit. He could then use that tally as leverage at his monthly meeting with Donkey leaders when they tried to get additional supplies from him.

Although it was repeatedly stressed to us in messages from Seoul that operations, not intelligence, was our primary mission, there was a great interest in what we sent back to higher headquarters. At first, I sent back to Seoul much of the information I received. Intelligence officers at the 8240th told me they wanted everything. The result was a flood of short-term tactical information about the movement of small units or truck convoys at certain grid coordinates that was largely useless to the intelligence types in Seoul. As I grew into the job I tried to analyze the intelligence reports from the standpoint of whether they would be useful from a strategic consideration.

Seoul was particularly interested in NKPA officers, their locations, and their movements. Vanderpool on occasion would decide it was time to capture a particular NKPA officer and would send up an order to have some of our people don NKPA uniforms and go in and snatch him. It was actually far easier than it sounds because of the convincing manner in which the partisans were able to play their roles as the enemy.

McKean and Dye were interested primarily in what the intelligence reports had to say about major shifts in troops. I was more concerned with possible immediate targets for ships or aircraft that might be in that particular area. As far as the Koreans were concerned, everything that came in was sent back to Seoul. But it was probably more like 30 to 40 percent, some of which went to the 8240th Army Unit and some to the Fifth Air Force for targeting or the rescue of downed pilots.

Our agents were responsible for at least 80 percent of the intelligence that came through Leopard Base from the mainland. We got the bulk of that information because we were the partisans' only source of supplies. They knew they had to come to us first with the information or risk being cut off. But that did not prevent them from later selling that same information to other American units on the island.

Because of the interservice rivalries that plagued American efforts during the Korean War, each unit on Paengnyong-do ran its own intelligence-gathering operation and shared that information only with its own higher headquarters. The Korean village on Paengnyong-do next to our headquarters was a hub of partisan activity and intelligence gathering by any number of agents. The army's Leopard Base operation controlled most of the agents, but we never had a complete handle on what they were sharing or selling to the other units on the island. All the Americans had their own way of digging out the information, as did the Koreans, and it was not unusual for an agent to sell the same piece of information four or five times.

We shared much of our intelligence on NKPA positions and strength on the mainland with the U.S. Marine Corps unit on Paengnyong-do. It had a need to know because it was responsible for the defense of the island. But the Marines were running their own agents in the villages and on the mainland and we saw virtually nothing of what they obtained.

It was the same with the air force and navy. They were running intelligence operations independent of ours and there was little coordination or communication as to who was going where or doing what. Most of the time there was little conflict because of the huge expanses of water and terrain in which we were working. But there were occasions when that lack of communication had disastrous results. The most serious of these involved agents from other services calling in air strikes on friendly forces. One such incident occurred in late May 1952.

An air force intelligence unit operating from a cabin cruiser in the Yellow Sea saw a fishing junk picking up some armed men on the mainland. Thinking it was an NKPA raiding party, an air strike was called in on it. The boat was hit and sunk, killing two of the men on board and wounding three.

Unfortunately, it was one of our partisan fishing junks. And to make matters worse, the boat was Mr. Pak's command-and-control vessel. Not only had two Donkey-4 partisans been killed, but much of the unit's communications gear was lost when the boat sank. We immediately protested through the 8240th Army Unit Headquarters in Seoul and the air force sent out a two-man team to investigate. To its credit, the air force admitted it was wrong. It agreed to replace Mr. Pak's boat and communications gear. The investigators also acknowledged that we controlled all small boat movements in and out of the mainland in this area and promised we would be consulted before any future air strikes were called in.

This type of cooperation was very limited, however. Throughout my tour at Leopard Base, Majors McKean and Dye and I continually emphasized to the other American units on the island the need to pool intelligence because it would benefit us all. But the other services were reluctant to do this because they were so protective of their sources. Every service was intent on running its own intelligence network. The turf battles were going on at several levels higher than us, but the differences filtered down and the result was that we all worked independently.

It meant more to the other services to cooperate with us than it meant to us because we controlled the bulk of the agents and information. But the representatives of the other services were reluctant to even come in for our briefings, find out what we were doing, or try to coordinate intelligence-gathering activities on the mainland.

The most reluctant of all to share was the CIA man on Paengnyong-do. He was young, probably no more than twenty-five, and was something of a loner. I never learned his name or who he actually worked for beyond some "government agency" that he never described or talked much about. We knew there was a CIA agent on the island, and by the process of elimination we figured it was he.

The agent lived in our compound when he was on the island and ate with us in our mess. He was curious about what we were doing and what we knew but never offered any information in return. Although he regularly tried to pump us for information we were as reluctant to talk as he was, and the conversations usually degenerated into small talk about the weather or events back home.

The CIA man worked a great deal with the air force helicopter crew and was often gone for weeks at a time. I never saw him leave and never saw him come in. He was just there.

Although we never encountered any opposition from the CIA or had problems stumbling over its agents, the same was not true in other parts of Korea, where different covert operations and intelligence-gathering initiatives kept bumping into one another, creating more than a little confusion.

There is much dispute over the effectiveness and efficiency of CIA operations in Korea but it is difficult to fully evaluate the agency's role because much of what it did there had larger strategic implications for the region and remains classified. Even those military personnel who worked for the CIA in Korea and later went into unconventional operations for the army are reluctant to discuss what they did for the agency.

It is no secret, though, that MacArthur had little use for any civilian agency that sought to conduct military or paramilitary operations in his theater. He had fought against the Office of Strategic Services during World War II in the Pacific, although that agency performed quite well in Europe and Burma before having the plug pulled on it at the end of the war. He also sought to keep the CIA from setting up shop in Korea, even though it had been running agents into China and North Korea since the end of the war and had a substantial amount of knowledge about the region.[3]

But, since MacArthur had no covert capabilities of his own in FEC early in the war, he reluctantly allowed the CIA to operate out of Japan.

It was initially run by Col. Richard G. Stilwell, the agency's director of Far East Operations, under whom I later served as a brigade commander in Korea.

The CIA came to Korea as an independent participant in the war, not only because of MacArthur's dislike for and distrust of it but also because of its unique mission. The CIA's scope was more global and of larger strategic interest. FEC was limited to events in Korea and the strategic considerations there.

The CIA operated under what was known as the Joint Activities Commission, Korea (JACK). Its primary missions were intelligence gathering, sabotage, kidnapping North Korean officials, and providing a network of escape and evasion safe houses for United Nations pilots shot down in the North.[4]

JACK ostensibly was part of CCRAK, the FEC's umbrella organization for covert operations in the theater; CCRAK was supposed to coordinate all special operations in Korea, and every army, navy, and air force unit involved in behind-the-lines activities was represented on it. But CCRAK had no command authority over the CIA. The CIA provided the deputy director for CCRAK but continued to take its marching orders directly from Washington because its mission transcended FEC. JACK had neither the responsibility nor the motivation to coordinate its covert activities with CCRAK and thus continued to operate as an independent player.[5]

While covert operations were not a priority consideration for the Eighth Army or FEC because of the reluctance of many senior officers in the regular army to get involved in them, they were exactly the types of things the CIA had been formed to do and was training its people to do.

To plan and conduct operations in Korea the CIA brought into its ranks a number of bright, young, eager, military and civilian personnel with extensive backgrounds in the Far East and covert activities. Among them were Jack Singlaub, then a young army major but a veteran of the OSS in China, who was to become the CIA deputy station chief in Korea; and Hans Tofte, a Danish-American who had served in the OSS in Europe but who had lived in Asia before World War II.

One of the first things Tofte did was develop an elaborate escape and evasion plan for downed fliers. It included a designated island off each coast above the 38th parallel that served as the destination for downed airmen, a string of trained guerrillas on the ground operating from fixed positions to serve as guides, and two fishing fleets, using involvement in black market operations as a cover, to facilitate escape and evasion.[6]

Tofte recruited about twelve hundred North Korean guerrillas and sent them to Yong-do, an island in the Bay of Pusan, off the southern tip of Korea, for training.[7] These agents were to be inserted into North

Korea by airdrop and amphibious landings to build the escape and evasion network, collect intelligence on Chinese and NKPA activities, and run raids in the North.

Singlaub, a former Army Ranger who chafed at the restrictions on Americans operating behind the lines, worked closely with the parachute operations. He started dropping North Korean paratroopers from high-altitude B-26 bombers to reduce the risks of their being spotted by observers on the ground and helped develop the HALO (High Altitude, Low Opening) concept of covert infiltration.[8]

From April to December 1951 the CIA sent forty-four teams of agents into North Korea to operate just below the Yalu River. They were to gather information, ambush truck convoys, and disrupt supply lines. Although Tofte considered this operation successful, the CIA has never made public any numbers to indicate just how successful these units were in terms of damage inflicted or information gathered. These guerrilla operations undoubtedly created some confusion behind the lines, but it likely was limited to specific areas and had no great deleterious effect on the ability of the NKPA and CCF to continue pushing troops and supplies south to the front lines.

There also are indications from others who worked closely with the CIA during this time that its covert operations were plagued by the same problems that plagued all such operations in North Korea. The airdrops of agents were quickly compromised. Radios were captured, stolen, or abandoned with their codes, and false information was sent back. Agents who successfully got onto the ground either by airdrops or amphibious insertions were often quickly captured because they did not know anything about the area they were being sent into or anyone in the nearby villages.

There was a certain ethnocentricity at work here that probably limited our ability to understand why the North Korean agents were being compromised so quickly. We generally assumed that any North Korean sent back to his homeland could quickly and easily fit back in, no matter what part of the country he was sent to. To us, a North Korean was a North Korean was a North Korean. But such was not the case. If a stranger showed up in a village he was immediately suspected of being either an infiltrator or a deserter and the local security police were notified. Only if that newcomer knew people in the village might he be accepted.

The Leopard Base operations sent agents back into the areas from which they had originally come in order to facilitate their assimilation into the local population. It was easier to develop a story that had some ring of authenticity to it concerning why the agent had been away from home for so long. And it was easier to find friends and relatives who knew the agent and would shelter him, feed him, and help him make that transition.

But, as we later learned, sending partisans into areas of North Korea where they were not known and expecting them to set up bases, collect intelligence, or aid in escape and evasion of downed airmen was incredibly difficult. North Korea was swarming with so many NKPA and CCF soldiers and security people that covert operations, whether by the CIA or the 8240th Army Unit, were often exercises in futility.

10

The Middle Ground: Baker Section and the Line Crossers

Of the three methods of inserting partisans and intelligence agents behind enemy lines—amphibious landing, airdrop, and line crossing—the latter two were particularly difficult in Korea. By the spring of 1951 the heavy concentration of troops on the main line of resistance, roughly along the 38th parallel, severely restricted the flow of refugees and other civilians between the lines, thereby greatly reducing the chances of infiltrating agents, while the security apparatus in North Korea prevented air-dropped partisans and agents from achieving any significant successes.

By all accounts, the airborne operations, known as Baker Section, were an unqualified disaster. Available records indicate that 393 armed partisans and agents participated in twenty-two airdrops behind the lines between December 1950 and April 1953. Of those, nineteen involved 389 partisans from Baker Section, originally organized in 1951 while the guerrilla operations were under Eighth Army control and later transferred to FEC, then to Army Forces Far East (AFFE).[1]

Little is known about those first three airdrops, done on what appears to be an ad hoc basis before the formation of Baker Section. The first occurred on December 8, 1950, and involved two agents dropped near Hwangju, about twenty-five miles south of Pyongyang, from a C-47 flown by pilots from the 21st Troop Carrier Squadron. Two more agents were dropped on February 22, 1951, one near Yonan, the

133

other near the west coast port city of Chinnampo.[2] What, if anything, they sent back or brought back is not known.

During 1951, while it was under control of the Eighth Army, Baker Section was primarily concerned with training, most of which was done near Pusan. But the airborne training for Korean partisans was rudimentary. Resources and facilities were lacking. Trainees were often taught how to land by jumping off the back of a moving jeep. Few aircraft were available for practice jumps. When practice jumps were permitted it was not unusual for the paratroopers to suffer serious injuries and deaths, because they had not had time to learn either how to shed their harnesses when they landed in water or how to steer away from trees and other obstacles on land.

For many of the Korean paratroopers, their first time in an airplane and their first parachute jump were on a combat mission behind the lines. There's no telling how many were badly injured or killed on landing.

Only two Baker Section airdrops took place in 1951. Both involved American, British, and Korean troops, but both were so unsuccessful that they should have provided the Eighth Army, and later FEC and AFFE, with sufficient warning about the difficulties inherent in such missions to force a reevaluation of the entire operation.

The first, code-named Virginia, took place on March 15 near the North Korean city of Hyong-ni. At least three Americans, one British officer, and twenty Koreans were dropped on a mission to interdict enemy supply lines, specifically a rail line running south from Wonsan. Although the British officer later wrote a rather embellished account of what he thought was a wonderfully successful mission, all but five members of the raiding party were killed or captured and there is no evidence that any significant damage was inflicted on NKPA or CCF troops or supply lines.

That same British officer reappears in the only other Baker Section operation of 1951, code-named Spitfire, which took place on June 18. He was a member of a five-man advance party that also included two Americans and two Koreans. Their mission was to set up a guerrilla base near the city of Karyoju-ri, in central North Korea. One week after the advance party landed, nine Koreans, one American, and one British soldier jumped in to join them.

It quickly became obvious to members of the group that establishing a guerrilla base behind the lines in North Korea would be far more difficult than anyone had realized. Group members, particularly the Caucasians, could not move freely among the local population. Even the Koreans had problems moving out of the isolated area without running into suspicious NKPA security forces. The infiltrators could not solicit help or food from local residents for fear of being exposed. There also seemed no popular support for a guerrilla uprising, primarily because of fear and intimidation by the security forces.

Shortly after the arrival of the main group, the British officer called for a helicopter so he could be extracted for reasons that are not totally clear. The first extraction effort, on June 27, failed—but alerted enemy forces that something was going on. By the time the extraction was made, on June 28, concentrations of enemy troops in groups of up to two hundred began moving into the area, monitoring houses and trails.[3] Unable to obtain food from local residents or forage off the land, the Baker Section group was forced to call for resupply by air. A late drop and radio problems compromised the group's position. In the ensuing fight, members of the group were widely scattered.

"Our radios were either destroyed [or] lost in the fight so we could not make contact for an evacuation or a resupply, we were without food and all houses in this area were being watched so we started for the lines on 13 July, passed [through] the 25th Division on 25 July," Capt. John Hearn, one of the Americans in the group, later wrote. Hearn reported that he lost twenty-five pounds while on the run from the North Koreans.[4]

Of the original group of sixteen to jump in on Spitfire, only eight survived, three of them American and British. Two enlisted men, one American and one British, were reported missing in action and presumed dead. They were never accounted for.[5]

Not only had the group failed to establish a guerrilla base, it failed to establish contact with any local guerrilla groups or provide any indication that future missions would be any more successful. Yet Baker Section pushed on with its mission of training partisans to parachute behind the lines to gather intelligence and set up bases from which guerrillas could operate.

The remaining seventeen Baker Section missions appear to have been as unsuccessful as the first two.

It was a full seven months after Spitfire before another airborne operation was launched. This one was code-named Mustang, the first of six Mustang operations numbered III through VIII (see figure 10-1).[6]

The second Mustang group, dropped on March 16, reported limited success in cutting rail lines and sabotaging enemy bases in the vicinity of Sinuiju, between Pyongyang and the Yalu River. But that sixteen-man group lasted only six days before contact was lost.[7]

The next three Mustang teams, totaling twenty-five Korean paratroopers, were lost immediately. The last two, in teams of five and six, were dropped on October 31, 1952. Each reported the destruction of a train before its radio went silent.[8]

Despite the lack of success of the airborne missions under first the Eighth Army and then FEC, AFFE pushed on with the program after it gained control of the partisan operations in December 1952.

Three teams of ten men each, code-named Jesse James I through III, were dropped north of Kaesong in late December and were believed to

Figure 10-1
Baker Section Operations

Code Name	Date	No. of men	No. of teams	Mission
Virginia I	15 Mar 51	24	1	Sabotage
Spitfire	18 Jun 51	16	1	Set up base
Mustang III	22 Jan 52	19	1	Sabotage
Mustang IV	16 Mar 52	16	1	Sabotage
Mustang V	14 May 52	10	1	Sabotage
Mustang VI	14 May 52	10	1	Sabotage
Mustang VII	31 Oct 52	5	1	Sabotage
Mustang VIII	31 Oct 52	6	1	Sabotage
Jesse James I	20 Dec 52	10	1	Sabotage
Jesse James II	28 Dec 52	10	1	Sabotage
Jesse James III	28 Dec 52	10	1	Sabotage
Green Dragon	25 Jan 53	97	1	Set up base
Boxer I	7 Feb 53	12	1	Sabotage
Boxer II	7 Feb 53	12	1	Sabotage
Boxer III	9 Feb 53	12	1	Sabotage
Boxer IV	11 Feb 53	12	1	Sabotage
Hurricane	31 Mar 53	5	1	Set up base
Rabbit I	1 Apr 53	40	20	Sabotage
Rabbit II	6 Apr 53	6	3	Sabotage
Totals		332	40	

Source: Cleaver, Frederick, et al. "UN Partisan Warfare in Korea, 1951–1954,"
Study, Operations Research office, Johns Hopkins University, 1956, page 93.

have been lost immediately. No contact was ever made with them. It was the same for four Boxer missions, all inserted in early February 1953 to run raids along the east coast in conjunction with naval missions, and for Rabbit I and Rabbit II, dropped near the east-west railroad between Hungnam and Pyongyang. Not a single radio signal was received from any of these groups and not a single partisan was known to have successfully exfiltrated.[9]

Two other missions, Hurricane and Green Dragon, were designed to establish guerrilla bases behind the lines. Hurricane, a five-man team dropped on March 31, 1953, was lost soon after the drop. Green Dragon turned out to be the largest and most unusual of all the Baker Section airdrops.

Green Dragon was a "stay-behind" mission. With the negotiations in Panmunjom drawing to a close and the loss of North Korea now inevitable, AFFE decided to insert a large guerrilla team that was to form the nucleus of a popular uprising against the Communist regime.

On January 25, 1953, ninety-seven men and fifteen hundred pounds of weapons and ammunition were dropped at five-minute intervals from three C-119s in an area about forty miles east of Pyongyang.[10]

For two months after the drop there was nothing but silence. No radio contact. No exfiltration. Nothing. Then, in late March, a radio report came in from Green Dragon that its strength had been reduced by nearly two thirds, down to thirty-one men, as a result of desertions and enemy action.

American intelligence and operations officers were immediately suspicious. Their belief was that the unit had gotten shot up on insertion and some of the paratroopers had been tortured into revealing information about their mission.[11]

Radio transmissions from the group continued to be sporadic. But in late April a report was received that indicated the group had rescued five downed U.S. pilots and was holding them for pickup. American officials were convinced the pilots were being held because they were able to establish voice contact with them.[12]

But instead of sending in a helicopter, as was requested by Green Dragon team leaders, fifty-seven more partisans were dropped on May 19 to assist in the rescue of the airmen. Dropped with them was equipment to lift the prisoners off the ground utilizing a snatch line that a slow-flying cargo aircraft could hook onto.

When the cargo aircraft flew into the area to attempt the rescue it was met by intense antiaircraft fire. The mission was aborted and an air strike was called in.[13]

Over the next six months the Green Dragon team continued to send back radio messages, but it was believed that the unit had been infiltrated and compromised. Despite warnings from American officials to the Green Dragon group to repatriate the pilots at the end of the war, none of the Green Dragon group returned to friendly lines and none of the five pilots was among the prisoners exchanged.[14]

For all the time, effort, and manpower spent on it, Baker Section was an expensive bust, expensive in terms of dollars but more expensive in terms of manpower. Successes were ill-defined or negligible. Personnel were quickly captured or killed, their radios confiscated, and their codes compromised. Those who survived and managed to return safely to friendly lines told terrifying tales of being on the run from NKPA security forces almost from the moment they hit the ground. These airdrops were virtual suicide missions for all involved.

One of Baker Section's great failings was that the agents usually were dropped into areas with which they were unfamiliar. The Leopard Base operation tried to insert agents into the same area they had lived in before the war. While that posed some risk of an agent's being identified as a refugee or a deserter, it also gave the infiltrator good knowledge of the terrain and the people who lived there. With friends and family in the area, an agent many times could find ready sources of food and shelter, whereas someone not familiar with the territory would not.

The line crossers ran as big a risk as the partisan paratroopers. They had to contend with NKPA and CCF troops in addition to the security forces in the North, then face the prospect of being shot by mistake when they came back through our lines.

When the lines were still relatively fluid in the first year of the war and tens of thousands of refugees were pushed in all directions up and down the peninsula, it was not difficult to send line crossers dressed in civilian clothes from a United Nations–controlled sector into an NKPA sector. Troops on both sides usually were more concerned with their own survival and often ignored refugees, even healthy males in civilian clothes.

Of course, young, fit Korean men used as line crossers ran the risk of being conscripted by the NKPA and therefore could not get back with the information they were sent to retrieve. The best infiltrators turned out to be children and women with babies. They were stopped and questioned less frequently, they could move more easily around the battlefield than men could, and troops on both sides seemed to have an aversion to shooting children and nursing mothers walking through their lines.

But once the lines stabilized and the front took on the look of World War I with its extensive bunkers, modified trench warfare, and a clearly defined no-man's-land between the warring forces, it became more difficult for civilians to infiltrate NKPA lines. What the 8240th Army Unit developed in response was an infiltration operation using line crossers run by American officers known as tactical liaison officers (TLO).

First Lieutenant John deJarnette of Atlanta, a friend and classmate of mine at North Georgia College, was TLO for the 7th Infantry Division for about four months before becoming commandant of the line crossers training school at 8240th Army Unit Headquarters in Seoul. John had been a schoolteacher before his Army Reserve unit was called to active duty during the war. Like most of us who found ourselves working for the 8240th Army Unit, John had no special skills for the job he was sent to do and was told very little about how to do that job. He, like the rest of us involved in partisan operations, had to learn as he went.

During one of my trips to Seoul in the summer of 1952 I ran into John in the headquarters building. After exchanging pleasantries and news about what was going on at home, he agreed to take me to the front and explain how the line crossers and TLOs operated.[15]

A three-man U.S. Army team of one TLO, two enlisted men, and about twenty-five Koreans was assigned to each United Nations combat division on the front lines, including the Marines. The ROK Army divisions were not given line-crossing teams because they would not accept them. The ROK soldiers did not like the line crossers and did not trust them. They considered the line crossers to be draft dodgers who had gotten out of dangerous combat duty in regular units simply because they volunteered to work for us. It was not unusual for line crossers to be shot at by ROK Army units, even when the units knew they were on a mission for us.

But line-crossing duty was extremely hazardous, probably more so than regular combat duty. First, the line crossers had to thread their way at night from friendly lines through the booby traps, unexploded ordnance, and listening posts in no-man's-land. Then they had to infiltrate NKPA or CCF lines without being shot. Then, usually dressed in NKPA uniforms (there were so few civilians around the front lines after mid-1951 that to put line crossers in civilian clothes would have been useless), they had to spend time, sometimes as long as three days, observing enemy movements and gun positions without being spotted as impostors. Finally, they had to make their way through enemy lines, no-man's-land, and back into friendly hands again that often were not so friendly.

The last part of the line crosser's journey probably was the most difficult. American and U.N. troops were always concerned about infiltrators and were quick to shoot at anything that moved or at any noise coming from no-man's-land. The line crossers were given specific times and places to return and a special signal with which they could be identified. Troops that passed them through the front lines got a good look at the line crossers before they went out, but it was amazing that more of them were not shot coming back in.

One of the biggest problems for line crossers involved coming back through the lines where there were no American units. The 7th Division had an Ethiopian brigade attached to it, and occasionally line crossers went out through it. All the Ethiopian officers had studied in England and knew English, but the enlisted men spoke only enough of the language to recognize passwords.

On one mission deJarnette was accompanying a five-man line-crossing team up to the front to pass them through the Ethiopians. The line crossers were dressed in full NKPA uniforms and were carrying loaded burp guns.

"For whatever reason I didn't get the password that night," deJarnette recalled. "It didn't dawn on me until we were coming up on the Ethiopian lines that I had a bunch of, for all practical purposes, North Korean soldiers around me. I told them to stay back and I crawled up toward the Ethiopian lines. The first thing I heard was a round being chambered. I thought I was gone. I started yelling 'G.I., G.I.' Luckily, an officer was in the bunker nearby and heard the commotion and came

over to find out what was going on. That was probably the only thing
that kept us from being shot by the Ethiopians that night."

The TLO and his line-crossing team essentially worked for the division G-2. He would get an assignment from the G-2, then pass it on to
the Korean interpreter. He in turn would pass it on to the team leader,
who would then study the maps to see if the mission was feasible based
on the disposition of troops.

Sometimes what seemed to be a particularly difficult mission turned
out to be unusually easy. One night one of deJarnette's teams was given
the hazardous task of identifying the separation between specific CCF
and NKPA units. A five-man team went out and was gone only a few
hours before it brought back the information higher headquarters was
seeking. The NKPA and CCF had been kind enough to paint signs
identifying which units had which responsibilities. The line crossers
simply brought back a sign.

On other missions team members were loaded down with cheap trin-
kets, which they could use to barter for information, such as Mickey
Mouse watches, cigarette lighters, and rings. There were boxes and
boxes of these things stored in the 8240th headquarters in Seoul and
regularly shipped to the TLOs for distribution to their teams.

As soon as the line crossers returned to friendly lines they were inter-
rogated by the division G-2. The information then went up through
that division's chain of command. It did not go back through the 8240th
Army Unit. The TLO got none of the intelligence to pass on. His primary responsibility was to ensure that teams were ready when the division G-2 needed them. The TLO simply decided which team would be
sent out on which mission. The G-2 provided all the specifics about
when and where the teams would go.

There usually were no more than two missions a week in any division
sector because of the difficulties involved. Trying to run too many people across one sector of no-man's-land would have provoked an increase
in security to cut down on the traffic.

There was some short-term tactical benefit derived from information
provided by the line-crossing teams. But the teams were never able to
stay in one area long enough to observe and report on trends and tendencies of the enemy forces. That was what several of the Baker Section
penetrations were designed to do, except that Baker was a disaster from
the outset. The lack of tangible success of these operations made it easy
for those opposed to the whole concept of unconventional warfare to
question the strategic value of utilizing them anywhere in the theater.

11

Flanking Maneuvers: Kirkland and Wolfpack

The tactical objectives of the three amphibious operations within the Guerrilla Division of the 8240th Army Unit—Kirkland, Leopard Base, and Wolfpack—were virtually identical. Their primary missions were to conduct quick strikes against enemy positions using seaborne troops and to gather intelligence about CCF and NKPA troop movements and gun emplacements near the coast. All were part of the overall strategy to keep enemy forces on the flanks and in the rear off balance while attempting to force a diversion of enemy resources and manpower from the front.

But geographical considerations and varying levels of support from higher headquarters, no matter whether the headquarters was Eighth Army, Far East Command, or Army Forces Far East, made the three operations quite dissimilar, not only in terms of how various missions were conducted but in their effectiveness.

The geographical differences in the areas of operations had the greatest impact. Leopard Base, as has been noted previously, conducted operations north and west of the Ongjin Peninsula in areas that were some distance from the front lines and from the enemy's main supply routes. Enemy positions were more widely scattered in this area and more vulnerable to partisan attacks.

There are numerous islands close to the coast in that part of Korea. But the major islands on which partisan units were headquartered were, for the most part, far enough offshore to provide some measure of protection from seaborne NKPA and CCF troops. It would have taken a sizable fleet of fishing junks to conduct a raid against one of the island strongholds. And by the time the attackers set sail one of the American,

Australian, British, or ROK navy ships patrolling the Yellow Sea could easily have intercepted them. Yet the islands were close enough to enable us to launch our own raids in fleets of fishing junks.

The geography in the Kirkland area of operations off the east coast was significantly different. Kirkland was initially organized in late April 1951 to serve as a counterpart to Leopard Base. While Leopard Base operated successfully from Paengnyong-do, only about fifteen miles from the mainland, there was no island in the Sea of Japan large enough or close enough to the coastline to support large partisan bases or Kirkland's headquarters. The largest island, Ullung-do, is nearly seventy-five miles offshore and well south of the 38th parallel. As a result, Kirkland's operations were split between two smaller islands, Sol-som and Nan-do.[1]

Another geographical feature of Korea that caused problems for Kirkland was the rugged mountains that closely hug the east coast in a jumble of rocky headlands, offering few landing areas for amphibious invasion fleets. This area of the peninsula also was heavily patrolled by NKPA soldiers and security forces because of the roads and rail lines running out of Wonsan.

Kirkland launched its first raids in June 1951 in conjunction with offensives by ROK Army I and III Corps. But high casualties, a high desertion rate, and occasional conflicts with CIA missions in the area relegated it to small raids and limited intelligence-gathering missions.

Even though resources allocated to Leopard Base and later to Wolfpack were minimal, Kirkland received even less. There seemed to be very little commitment to the east coast operation. Only two American officers and two enlisted men were initially assigned to Kirkland, and the number of advisers did not increase significantly over the next two years. The average number of Americans assigned to Kirkland during 1952 was only ten, four officers and six enlisted.[2] By 1953 the numbers increased slightly, to thirty-two (eleven officers and twenty-one enlisted men), to oversee forty-eight hundred partisans.[3]

While Kirkland served as the east coast flank protection for United Nations forces, Wolfpack was carved out of Leopard Base operations to perform much the same function in the west. Wolfpack was organized in December 1951 at the time when control of the partisan operations was switched from the Eighth Army to FEC/LD (K). Its area of operation was roughly east and south of the Ongjin Peninsula and included the Han River estuary and all the offshore islands near Inchon. The Donkey units that had been operating in this area simply underwent an administrative name change to Wolfpacks and came under command of Capt. George Lamm, a short, stocky native of Massachusetts who carried a nickel-plated .38-caliber revolver in his hip pocket.

The geography in the Wolfpack area of operations was such that units were much more susceptible to raids launched against them from the mainland than were Kirkland and Leopard Base units. Wolfpack units operated from numerous small islands so close to the coastline they could be reached on foot at low tide. Wolfpack-6 was on Mu-do, only about four hundred yards from the mainland. Wolfpack-4 was on an island known as So-Suap, which sat in the mouth of Haeju Harbor and controlled access to the city.

There were frequent battles for control of some of these islands throughout 1952 and 1953. It was not unusual for a Wolfpack unit to be driven off a small island only to reclaim it a few days or weeks later. One of the largest of these battles occurred in late 1952 at Sunwi-do, less than three miles off the southern tip of the Ongjin Peninsula, the northern edge of the Wolfpack area of operations.

Wolfpack-8, with about eight hundred partisans under the command of Lieutenant William L. Givens, a no-nonsense paratrooper, controlled Sunwi-do. Givens and his partisans were a constant irritant to the Chinese commander opposite him. In an effort to rid himself of Givens, the Chinese commander put a $25,000 bounty on the American. Givens retaliated with a slap in the face: He put a $25 price tag on the head of the Chinese commander.

But Givens did not let it stand at that. After each successful raid by one of his Wolfpack units Givens lowered the bounty by $1. When it reached $16 the Chinese commander reportedly was relieved and sent elsewhere.[4]

In late 1952 the CCF and NKPA decided to run Wolfpack-8 off Sunwi-do and launched a low-tide night raid in freezing weather with about three thousand men. The defenders on Sunwi-do were well entrenched and had excellent fields of fire on the exposed mudflats and land bridge. A number of fifty-five-gallon drums filled with napalm that could be command detonated had also been employed for defensive measures.

When the attackers got within range they were raked with mortars and machine guns. When they reached the napalm canisters those were ignited. Air force planes then were called in to help beat back the attack. They dropped parachute flares, then flew up and down the mudflats, bombing and strafing the attackers.

About midnight the tide started to change, catching survivors well out on the mudflats. Tidal surges can run at up to seven knots in this part of Korea, and the attackers found themselves not only being pounded by U.S. Air Force planes but being swept away by a rising tide of water so cold it contained ice chunks.

The air force planes continued their attack until there appeared to be no survivors, then withdrew. The next morning at high tide naval vessels cruised through the channel looking for survivors but found none. By all estimates, the entire three-thousand-man attacking force was wiped out. Sunwi-do was never hit again.[5]

Despite its strategic location as western flank protection for all the United Nations forces, Wolfpack suffered many of the same manpower problems as the rest of the Guerrilla Division operations. It had nearly three hundred boats at its disposal but there were never enough American advisers for the number of partisans who used the boats. The average number of Americans assigned to Wolfpack operating units during 1952 was fifteen, seven officers and eight enlisted.[6] Captain Archie B. Johnston, who took command of six Wolfpack units, 3 through 8, in October 1952, found he had only two lieutenants and five sergeants to work with three thousand partisans.[7]

The numbers of American advisers increased slightly as partisan forces were beefed up near the end of the war. By May 1953 there were sixty-six Americans assigned to Wolfpack (which by then had been reorganized into two Partisan Infantry Regiments, a subject to be covered in more detail in Chapter 14). But the sixteen officers and fifty enlisted, not all of whom were assigned to operating units, were responsible for more than seventy-two hundred partisans.[8]

And, like many Americans assigned to the Guerrilla Division of the 8240th Army Unit, they had neither the experience nor the training necessary to work in unconventional warfare. They had to learn on the job. While many learned well, they never had an opportunity to pass on what they learned to their successors before their year's tour of duty was up and they were sent home. Each new captain or lieutenant or sergeant assigned to the Guerrilla Division had to start from the beginning and relearn lessons that had been learned several times previously.

It seemed at times as if we were trying to do all the right things but in all the wrong ways.

12

Recruiting Agents

By August 1952 the intelligence reports filtering through my S-2 office at Leopard Base were beginning to show an ominous trend among the enemy forces in our area of operations. A steady and sizable buildup of coastal defense forces, particularly in Hwanghae Province, was being reported by Donkey units coming back from raids and by our intelligence agents in the interior.

Throughout much of 1952 the NKPA I Corps and IV Corps, with a combined strength of about 77,700 troops, had been responsible for coastal defense from Pyongyang south through Hwanghae Province and into Wolfpack's area of operations. The CCF 40th Army had remained near Sariwon, out of the fight and well away from the areas we were raiding. But now, elements of three Chinese armies—the 42nd, 63rd, and 64th—plus the NKPA's 81st Army Unit of the 9th Brigade, were being brought in to counter the partisans.

Mr. Pak had spoken to me several times in late July and early August about the difficulty he was having finding enough trustworthy agents who could supply us with information we needed about the buildup. The NKPA was severely hindering recruiting by going from village to village and threatening to kill all the members of any family whose husbands or sons joined the partisans. The NKPA soldiers said double agents had infiltrated partisan units and knew the names of all the members.

There was another concern of the potential recruits, Mr. Pak said. They were wary of what support they would receive from the United States and the United Nations if they joined the partisans. They were not sure it was worth the effort to leave their homes and families and risk their lives to fight a war that at this point many considered unwinnable. They wanted some assurance that the U.N. would not abandon them at the end of the war and would come to their rescue if necessary.

145

Despite their isolation and the limited amount of information the people of North Korea received, they were aware of the slow pace of the peace talks at Panmunjom. They knew what was in the offing for them if the war ended with the lines as they were. Their reluctance to join the partisans was pragmatic, not unpatriotic.

At that time neither Mr. Pak, nor the members of Donkey-4, nor I fully realized we were doing little more than fighting for time and space for the negotiators. All I knew about the strategic situation was what I read in the *Stars and Stripes*, which we received only occasionally. I knew peace talks were in progress and there were occasional surges across the lines by both sides. From my limited view of the war, well out of the information loop concerning the progress of the truce talks, I still saw the potential for another offensive to reclaim the North.

At least I wanted to believe the potential was there. The partisans wanted to believe it, too. I might have deceived myself, and deceived the partisans in the process, into believing that what we were doing was not a waste of time and manpower. Whenever the partisans expressed doubt about the outcome of the war and what would happen to them I deflected the questions as best I could. I had no more answers than they did. Besides, the overall picture was lost in a blizzard of daily tasks that permitted no great introspection on the war's final outcome or what would become of the partisans when the negotiators reached an agreement. Thus, we continued to press on with the raids and intelligence gathering, and that caused the need for more agents.

In mid-August Mr. Pak decided that the recruitment of agents had become so critical he needed my help. I felt I could not refuse him, no matter what the request, because of the effort he had put forth to make Donkey-4 Leopard Base's most active unit. But this particular request gave me some pause. Mr. Pak wanted me to accompany him on a recruiting trip to a small village about twelve miles inland as a representative of the United States and the United Nations. My presence was needed to convince reluctant recruits that they were not alone in this fight.

The risks were all too obvious. We would be traveling in areas controlled and heavily patrolled by NKPA and CCF troops. We would have no air cover, no naval gunfire, no artillery support. There would be no backup units available to rescue us if we got into trouble. We would have to travel in a small group at night in order to hide me. If the mission was compromised there was no place for me to run or hide. The partisans could shed their uniforms and blend in with the local populace. I could not.

Although there were far more negatives than positives, I agreed to accompany Mr. Pak. But because of the risks involved, I decided not to tell Major Dye about it. I'm sure a formal request would have been denied. In lieu of standing orders not to participate in such missions, I did what I thought necessary to help Mr. Pak. I could cover my absence by telling Major Dye I was going to Wollae-do for a few days, something I did frequently.

The recruiting trip was planned for August 23 in an area of the mainland northeast of Wollae-do near the village of Sokkyo-ri. The village had only about two hundred to three hundred people but was a key choke point on the road network that led east and north from Changsan-got to Changyon and Chinnampo. Donkey-4 had been gradually losing control of the area and was having difficulty getting information about the movement of troops, convoys, and supplies. If we could not cut off some of those convoys the NKPA would be able to reinforce their troops on Changsan-got, reclaim the tip of the peninsula, and have a better base from which to harass our boat movements off the coast. Mr. Pak wanted to make it difficult for the convoys to move. He wanted the drivers to start worrying from the moment they climbed into the trucks that they might be ambushed. To do that he needed to hit some convoys, and to learn the schedule of the convoys he needed some reliable agents. To get agents he needed me to convince them they would have the backing of the United States and the U.N.

I did not want to portray myself as a United Nations emissary. I looked at this mission as a means of helping Mr. Pak expand his operations. I had been assigned to him and it was my job to help him. If that meant recruiting agents, so be it. But I never considered myself as the advance guard for the U.N. and could not tell people about policy I knew nothing about, although that's essentially what Mr. Pak wanted me to do.

The plan called for us to go ashore at about ten-thirty P.M. on August 23. We would be met on the beach by one agent who would lead us inland for about two miles, where we would rendezvous with another agent. The second agent would then lead us the ten-plus miles through the mountains to an area near Sokkyo-ri. There, a third agent would bring the potential recruits to meet us. The only people who knew an American would be on the trip were Mr. Pak, myself, and the six bodyguards who would accompany us. If anyone else knew the mission might be compromised.

By four P.M. on August 23 I was sitting in Mr. Pak's bunker on Wollae-do, drinking coffee, going over the plans for the trip, and rechecking my equipment. I was carrying the same combat load as I had on the raid on the 76mm gun in July: my carbine, ten clips of ammo, my .45, and two hand grenades. I wore my short-sleeve fatigue shirt with U.S. Army insignia underneath a black Korean jacket, black Korean pants taped at the ankles, Korean tennis shoes, and a black, short-billed Korean cap. With burnt cork rubbed into my face it was difficult to distinguish me from the Koreans in the dark except for my height.

We left Wollae-do at nine P.M. with a light breeze behind us and a three-quarter moon to light our way. By ten-thirty we were in position just off the coast about one thousand yards north of the area where we had landed for the raid on the 76mm gun. The sails were lowered as we waited for the signal to land.

The first light we saw was red, which meant the landing area was not clear. Twenty minutes later we saw the white light, and the skipper of the junk directed it into a small cove, where the boat promptly ran aground on a sandbar. Luckily, the junk floated free when Mr. Pak, I, and the six partisans slipped into the water and waded ashore.

The agent who met us on the beach said that a four-man NKPA patrol had just cleared the area but should be no problem because it had been moving in the same direction as we planned to go. Mr. Pak did not like the idea of following the patrol. After a brief discussion we moved down the beach about five hundred yards to another trail that would lead us to the road where the second agent would be waiting.

It took us less than thirty minutes to cover the two miles to the road. The first agent passed us off to the second agent and we immediately set off at a fast walk. We still had ten miles of difficult terrain to cover. I was fifth in the column, Mr. Pak directly in front of me, one of the partisans who served as my interpreter directly behind me.

The rocky, little-used trail led up through stands of pines to steeper elevations where the path was cut out of the side of the mountain. It was just wide enough for an oxcart but obviously was a secondary trail, not used frequently by either woodcutters who lived in the area or NKPA patrols. With our gear tied down or strapped down the only sounds we heard were our feet hitting the ground and our own breathing as the trail climbed and dipped and switched back on itself.

At about four A.M. we approached a trail junction in the mountains overlooking Sokkyo-ri. The junction was about halfway up the mountain in the middle of a stand of fifty-foot-tall pines. Mr. Pak motioned for me to hang back, then dispatched guards down each of the four trails as he and the first agent, who had been walking point, went to the intersection. I scanned the trees looking for trouble. If we were going to get hit, this would be the time.

As Mr. Pak and our guide approached the intersection I could see five shadowy figures, one of Mr. Pak's men and four potential agents, emerge from the trees. There were bows and handshakes all around. I let out a deep breath, loosened the grip on my carbine, and wiped the sweat from my face.

Mr. Pak spoke to the four potential agents for a few minutes, then motioned me forward. I straightened up from the slouch I adopted while walking with the Koreans so I was not so conspicuous, took off my cap, and in a firm voice said in English: "Hello."

Even in the shadowy darkness beneath the trees I could make out the looks of shock on the faces of the four men when I spoke English. They were startled into silence for a few seconds. Finally, one of the men said something to Mr. Pak in Korean.

"They want to see some identification," the interpreter said.

These guys were taking no chances. They were smart and wary of both Mr. Pak and me. I pulled out my dog tags and military identification card and held them up for inspection. Each man looked at them closely, then looked up at me to confirm that I was the man in the photograph on the ID card.

Apparently convinced that I truly was an American, the four men began tossing questions at me through Mr. Pak and the interpreter.

Where were the front lines?

What had happened when the U.N. forces were pushed back into South Korea?

Would we push north again and liberate their village and North Korea?

Would their families be safe if they joined Donkey-4?

"They say they are interested in joining us but are worried that a secret agent will join our unit and endanger their families," Mr. Pak said.

I tried to answer their questions as truthfully as I could without making wild claims or promises for the U.N. or U.S. forces in Korea that would be impossible to keep. I told them I did not know if there would be another offensive but that if our efforts could relieve some of the pressure at the front lines it would make it easier for those running the war to make that decision.

When I questioned the four recruits about their jobs I understood why Mr. Pak wanted them to join Donkey-4.

Mr. Kim had a municipal job in Sokkyo-ri that gave him access to records of supplies delivered to a dozen towns and villages in a fifty-mile radius. Over the next few months information from Mr. Kim enabled us to compile lists of supplies delivered to each village and the times and routes of the trucks carrying them. Once the supply center was located that information was passed on to the Fifth Air Force, which sent in an air strike to destroy it and several trucks.

One of the other men owned a tobacco shop on the south side of the village and was able to keep a detailed record of all truck traffic and troop movements in and out of the village. Over the next few months his information enabled us to target and destroy five convoys leaving the village. In order to keep our agent from being compromised the attacks usually took place at least ten miles from Sokkyo-ri.

Another of the new men was a blacksmith and mechanic who at that time was repairing truck motors and weapons for the NKPA and local security officials. Mr. Pak desperately needed a good mechanic on Wollae-do, and he set up an elaborate scheme to get the man off the mainland without endangering any of his, or his wife's, relatives. The scheme, which took more than two months to set up, involved getting official permission for the man to move from Sokkyo-ri to another village. En route to the new village the mechanic, his wife, and their one child simply disappeared. Officials in the new village had not known they were coming so they were not missed. The man and his family were last seen living and working on Wollae-do.

After about thirty minutes of questions the four men agreed to join Donkey-4. They said they could recruit eight more men.

The other men recruited by these four were woodcutters, rice farmers, or laborers working for the NKPA. Each bit of information they furnished was valuable because it gave us a larger picture of the enemy buildup in the area.

Before departing we gave the four men a radio, some extra batteries, and a plastic cover they could store it all in. After a brief demonstration of how to call D-4 on Wollae-do we shook hands, wished them luck, and gathered up our gear. The plan called for us to move up the mountain about three miles to a safe area, rest and hide out during the day, then move back to the coast after dark, and rendezvous with a pickup boat at midnight.

The first hints of sunrise were beginning to appear on the horizon as the four new agents went down the mountain to their village and we began moving higher, looking for the safe area.

After a little less than an hour of fast walking the agent motioned us off the trail and into a thicket of scrub pines and heavy vegetation. Mr. Pak called for two guards and dispatched one in each direction along the trail.

The safe area had been carefully chosen. The mountain behind us was steep and rocky, making a quiet approach from that direction all but impossible. We had a good view of several hundred yards of the trail in each direction and could see another trail about five hundred yards down the mountain. The undergrowth was thick enough to hide us from all but the most persistent of eyes, and it was unlikely that any NKPA patrol would venture this high.

I flopped down on the soft ground, took off my cap, and breathed deeply. The danger was over for the time being and I could relax. Suddenly, I discovered that I was famished. I had not eaten anything since the morning before. I rummaged through my backpack, pulled out a can of C rations, opened it quickly, and began gulping down the contents without ever tasting them. Mr. Pak and his men put a small cloth on the ground, sat in a circle around it, pulled out their rice and sauces, and had their own small feast.

We spent most of the day sleeping or standing guard. The sun was warm and comfortable and the traffic on the trail below us was light. We saw several farmers and a few oxcarts but nothing else. We relaxed and conserved our energy for the trip back to the coast.

As soon as the sun started to slip behind the mountains we gathered our gear and started down the mountain. We were able to move more quickly than on the trip in, and by ten P.M. we had reached the road where we were handed from one agent to another for the remaining two-mile trip to the beach. By eleven P.M. we had reached a small stand of trees just off the beach. We went into a defensive posture with guards in all directions and began watching for the pickup boat to appear offshore.

At eleven fifty-five P.M. we could see the dark outline of the boat bobbing gently on the waves about five hundred yards offshore. The NKPA beach patrol was not due for some time, but we looked up and down the beach, saw nothing, and flashed the white light indicating it was safe to land.

The boat began moving toward the beach and we gathered our gear, ready for the trip home. But just as we started to move out of the protection of the tree line, the area off to our left erupted in gunfire. We jumped back into the trees, startled and unsure just what had happened. It took only a few minutes to realize that the NKPA patrol apparently had doubled back on its route, seen the boat offshore, and set up a hasty ambush.

The NKPA were laying down a good base of fire with long bursts from their burp guns interspersed with sharp cracks of semiautomatic rifles. We could hear the bullets hitting the sides of the boat and knew the crew was in trouble. As soon as the firing started the boat started into a long, slow left turn out to sea. But it was so slow that the boat must have taken at least three hundred rounds before it got out of range.

We were in a difficult situation. We could jump into the middle of the fight and hope we killed or wounded all of the NKPA soldiers before they called for reinforcements with the radio we were sure they were carrying. Or we could stay out of the fight, let the smoke clear, and see what happened. We had a backup pickup plan scheduled for three A.M. five hundred yards down the beach. We decided to hold our fire.

As the boat eased out of range, its little two-cylinder motor pumping furiously, the ambushers emerged from hiding. Just as we had suspected, it was a four-man patrol with a radio. They walked up and down the beach, watching the boat move offshore, congratulating one another for keeping an agent from coming ashore. The NKPA obviously never thought the boat was there to pick up people or they would have come looking for us.

The NKPA came within just a few feet of us during their impromptu celebration. We were close enough to smell the kimchi on their breaths and the odor of the strong Chinese cigarettes they smoked. But none of the partisans moved. The fire discipline of Mr. Pak's men was incredible. They would not fire in a situation like this unless they were literally stepped on or physically identified. No matter how close the NKPA came, the partisans would lie motionless, barely breathing. They had the best fire discipline of any unit I have ever served with—American, Korean, or South Vietnamese.

After the NKPA soldiers finished congratulating one another and moved out of the area, we remained in hiding, listening for the sounds of approaching troops, watching up and down the beach. After seeing and hearing nothing for about an hour, we finally crept out of our hiding places and moved toward the secondary pickup point.

By two forty-five A.M. we were in place but could not see the boat. If it did not arrive shortly we would have to make other plans to get away from the beach area, find a place to hide for the day, and wait for a pickup the next night. But that was incredibly risky because this area was heavily patrolled.

Finally, after thirty anxious minutes, the junk appeared on the horizon. We flashed the white light and the boat cautiously approached the beach. It was moving so slowly we began to wonder if it had suffered serious damage or if there were wounded on board.

When the boat got close enough we ran down to the water and waded out to it, pulling ourselves over the gunwales and flopping down on the deck, dripping wet and exhausted.

Two members of the five-man crew had been wounded in the ambush. One had a minor arm wound, the other a serious chest wound. We took the partisan with the minor wound to Wollae-do for treatment and the other to Paengnyong-do for transfer to Seoul.

My report to Major Dye that afternoon was brief and to the point. I simply told him that I had gone ashore with Mr. Pak, that we had recruited several agents and had returned without incident. I never told him I had been twelve miles inland. Or that I had gone onto the mainland dressed as a North Korean.

He just said, "Good job" and let it go at that. He probably figured the less he knew about what I was doing the less he would have to worry about. He was so concerned about the overall operation and dealing with sixteen-plus partisan leaders and the allocation of weapons and supplies that this was just a small item in his daily list of activities. He had given me responsibility for Donkey-4 and I saw it as my job to keep the unit functioning and growing as best I could.

Mr. Pak never missed an opportunity over the next few weeks to tell me how pleased he was with the results of our recruiting trip. He told me that he had made two more trips into the area, taking weapons, rice, and radios to the group of partisans that had grown from the four we had seen to twelve and finally to sixteen. He told me he never could have done it without my help.

What I did not realize at the time was that Mr. Pak was lavishing all this praise on me because he was planning another recruiting mission and wanted me to go along. After the initial success and all this praise, how would I be able to refuse him?

In mid-September, about three weeks after the first trip, Mr. Pak came to me with details for the second trip. This one would be to the city of Changyon, about twenty-five miles inland. Mr. Pak had some agents in Changyon but the security police were going through the city block by block, ferreting them out. He wanted additional agents in the area and needed my help to get them.

Once again, the risks were clear. The trip would take three days, all of it through heavily patrolled enemy territory, again without any fire support or backup. Mr. Pak figured the odds of completing the mission without running into an NKPA patrol were rather slim.

I told Mr. Pak we could improve our odds by targeting some of the NKPA units in the area for air strikes while we were on the move. That would divert attention from us. I told him to come up with a detailed plan and give it to me at least three days before departure so I could study it and arrange for the air strikes. Meanwhile, I would go through our files on units of the NKPA 23rd Brigade, stationed near Changyon, and pick some targets from our most recent intelligence.

About a week later Mr. Pak called from Wollae-do and said he was on the way to Paengnyong-do with his plan. For a man who had spent much of his life as a fisherman, Mr. Pak had great military instincts. He knew the strengths and weaknesses of his own troops and those of his enemy and planned accordingly with great attention to detail. Some of the partisan commanders planned to excess and had to be pushed into executing a mission. Others planned too little and jumped into an operation without considering what might go wrong. Mr. Pak had a sense of when to plan, when to pull the trigger on that plan, and when to be flexible if the plan did not work.

This second recruiting trip called for us to land on the south coast of Changsan-got and move about ten miles inland through the mountains before daylight. Although Changyon was closer to the north coast than the south, we chose to land in the south because defenses were lighter, we had a better chance of getting ashore undetected, and we were more familiar with the area. We would rather walk twenty-five miles through the mountains than land on the beach on the north side of the peninsula and have to fight our way through coastal defenses.

The second night we would travel the remaining fifteen miles, meet with the potential agents, then find a place to hide. The air strikes would come the next morning. We would take advantage of them to move during the day and continue walking until we reached the coast.

Once again we would be traveling light. In addition to me and Mr. Pak there would be only six partisans, one armed with a Browning automatic rifle, two with M1 Garand rifles, and the remainder, like me, with M1 carbines and .45-caliber pistols. We each carried several hand grenades and three days worth of rations. We all dressed in black Korean jackets and pants, tennis shoes, and black Korean caps. I had my dog tags around my neck and my ID card in my pocket. If I was captured, my story would be that I was a downed pilot trying to get to friendly lines. But I knew that story would not hold up long.

I realized this would be a difficult operation and chances were good some members of the group would be killed or captured. But I never considered myself one of those at risk. General S. L. A. Marshall, the famous military historian, had spoken to our class during infantry training at Fort Benning about such dangerous missions, and I never forgot his words. He said if a commander asked for ten volunteers for a tough mission and told them only one would return alive, the ten would still volunteer and each would feel sorry for the other nine because they would not be coming back. I always felt like that tenth man, the one who knew he was coming back. I believed I could change the odds and improve our chances of success simply by participating in the mission, no matter what the risks involved.

I always approached these missions as a challenge, not something to be feared. Infantry training had taught me to remain calm and to control my fears under the worst conditions. And while I have experienced fear many times in my life—from combat in Korea and Vietnam, to a motorcycle wreck, to a car accident, to jumping out of an airplane with a faulty parachute, to having a helicopter engine go dead and being forced to autorotate to the ground—I have always sought to use the powerful energy created by fear to my advantage. Fear can be controlled and harnessed. That surge of adrenaline can be used to do things not otherwise physically possible. In my case fear produces a burst of energy that compels me to do something immediately to reduce the source of the fear. But I knew that on this trip to the mainland my control over my fears would be severely tested.

On the day the operation was to begin Mr. Pak sent his boat to Paengnyong-do to fetch me. I arrived on Wollae-do at about four P.M. and went straight to Mr. Pak's operations bunker for some intelligence updates and a last-minute equipment check. There had been an increase in troop movements in Changyon, but Mr. Pak's agents attributed it to a position swap by platoons north and south of the city. Since we would be approaching Changyon through the mountains to the south we were concerned that the new platoon might change its patrol routes and times. But the intelligence was not strong enough to convince us to cancel or delay the trip. Either we went now, while everything was planned and in place, or we postponed and ran the risk of not being able to put all those assets together again for some time. We had to take the chance that our agent in the area was aware of the situation and would make changes in his plans accordingly.

We left for the mainland at about eleven P.M. and made the crossing without incident. We arrived on the beach on schedule, met the first agent as planned, and were well inland and in hiding by the time the sun began to rise. The only problem I encountered was a blister on my right foot caused by the wet tennis shoes. A small bandage and a dry pair of socks and I was back in business.

We slept for a few hours, then rechecked the maps for our routes to the rendezvous site that night with the potential agents. We had fifteen miles to cover, according to the map, although the actual distance was more like twenty if you counted all the switchback trails we would be traveling.

We left at dusk, moving out at a fast walk. Twice the point man stopped us and motioned us off the trail as civilians, one with an oxcart, came past us. We slid into the darkened bushes until the civilians were well past, then resumed our journey.

We thought time was against us but somehow we underestimated our speed and reached the rendezvous site a good thirty minutes ahead of schedule. The Donkey-4 agent from Changyon who met us seemed surprised and said it might be some time before the others arrived.

I sat down by the trail and breathed deeply of the cool, pine-scented mountain air. I was tired and stiff from the two days of tough walking but my senses remained on full alert. I was still a lone American in the midst of a lot of Koreans.

About fifteen minutes later the four men we were to meet came walking up the trail. They also seemed surprised that we had arrived early. But they exchanged greetings with Mr. Pak and he brought them over to the area under the trees we had chosen for the meeting.

Mr. Pak introduced me as a U.S. Army lieutenant in charge of special forces. I shook hands with them and greeted them in Korean. Unlike the previous group, these men seemed not at all interested in me. Instead, they turned to Mr. Pak and began questioning him about Donkey-4's operations.

I was a bit curious about their behavior but tried to push it out of my mind and catch what they were saying to Mr. Pak. Then one of the men turned his back to me. Even in the dim light I could see the outline of a pistol tucked into the waistband of his pants. These men were to have brought no weapons to the meeting. Something was not right here.

I turned and mentioned the pistol to the partisan in charge of security for the trip. He tensed, slowly dropped his carbine into firing position, and moved to get a better view of the man carrying the pistol. I started backing away from the group, feeling for my carbine, waiting to see what would happen.

Mr. Pak continued to talk to the four men and offered them cigarettes. As he moved around the group, one of them, a man named Mr. Kim, slipped something into Mr. Pak's hand. It was a note. Mr. Pak palmed the note, then turned his back as if to light his cigarette. By the light of the match he could read the Korean words scrawled on the scrap of paper: "I am a prisoner—this is ambush."

Everyone seemed to react at once. The security chief yelled to Mr. Pak that one of the men had a gun. Mr. Pak yelled "Ambush!" and dived for cover as he reached for his weapon. Mr. Kim hit the ground. Three of the men pulled pistols from under their shirts and started shooting. I jumped into the underbrush, found a small ditch, and fired off a few rounds. The rest of Mr. Pak's men opened up on the three agents, knocking down two in the first burst. The third man ran off down the mountain to the north.

Two of Mr. Pak's men ran after him but had gone only a few yards before they ran into a ten-man NKPA patrol. The mission had been compromised. We had been set up for an ambush. Only our early arrival and Kim's note to Mr. Pak had upset the plans.

We tossed about a dozen grenades down the trail to the north and began pulling back along our escape route to the south. But we immediately ran into about twenty NKPA moving up the mountain along that trail to intercept us. They opened fire and quickly had us outgunned. Rounds were snapping past my head and thunking into the trees around me as I sought cover.

The situation was not good. We were outmanned, outgunned, and had NKPA coming at us from three sides. With our limited firepower we didn't stand a chance in a lengthy fight. There was no telling how many more NKPA were converging on this position or how quickly they could reinforce the soldiers in the ambush. It was either fight, and probably die, right there on that remote mountain—or try to get away and live to fight another day.

In combat situations like that, while things are actually happening at a frenetic pace, they seem to be occurring in slow motion. I could see the muzzle flashes of the NKPA weapons in the trees on three sides of us. I could hear the rounds hitting the trees and cracking past my head. I could feel pieces of bark and leaves showering down on me as the NKPA soldiers fired too high. And I could sense Mr. Pak's men around me, carefully picking their targets, firing at the muzzle flashes, not panicking, conserving their ammunition. I was still thinking clearly and I knew we had only one chance to get out of this.

"Follow me!" I shouted to Mr. Pak and his men. "Follow me!"

I tossed one grenade down the trail to the south, another to the north, then took off through the thick brush to the west.

Tree limbs clawed at my face. Briars and thorns ripped at my pants and shirt. Mr. Pak and his men were right behind me, running at full speed, up and down hills in complete darkness. We bounced off low-hanging limbs. We stumbled and fell when the ground dropped away from us. We tripped and went sprawling over rocks and tree roots.

Behind us we could hear the NKPA continuing to fire. But they were not shooting at us. They were shooting at each other. We had broken out of the trap so fast that the units converging on us thought we were still there. When they discovered what had happened we heard a great deal of shouting, but in the darkness they could not tell we had headed west.

We ran in single file, avoiding all the trails we crossed, although we crossed very few of them. I was concerned that if we turned south too soon we would run into NKPA ambushes. Since the mission had been compromised the NKPA knew we had come from the south and most likely would be waiting for us there. Our best hope was to keep moving west.

After forty-five minutes of full-throttle running, when I was reasonably sure the NKPA were not pursuing us, I stopped to gather our forces, tend to our wounds, and plan our next move. We were all bruised and sore and cut up. I later counted more than two dozen cuts on my face and arms from tree branches.

The situation was not good. We were essentially surrounded deep in enemy territory. Enemy patrols had a fairly good fix on our location, and it would not be long before reinforcements were called in. But without fire support or backup, we would have to work our way out of this on our own.

Just as I was beginning to catch my breath and starting to sort out what to do next, I discovered that our group had a new member—Mr. Kim. He had run into the bushes with us and followed us on our cross-country dash. He said he could not return to his village but now feared for the safety of his family.

Mr. Kim quickly explained how the mission had been compromised. He said North Korea security police had suspected him of being an informant for some time. They watched his house and followed him to the meeting in the mountains with the Donkey-4 agent in which plans for the rendezvous with Mr. Pak were finalized. Mr. Kim found four security police waiting in his house when he returned. He said they beat him and threatened to kill his wife and seven-year-old son if he did not cooperate with them.

The four stayed in the Kim house until the night of our meeting. Three of the agents accompanied Mr. Kim. The other agent stayed at his house with his wife and child. Mr. Kim had had just enough time to write a note to slip to Mr. Pak warning him of the ambush. His plan had worked. But, as a result, his family was in danger.

"I am going back to try to get my wife and son before the soldiers return," Mr. Kim announced. He said he would move them into the hills, work his way to the coast, and try to join Donkey-4 at a later date.

I listened to Mr. Kim's story without interrupting. It had taken a great deal of courage to write the note and slip it to Mr. Pak right in front of the NKPA agents. Now he planned to return alone and unarmed to his home, where another agent was waiting for him.

Mr. Pak said he felt an obligation to Mr. Kim and his family because of what he had done to warn us of the ambush. I, too, felt an obligation, although I was not quite as ready to act on it as Mr. Pak.

"How far are we from Mr. Kim's house?" I asked.

"About thirty minutes," Mr. Pak replied.

"What direction?"

"Northwest."

I thought about the risks of trying to get in and out of the village without being spotted. They were probably far greater than the rewards of helping Mr. Kim and his family. But the NKPA were looking for us to the south. And the more I thought about it, the more I saw it as a challenge to rescue Mr. Kim's family. We were in enough trouble already. A little more wouldn't hurt at this point.

We quickly cobbled together a plan and headed for Mr. Kim's village. We arrived before daybreak and surveyed the situation. Mr. Kim's house was the second from the end of the street. The house next to his was occupied by an NKPA security official responsible for that street. We had to take out the agent in Mr. Kim's house quietly so we did not disturb the security official next door.

We could see a light from Mr. Kim's house and figured the agent was waiting for him. We positioned a partisan on each side of the door, then told Mr. Kim to knock and announce: "We are back."

He did as instructed and the agent stepped outside to greet his friends. The two partisans jumped him, knocking him to the ground. A knife flashed, there was a slight groan, and then silence. We looked at the house next door and listened. There was no noise or light. Mission accomplished.

Mr. Kim rushed into his house and in less than a minute had gathered his family and their meager belongings and joined us for the trip to the coast. We carried the body of the agent about two hundred yards into the underbrush, threw it into a ditch, covered it with leaves, and headed into the mountains.

We continued moving west. We were dog-tired but knew we could not stop for even a few minutes of rest. The NKPA would soon discover the dead agent and figure out that we were moving west. By dawn we were so far into the mountains we saw no signs of civilization. There were no fields, no animals, no trails, no troops, no civilians. We were still moving cross-country at a fairly good pace. Mr. Kim and his family kept up without complaint. They were used to the terrain.

After a few hours, we decided to turn south. If we moved too far west we ran the risk of bumping into one of the coastal defense units on the north side of Changsan-got. Turning north or east would simply take us deeper into enemy territory and back into the hands of the NKPA patrols that by now were in full pursuit.

By dark we figured we were ten miles north of the pickup point on the beach. If we walked all night we could still make the rendezvous. But we would not be able to meet our agent at the designated check-point. Mr. Pak decided to break radio silence. We climbed to the top of a mountain and Mr. Pak broke out the radio. He contacted the agent and simply told him to leave the area where he was waiting for us. He did not tell him to meet us at the pickup point on the beach but it was understood he would.

We walked on through the night, up and down mountains, guided by the knowledge Mr. Pak and his men had of the area, hoping we would come out on the beach near the pickup site, hoping the boat would be there on time, fearing it would not be.

Despite our bad luck early in the operation we came down out of the mountains onto the beach not far from where we were to meet the boat. We quickly found the agent and he signaled the boat to come ashore. We waded out, climbed aboard, and flopped onto the deck, bone-tired, hungry, and sore from the cuts and bruises.

Only one man had been wounded in the ambush. He had taken a round in the arm, and although he lost a lot of blood he never complained and never lagged behind on our wild dash through the mountains. The partisans amazed me with their stamina and seeming indifference to pain. We had lost one rifle, two pistols, some ammunition, a radio, and a few canteens, but I considered us very lucky to have escaped with anything, much less our lives.

The mission had not been a success. The only thing we were able to do was get in and out without getting any of us killed. We had planned it as well as we could, based on the intelligence available to us. But we could not have taken into account the fact that Mr. Kim had been compromised. Only Mr. Kim's courage in slipping the note to Mr. Pak, and our own blind luck in arriving before the ambushers, prevented all of us from being killed or captured.

But that was the nature of partisan warfare. It was small unit actions, usually very personal and very deadly. It was luck and timing and training overcoming superior manpower and firepower. It was knowing the terrain and being able to use it to our advantage. It was being able to reach down deep when you're dead-tired and hungry and scared and being able to think and react more quickly than the other guy. It was believing that what you were doing was morally right, strategically significant, and tactically proper, even if the guys who ran the war from Seoul and Tokyo did not.

Eventually, we were able to get some agents into the area around Changyon. Mr. Kim led a group back in several weeks later and helped establish a supply area in the mountains south of the city. That group also was able to recruit several more agents and provide targets for air force and navy jets.

When I reported to Major Dye about the trip I simply told him I had gone on another recruiting mission to the mainland with Mr. Pak but it had not been as successful as the previous one. I did not mention that I had gone twenty-five miles inland, that we were nearly caught in an ambush, or that we spent two days running through the mountains to escape the NKPA patrols hunting us.

"Too bad," he said, barely looking up from his paperwork.

13

Special Missions

The longer I stayed in Korea the more missions to the mainland I wanted to participate in. Each time I returned safely from a trip inside North Korea I wanted to go back and do it with bigger challenges, just to see if I could do it. I wanted to be there when the missions I helped plan were carried out. I wanted to make adjustments in the attack plan on the run and call in air strikes and naval gunfire. When my plans were being executed I felt almost a parental obligation to be there to watch them unfold and make sure they succeeded.

I knew I was pushing my luck and the bounds of good sense by making frequent trips to the mainland and going deeper into NKPA territory. I also knew I was testing the patience of Maj. Tom Dye and creating problems for Mr. Pak and his men. The men of Donkey-4 had the task of protecting me and making sure I returned safely from these missions.

Mr. Pak's reasoning on my participation in the raids on the mainland was that there had to be a compelling need for my presence and reasonable assurances I could make it back alive. Mr. Pak and the other partisan leaders made it clear they did not want me risking my life unnecessarily. They, perhaps more than I at that time, realized how vulnerable I was behind the lines. And they knew far better than I what would happen if I were captured. So there were some occasions when their experience and maturity won out over my youthful exuberance and desires to go everywhere and do everything with Donkey-4 units.

One such mission involved a raid on a hydroelectric plant near Pyongyang in August 1952, one of our more ambitious and daring operations because of the depth of the penetration. The hydroelectric plant was about forty miles north of Pyongyang and thirty miles inland from the Yellow Sea. Agents from Donkey-10 operating off Cho-do, north of Changsan-got, had tried on several occasions to knock out the plant but

161

were unsuccessful. On one of those raids three Donkey-10 agents were killed when they were discovered placing explosives around the plant.

In early August I met with the leader of Donkey-10 to identify terrain features that might aid the air force in pinpointing the hydroelectric plant. We reasoned that rather than risking more agents we could put a large X on the map in the middle of those features, show the map to the pilots, and tell them: "Bomb there."

But the air force had as little success as we did, failing three times to hit the target. The plant was well camouflaged and heavily defended by antiaircraft artillery; D-10's agents on the ground said they could hear the planes and see the bombs exploding but they were well off the mark. Since the agents had no radio communications with the pilots they could not adjust the air strikes. Even with radios it would have been difficult to communicate because the agents did not speak English.

The simplest and quickest way to solve the problem, I thought, was for me to go in with a radio and adjust the air strikes. I would go ashore dressed in my Korean outfit with a small group of partisans, move cross-country to the plant, adjust fire on the target, then exfiltrate. As I planned it in my head, it sounded relatively easy.

But D-10 found nothing simple or easy about the idea when I proposed it to him. He bluntly told me he did not think it was possible for me to survive such a trip and began describing the problems I would face.

I would have to go ashore north of Cho-do in an area heavily defended by the NKPA. If I made it ashore safely I would still be faced with a sixty-mile trip on foot through numerous checkpoints: D-10 could fix me up with a fake ID card, tint my exposed skin, and dress me in Korean clothes, but I was too tall and did not speak Korean well enough to fool even the most slovenly of NKPA checkpoint guards. Most likely I would be spotted and nailed at the first stop. And even if I succeeded in getting to the hydroelectric plant, getting out would be extremely difficult because of increased security after the raid.

Reluctantly, I had to agree with D-10. I was setting myself up for a suicide mission if I insisted on going along on this raid. After much thought I abandoned the idea and began concentrating on how to use D-10's agents to take out the plant.

We eventually came up with the idea of sending in four agents to light flares on each of the four sides of the plant so the planes could see where to bomb. It was terribly risky for the four men, as were most of those types of missions, but we reasoned that in the confusion of the bombing the agents could slip out of the area.

Getting the agents into position near the plant was no problem. Doing so with the flares was another matter. Personal belongings were rigorously searched at all checkpoints, and it would be difficult sneaking anything through. We decided to use D-10's two agents in the mountains and send in two more from Cho-do with the flares. The two from Cho-do would be disguised as farmers and would carry the flares hidden in the bottom bag of several bags of rice stacked on an oxcart. The four agents would not meet until the day before the raid. That way if the two coming from Cho-do were discovered we would lose only two agents, not four.

While D-10 made the preparations for the agents to go ashore I coordinated with the air force. We planned the raid for the morning of August 11. The four agents would move separately to within about one hundred yards of each side of the plant and be in place by two A.M., when the bombers were due. They would remain in place until they heard the bombers approaching. Then they would pop their flares and scatter into the mountains.

If all went as planned the bombs would hit in the area between the flares and destroy the plant.

D-10 would remain on Cho-do during the raid to monitor radio calls from the agents. I would be in the radio shack at Leopard Base to coordinate with D-10 and the air force.

At about ten P.M. on August 10 D-10 called to inform me that his two agents had gotten through with the flares, met up in the mountains with the other two agents, and were proceeding to the plant.

I was like an expectant father sitting in that radio shack listening to the hiss and crackle of the radios, trying to visualize what was happening, wishing I was there to assist.

At about one-thirty A.M. I heard the low, steady drone of the bombers flying over Paengnyong-do headed for the target. Several hours later, I heard them returning.

It was not until about five A.M. that D-10 called to report that the mission had been a complete success. Guided by the light from the flares, the bombers had blown away the camouflage, destroyed the plant, and started a number of electrical fires in the area. And all four agents, after some initial problems, got away safely.

Later in the day I radioed the air force operations office in Seoul to get their assessment. They said there had been some problems with the flares but they were generally pleased with the results. The fires started by some of the first bombs lit up the area and provided a wonderful target for later planes. It was one of the few times I had received any feedback from the air force on a mission. We provided them with hundreds of targets during my time in Korea and only occasionally did we receive reports of whether those targets had actually been hit. Our primary source of bomb damage assessment came from agents responsible for pinpointing the targets, but often it was weeks before an agent was able to get out of the bombed area and report to us.

In this case it was several weeks until the two agents sent in from Cho-do were able to work their way back to the coast and get off the mainland. The other two agents remained behind.

The two who returned said there had been some problems getting into position to set off the flares because of NKPA guards around the plant perimeter. One of the men ignited his flares late and another was out of position, but the agents still succeeded in pinpointing the plant for the bombers. Once they set off the flares the agents found ditches to crawl into and only barely survived the chunks of concrete from the destroyed dam hitting all around them.

After listening to the agents talk about their numerous narrow escapes I was convinced that I had made the right choice by not going with them. I would have been far more of a liability than an asset. My presence could easily have compromised the mission.

There was little time to reflect on that operation because we were in various stages of planning several others. August generally was our busiest month because of the good weather. Things began to deteriorate in late September. October brought the first snows. By November it was so cold and snowy that movement was greatly restricted. Winter reduced partisan operations by at least 80 percent, so before its onset we tried to visit some of our more remote Donkey units to assess their operations and give them some extra supplies.

Our most remote operations were in the North. We had several Donkey units operating in and around islands on the west end of MiG Alley and the Yalu River. This was cold, lonely, and dangerous work. It required the partisans to spend days on end in their rickety fishing junks. They were battered by the cold, the wind, and the salt air, and were constantly under threat of attack from NKPA and Chinese patrol boats in the area. When the partisans landed on an island they often had to fight to stay. If they stayed too long they often had to fight to get off. By December the Yellow Sea was frozen over in the shallow waters around the islands, making boat travel terribly difficult. These northern Donkey units were able to slip a few agents in and out of North Korea on occasion, but the closer they got to the Yalu River, the heavier the coastal defenses and the more problems penetrating the area.

The primary responsibilities of the northern partisan groups were to search for downed fliers, gather intelligence, and run small patrols on the dozens of islands in the area, many of which were uninhabited. Lieutenant Jim Mapp, a tough, pugnacious Georgia native, was the Leopard Base adviser who had the unenviable task of riding herd on those Donkey units. We saw him infrequently on Paengnyong-do. He was either on Cho-do or on the boats with his Donkey units. He would disappear for weeks at a time, our only contact with him an occasional radio message about some operation.

Mapp used the code name Himong, which, roughly translated, means "hope." Whenever we received operational summaries from Himong they were generally short, to the point, and devoid of any descriptive analysis that would give us some indication of what had actually happened.

On June 10, 1952, we received the following operational summary from Mapp concerning a mission the previous day: "Pilot, friendly, rescued by Himong from Taewha-do. 9 Jun 52. Air Force colonel, 33 years old."[1]

What we did not realize was that this pilot, Col. Albert W. Schinz, was a deputy wing commander who had been missing for thirty-seven days. Nor did we realize that his own unit had given up trying to find him. But his rescue by Mapp's partisans would almost blow the cover on the entire Leopard Base operation because the story found its way into *Life* magazine in great detail two months later.

Schinz's F-86 had been shot up in a raid over MiG Alley on May 1, 1952. He had been forced to bail out into the Yellow Sea but landed close to a small island and was able to make it ashore safely. On the island he found a deserted village and enough rice, boiled corn, and onions to sustain him for several weeks.

He fashioned large "SOS" and "MAYDAY" signals from some raw cotton left in one of the huts. He lit signal fires and shot off emergency flares whenever aircraft came near. But none of the pilots apparently saw his signals, because no helicopters were sent to rescue him.

The rescue was left to Mapp and his partisans. They knew nothing about the downing of Schinz's jet and were actually searching for the pilot of an F-51 they had seen go down on June 8 when they passed near the colonel's island and saw a fire. Thinking that an NKPA unit might have been sent to the island, Mapp and his partisans waited until early morning before investigating.

What they found surprised them almost as much as it did Schinz. They were not expecting a full colonel in the U.S. Air Force, and Schinz was not expecting a group of armed partisans, one of whom told him: "We are friends. We help."[2]

Mapp had some eggs on his boat, and Schinz wolfed down more than a dozen of them plus a healthy portion of a bottle of Scotch on the trip back to Cho-do. Once there, Schinz blistered every air force ear within radio range for abandoning him.[3]

For his part in the rescue, Mapp was awarded the Bronze Star with V device. It was a much-deserved reward, not only for the rescue but also for working those thankless missions under incredibly brutal conditions on the northern edge of our area of operations.

Despite the numerous details about the rescue in the July 28 *Life* magazine story, the Leopard Base operations were not compromised because no mention was made of Mapp or the partisans. The article simply said that Schinz was rescued by "Koreans."

The rescue of Schinz again demonstrated the value of the partisans. We not only had seaborne units behind the lines searching for downed pilots, we had agents and safe houses on the mainland, and island bases such as Cho-do and Paengnyong-do where pilots could land crippled aircraft.

The Fifth Air Force reported that of ninety-three of their pilots shot down between July 1950 and January 1952 who managed to evade capture, twenty-nine of them, or 31 percent, were rescued by partisans.[4]

On Paengnyong-do we seemed to be constantly plucking pilots out of the waters surrounding the island or pulling them out of their damaged aircraft after they landed on the beach. We were a safe haven in hostile territory for many pilots.

If a plane was not too badly damaged but the pilot had doubts about making it back to his base, he could land on Paengnyong-do and either the U.S. Navy or Marine Corps or the British navy would send out technicians and pilots to repair it and fly it out.

If the planes were in bad shape or crashed on landing at Paengnyong-do, we either hooked them up to a bulldozer and pulled them off the beach or used a few thermite grenades to destroy them in place before bulldozing the metal scraps off the landing strip.

The air force helicopter on the island was on call around the clock for rescues of pilots in trouble, and I occasionally went along to assist.

One day in early November 1952 I stopped by the helicopter pad to talk to the pilot. As we were chatting he received a Mayday call on his radio from the pilot of a damaged Corsair. The pilot cranked up the chopper, I climbed on board, and we were off the ground in just a few minutes.

The helicopter pilot established radio contact with the Corsair pilot and learned that he had been wounded and the plane badly shot up. He would not be able to make it to the beach at Paengnyong-do. He was directed to fly toward the nearest ship in the area, the British frigate *Cardigan Bay*.

We never saw the plane but maintained radio contact with the pilot until he ditched, then established communications with the ship. The pilot was close enough to it to be rescued as his plane was going under.

Three days later the *Stars and Stripes* carried a story on the rescue. The pilot, Maj. Alexander Walker, Jr., of Leander, Texas, had been wounded in the arm and leg by NKPA ground fire and his plane badly damaged. The story mentioned our efforts, although not by name or unit, to stay in contact with him and direct him toward the *Cardigan Bay*. He was treated for his wounds, passed from ship to ship, and eventually returned intact to the carrier *Bairoko*, although he was wearing a borrowed Australian naval dress uniform.

While the partisans were fairly successful at rescuing downed pilots, we did not have any luck at all while I was there with rescues of POWs. The problems with POW rescues were numerous. The North Koreans moved the camps frequently. The camps were heavily defended and could be easily reinforced. Getting there and breaking in was no problem. Getting out with the POWs, many of whom undoubtedly were crippled and malnourished, would have been extremely difficult without a numerically superior force.

On one occasion one of the Donkey units operating in the area of Pyongyang discovered what appeared to be a semipermanent POW camp. Our agents were able to maneuver close enough to use a slingshot to shoot messages wrapped around steel balls and covered with plastic inside the fences. The messages instructed the POWs to give us a signal whether they could travel three to five miles for a helicopter pickup. But before we could get a reply the POWS were moved and the camp was shut down.

In early August we got a call from Mapp that he was running short of supplies. Major Dye decided he and I would both make the trip up north with the supply ship. In addition to carrying supplies to Mapp, we wanted to personally reassure him that we were still there, still fighting the war, still supporting him.

Getting up there proved to be more of a problem than we had thought. We could not make the trip in our fishing junks. They were too slow for the distance we had to travel. At that time special operations forces had no dedicated naval vessels or aircraft, a situation that has been partially rectified only in recent years. But without those dedicated assets we were forced to borrow or beg what we could from the U.S. Navy and Air Force. When we were not successful there, we had to turn to other sources. Since no American ships were available for this trip we had to somehow convince the British to send one of their ships.

The British were very reluctant to cooperate on this mission because of where we wanted to go. They could not spare more than one ship and thought it extremely hazardous to send a lone vessel north of Cho-do. Not only were the beaches more heavily defended, there were always risks of being attacked by MiGs or by the coastal patrol boats that roamed the area.

It took nearly two weeks to convince the British naval commander in the Yellow Sea that the situation with Mapp and his partisans was getting desperate and we needed to supply them quickly. He finally agreed to send a frigate to Paengnyong-do in mid-August to pick up Dye, me, and the supplies and take us to meet Mapp.

We radioed Mapp the grid coordinates for the rendezvous off one of the northern islands, arranged to meet him at twelve-thirty A.M. the next night, then put together a large supply of food, ammunition, a radio, plenty of batteries, and other needed items.

The frigate picked us up as scheduled late in the morning, then headed west, away from the coast, out into the Yellow Sea. The captain said he wanted to be well off the coast and out of NKPA radar range to reduce the chances of being spotted before we met Mapp that night.

By sundown we were still several hours from the rendezvous. But we were north of Cho-do and the heightened tension on the ship was evident. Gun crews went on full alert and lookouts were perched all over the ship watching for aircraft and patrol boats.

Near midnight we approached the rendezvous point. There was a stiff wind out of the northwest churning the sea into a white froth. In that kind of weather Mapp and his small fleet of fishing junks would undoubtedly be late. At twelve-thirty, the appointed meeting time, there was no Mapp. At one A.M. he still was not there. Finally, at one-thirty A.M., some small blips appeared on the frigate's radar screen. From their size and direction and the speed at which they were approaching, the British crew concluded they were Mapp's boats. About thirty minutes later several of the junks emerged from the darkness, bobbing wildly on the whitecaps.

When we finally hauled Mapp and about ten partisans aboard, he greeted us like long-lost brothers.

The British crew and some of the partisans quickly went to work loading the supplies into the junks. Mapp warmed himself, had something to eat, and filled us in on some of the details of his operations. He told us about the rescue of Schinz and talked about having problems getting the partisans to stand and fight on occasion. He expressed his frustrations with the limited resources he had to work with and the problems with the logistics system, to which we could only nod our heads in sympathy. We were all frequently frustrated by what appeared to be Far East Command and Eighth Army indifference to our operations.

After about an hour Mapp climbed back down the rope ladder to his junk with his partisans and slipped off into the night. The vessels danced away from the frigate on the wave tops before they were swallowed by the blackness of night on the open sea.

The captain of the frigate immediately turned south at full speed to put as much distance as he could between the North Korean mainland and his ship before dawn. Dye and I caught a few hours of sleep belowdecks but were up and on the bridge to watch the sun rise. We were back at Leopard Base by noon, the only casualty of the trip one of the four bottles of Scotch I had purchased from the ship's store.

Despite careful wrapping it shattered during the leap from the ship's launch to the rock jetty on Paengnyong-do.

Even though we were more than 125 miles behind enemy lines on Paengnyong-do, and a mere 15 miles from the North Korean mainland, there was a sense of security on the island that Jim Mapp did not have where he operated. His existence was terribly lonely and extremely dangerous, and it was quite understandable for him to be so frustrated with his role in that war.

Not long after our trip to visit Mapp, he came back to Leopard Base for some rest and to catch up on his mail and what little news we could get on what was going on with the rest of the war.

Mapp got to Leopard Base about the time Mr. Pak was completing plans for another raid on the mainland, this one on the north side of Changsan-got. The targets were two heavy machine guns blocking Donkey-4's beach landings in that area. The guns were manned by regular NKPA troops who had been brought in to replace the reserve coastal defense forces. Mr. Pak asked me to accompany him and I asked Mapp if he wanted to go along. Since he had few opportunities to get onto the North Korean mainland he jumped at the chance.

The plan called for a twenty-man Donkey-4 team to land on the south side of Changsan-got and infiltrate across the mountains to the rear of the machine-gun positions. At midnight on the appointed day a small boat, its sides reinforced with heavy timbers, would pull close to shore to draw fire from the guns. At that point the twenty-man team would attack the guns from the rear.

While that battle was in progress one boat with eight men would land north of the guns and another eight-man boat would land south of them. They would then attack from the flanks.

Mr. Pak, Jim Mapp, and I would be in the last boat. We would land about ten minutes after the main attack. We were prepared to reinforce either of the attacking units—or, if they were doing well, slip about five hundred meters north and blow up an ammunition dump.

At about eight P.M. the day of the raid Mr. Pak picked up Mapp and me in his boat at Paengnyong-do. We each carried our usual combat load of carbine, ten clips of ammunition, .45-caliber pistol, and several grenades. Mr. Pak said the twenty-man team was in position behind the guns while the two attack boats and the decoy boat were sitting a few miles off the coast waiting for midnight. We were scheduled to rendezvous with the three boats at about eleven-thirty P.M.

Under normal circumstances three and a half hours was more than sufficient time to reach the north side of Changsan-got. But this night was not normal. There was a full moon, and an unusually strong tidal surge hit us just as we rounded Changsan-got. The tide was running four to five knots against us while Mr. Pak's boat could barely make six knots. We were virtually creeping along. Mr. Pak screamed at the boat operator to make the thing move faster but there was little he could do against the forces of nature.

We were so dependent on those sail junks that the tide, the moon, the wind, and every capricious act of nature had to be factored into an operation. This was warfare at its nineteenth-century worst, and yet it could easily have been brought into the twentieth century with just a few extra dollars.

We fretted and chewed our fingernails while the old boat and its puny motor labored against the tide. It was eleven forty-five P.M. by the time we rounded the cape, and we knew we would never get into position in time to be a part of the raid. But we pressed on.

From what we learned later the raid went off exactly as Mr. Pak had planned. The first boat went in fast and drew fire from both machine guns. The twenty-man team jumped the gun crews from the rear, and when the NKPA turned to fight them, the amphibious raiding parties hit the beach, flanking the gun positions north and south.

We could see the muzzle flashes of the guns against the dark background of the mountains long before we heard the sounds of firing. We pulled close to the beach to provide what late assistance we could, but the guns had already been knocked out and the raiding parties were beginning to break contact. Had we been in position on time we could have gone after the ammo dump. Now, all we could do was watch.

The NKPA reinforcements quickly began moving into the area, making the withdrawal to the boats somewhat difficult for the two landing parties. The team that had gone overland was cut off from the beach by these reinforcements and was forced to flee back into the mountains. Its escape route was southwest through the mountains to Donkey-4's safe area on Changsan-got. We could do little to help at that point, so we decided to head for the safe area and give the team some extra firepower if it was needed there.

Since we were running with the tide on the return trip we were clipping along at ten or eleven knots. We rounded the cape in short order and eased into the beach at the safe area. Mapp was surprised that we could go ashore without being shot at. He kept looking around, waiting for a surprise attack—as I had on my first visit to the safe area.

We heard the distant pop and clatter of gunfire echoing back in the mountains and knew that the Donkey-4 team was fighting a running gun battle. We scrambled up the path through the trees to the edge of the minefield and no-man's-land.

Just as we got there the first of the raiders reached safety. He and the rest of the Donkey-4 team knew where the mines were and quickly tiptoed through. The NKPA were right on their heels but stopped at their edge of the minefield. They fired a few last shots in our direction, then turned and headed for home. They were not about to risk their lives in the minefield.

The raid, while not a major strategic initiative, nevertheless demonstrated just how quickly and easily the partisans could strike the NKPA. From a tactical perspective, it had been important to knock out those two machine guns. But from a psychological perspective, it had been even more important to Mr. Pak to let the NKPA and the civilians in the area know that the partisans could strike wherever and whenever they chose.

Of course, not all combat operations involving partisans were as successful as our raid on the 76mm gun or the raid on the machine guns. If something could go wrong, it often did, as was evident in the tide's playing havoc with our boat. Without good planning and a lot of luck, there were a million things that could go wrong with partisan operations. The biggest problem was the possibility of an operation's being compromised. The aborted recruiting trip in which I had been nearly killed was a prime example. In that case we were surprised that the operation had been compromised because information about it was restricted to a very few people. On larger raids involving more people the risks were far greater. One such compromised operation in late October nearly resulted in the deaths of two American advisers.

Captain Don Seibert and M.Sgt. Roy Meeks were advisers to Donkey-1, which operated along the coast east and southeast of Paengnyong-do. In October 1952 Meeks and D-1 developed a plan to hit an NKPA staging area where there were usually 500 to 600 troops. The plan called for 200 partisans, a 150 led by Meeks and the rest by Seibert, supported by air and naval gunfire, to launch a two-pronged attack before dawn on October 29.

The raiders had barely landed before both elements were ambushed. The NKPA knew the planned routes of attack and raked them with mortars, machine guns, and small arms. Seibert's interpreter was killed and the radio was lost, making it impossible for him to communicate with Meeks, the Korean leader of his element, or the naval and air fire support centers. Pushed onto the beach by the pursuing NKPA, the partisans discovered there were no boats waiting for them. Many jumped into the water and began to swim. Seibert found a log floating in the surf and was able to stay afloat until the boats returned.[5]

Disaster was averted when Meeks called in the air support and naval gunfire, keeping the NKPA at bay long enough for most of the partisans to be rescued. Still, they suffered 10 dead, many of whom had to be left behind, and 17 wounded.[6] Enemy losses were put at 184 NKPA and 88 CCF killed.[7]

Most of our operations were not this large. Much of what we did utilized small groups of partisans, usually fewer than ten men. On occasion we even did detailed planning for a mission involving just one agent. Missions that small sometimes involved efforts to assassinate a local Communist official. We had been instructed by Vanderpool in April 1952 to have our Donkey units target for assassination Communist leaders and village chiefs not sympathetic to partisan efforts.

"If succeeding Communist leaders are assassinated," Vanderpool wrote, "the ambitions of minor leaders will be dampened. This has already been demonstrated by our efforts in some sectors. Terrorist tactics of focussing attention on the high mortality rate of enemy leaders are to be encouraged. Only selected Soviets should be assassinated. . . . Soviets should be assassinated in areas that abound with pro-Communist(s). This creates suspicion and doubt between the Soviets and their satellite Korean followers."[8]

Vanderpool knew from his experiences in the Philippines the value and the risks associated with assassinating enemy political leaders. It was a tactic the Viet Cong would use so effectively against us and the government of South Vietnam little more than ten years later. We could never come to grips with it there because we did not take advantage of what we had learned about the use of these terrorist tactics during World War II and Korea.

There was only one occasion during my tour in Korea when D-4 specifically targeted an individual for assassination. That was a village chief, a hard-core Communist, who had exposed one of Mr. Pak's agents. The village chief pointed out the agent to the NKPA, who arrested him and executed him in the middle of town. The exposed agent been one of Mr. Pak's best men and now Mr. Pak wanted revenge.

Mr. Pak wanted the assassination done in a public place. But it had to be done quickly, with little noise and no indication of who the assassin was.

"Do you have a weapon to do this?" he asked me.

A knife was too messy and too obvious. A .45-caliber pistol was too loud and also too obvious. Mr. Pak needed a smaller caliber weapon, possibly with a silencer. I sent his request on to Guerrilla Division Headquarters in Seoul. Vanderpool replied that he would send a .38 Special with a silencer.

Two weeks later Vanderpool's office radioed Leopard Base and said the item we had requested would be on the C-47 supply flight, due the next day, in a box marked "Leopard Special Request." The box was in the mailbag and contained three .38 Special snub-nosed revolvers, three boxes of ammunition, and three screw-on silencers.

I test fired each of the weapons and found they were just what Mr. Pak wanted. When fired the weapon made a slight ping, followed by a hiss, both of which could be easily drowned out in a crowd.

I gave one of the weapons to Mr. Pak and the others to Donkey units I thought had agents who might be able to use them. But only Mr. Pak's man was able to get close enough to make a hit. As the story came back to us, Mr. Pak put his agent with the .38 into the village as a laborer. One day, while the agent was loading rice onto trucks, the village chief showed up and began shouting at the workers. There was a great deal of confusion and noise from workers and trucks in the area.

The agent moved behind the village chief, pulled out the silenced .38, and shot him through the heart at point-blank range. The village chief fell face-first onto the street. The workers rushed to him, thinking he had suffered a heart attack. The agent offered to get the village doctor and was able to escape in the confusion. When the doctor arrived and discovered that the chief had been shot, the death was blamed on a sniper in the mountains since no one had heard the shot.

As we pressed on with the partisan campaign through September and on into October, we found we were having a profound effect on enemy forces. The NKPA and CCF forces continued to reinforce in our area of operations. Troops were being repositioned from the static front lines because of the increase in the tempo of our operations, and we were beginning to feel the pressure.

The numbers of the partisans also were being increased. Even as the hard-core partisans who had been fighting for nearly two years felt the U.S. and U.N. commitment to them waning, they saw their depleted ranks being filled by recruits who did not have the same fire for freedom burning in them. We all knew the end was coming and likely would be there before the partisans could reclaim their homeland. The question being raised in many minds was how to deal with thousands of heavily armed North Koreans on South Korean soil who liked neither the Communist government of Kim Il Sung nor the U.S.-supported government of Syngman Rhee.

The answers were not long in coming.

14

On Leaving Korea

In early October the Korean winter began closing in around us. The tempo of operations slowed and our intelligence-collection capabilities declined. Raiding parties were hampered by deep snow and cold, and partisan agents who had been able to move freely through the higher mountains on the peninsula and keep tabs on enemy troop movements were forced to seek shelter in villages and maintain lower profiles.

October also brought the next round of major organizational changes in the partisan operations. By the time I completed my tour in December these changes had drastically altered the structure and impact of the units and had set in motion events that would bring an ignoble end to this noble group of warriors little more than six months later.

Enemy strength in the Leopard Base and Wolfpack areas of operations had more than doubled from the previous October, when it had been estimated at 77,700. Now we were facing roughly 160,300 CCF and NKPA troops. The enemy had positioned four Chinese armies—the 40th, 42nd, 63rd, and 64th—the NKPA IV Corps, and three NKPA brigades along the west coast opposite us.[1]

Much of the buildup had taken place in little more than three months, and the flow of information through my S-2 shop reflected the rapid increase in enemy troops. Since July I had been receiving frequent intelligence reports about new and larger concentrations of CCF and NKPA troops in Hwanghae Province. When I was not running operations with Mr. Pak and Donkey-4 during that time, I was kept busy providing target information to the navy and air force.

This increase in enemy troop strength served not only to counter our operations but was a clear indication of concern among the North Korean leadership that U.S. and U.N. forces might try to open a second front on the west coast. Although that was never the intention, the implication was there.

To further exploit that North Korean concern and make it appear that something big was brewing, which would be an unstated bargaining chip at the peace talks, Far East Command decided in early October to quadruple the number of partisan fighters from the 9,000 we had then to about 40,000. At that time Leopard Base and Wolfpack had the bulk of partisan fighters, 4,600 and 4,100, respectively.[2]

A wholesale recruiting drive was launched to fill these slots. At one point there were reported to be more than six hundred recruiters traveling throughout South Korea promising food, clothing, and money to any able-bodied male who would sign up.[3]

But the program was flawed in its concept and execution. The integrity of the partisan units, particularly those operating under Leopard Base command, was maintained by a relatively strict policy of admitting only members who came from the same geographical area. That reduced the risk of infiltrators and double agents while it strengthened unit cohesion.

But that also made it difficult for us to recruit new men as the war dragged on. The North Korean security apparatus targeted families of those who joined the partisans, and our reputation in Hwanghae Province was such that replacing our losses with fresh recruits was a constant struggle. Although North Korea seemed to have a virtually inexhaustible supply of manpower, the people were reluctant to join our cause. And those who had fled south and had somehow avoided being swept up in the ROK Army draft were not about to suddenly find a large measure of courage or patriotism at that point in the war.

As a result, the South Korean recruiters were doing little more than signing up draft dodgers and deserters. They were plucking bodies from the ranks of refugees to fill their quotas. There were plenty of men but good fighters were in short supply. Joining the partisans earned these recruits an exemption from the ROK Army draft and many signed up because they thought that by doing so they could avoid front-line duty.

Mr. Pak had taken an active hand in the recruiting process and brought in about one hundred new men from the North Korean mainland for training. Another one hundred, a mixture of South Koreans and North Koreans, were sent to us from the south. The new men recruited by Mr. Pak worked out well. Those from the South did not.

The mix between these men and the veteran partisan fighters was not good from the beginning. The new recruits were not as committed, not as loyal, and not as physically able to withstand the rigors of partisan life as were those men with whom I had been working for the past nine months. During the early stages of training I estimated that at least 60 percent of the new recruits were unsatisfactory.

Kirkland, the east coast operation, had the largest increase in partisan strength and the most problems during this time. From fewer than three hundred partisan fighters in October 1952, Kirkland grew to nearly six-teen hundred by the end of the year. Most of these recruits from South Korea were of questionable motivation, as was evident in a desertion rate of more than one a day. The closer the unit got to combat, the more desertions occurred.[4]

Since Donkey-4 recruits were relatively handpicked compared to those in some of the other units, we did not experience the same prob-lems with desertions, although there was a noticeable dip in the morale of the men. More and more they began to question what would happen to them at the end of the war. We had no answers for them because there were no answers. No one knew what would happen to the parti-sans. We simply continued training as if the war would go on forever, even though all of us knew it was slowly and painfully drawing to a close.

Things were changing rapidly as individuals, units, and ships that had worked with us closely over the past year rotated home.

On October 30 we received the following message at Leopard Base from the British ship *Ocean* as it prepared to leave the theater:

> On completion of our tour of duty in this theater would like to express the great admiration felt by all air crew men in HMS Ocean for your splendid organization. The intelligence supplied often at great personal risks, by your units has played a major role in the direction of our air support. It is [*sic*] always been a great pleasure to support your daring raids against the enemy mainland and all on board wish you every suc-cess in your future operations. Good bye good luck. . . .

One curious change to our training routine that October ordered by the Guerrilla Division of the 8240th Army Unit in Seoul was to begin train-ing some of the new men for airborne operations. We were not told why this was being done at this time. Nor were we told how these men were to be used. The only explanation we received was that headquarters wanted the capability to have airborne units in each partisan group for possible future use.

Lieutenant Lex Watson was responsible for the airborne training. He recruited an American sergeant who was jump-qualified to direct the training and design the necessary facilities. I had previously built a twenty-foot tower and installed a set of flying rings for the soldiers to exercise on. We were able to convert that into a twelve-foot jump tower where the Koreans were instructed how to jump with their feet together and knees bent to absorb the shock when their chute opened. The tower cables stopped them two feet from the ground and gave them more real-istic jump training than many airborne partisans received in other parts of Korea.

We were still in the early stages of the airborne training in late November when we finally understood the reason for it. On November 25, 1952, the Guerrilla Division of the 8240th Army Unit was redesignated United Nations Partisan Forces, Korea (UNPFK), later changed to United Nations Partisan Infantry, Korea (UNPIK). Each major command within the Guerrilla Division of the 8240th Army Unit was redesignated as a Partisan Infantry Regiment (PIR). Leopard Base became the 1st PIR, Wolfpack the 2nd PIR, and Kirkland the 3rd PIR. Baker Section became the 1st Partisan Airborne Infantry Regiment (PAIR) and our airborne-trained men were sent to that unit. In April 1953, as a result of the manpower increase, the 5th PIR was added in what formerly had been the Wolfpack area of operations and the 6th PIR in the former Leopard Base area of operations.

Although my job did not change, I was redesignated as a Special Forces Commander and became the commander/adviser of the 4th Partisan Infantry Battalion, 1st PIR, which was how Mr. Pak's Donkey-4 unit was now known.

It seemed at first to be merely a cosmetic name change because there was little immediate impact at our level. We continued to collect intelligence and run a number of small-scale operations on the mainland. Most of those operations targeted the North Korean rice harvest. We employed something of a scorched earth policy that fall, burning rice, killing and stealing oxen, blowing up rail lines, and ambushing truck convoys to make it increasingly difficult for the North Korean leadership to keep its people fed. We also captured more North Korean prisoners by using Vanderpool's tactics of dressing partisans in the uniforms of North Korean security police. They would stop an unsuspecting convoy, find an officer, arrest him on some trumped-up charge, then send the convoy on its way without anyone's knowing what had happened until the convoy reached its destination.

Not until much later did we understand the reason for all these changes. They were an effort by FEC, and eventually the ROK government, to get a better handle on the partisans and their operations. The reorganization of the partisan units into combat battalions provided a structure that higher headquarters could understand. Having Donkey and Wolfpack units operating within the framework of the U.S. Army command structure just did not go over well with the regular army types for whom unconventional warfare and all its trappings were distasteful aberrations. Restructuring the partisans into regiments and battalions made it easier for the headquarters types to understand what we were doing.

This reorganization also provided a structure that could be more easily integrated into the ROK Army, which had been fashioned along the same lines as the U.S. Army. But this was a particularly sensitive issue for the North Korean partisans, the ROK Army, and the ROK government. The partisans were not particularly fond of Syngman Rhee or his government. And Rhee's ROK Army was wary of thousands of armed North Korean partisans becoming a part of the country's military forces.

More changes occurred in the overall structure of partisan operations in early December that only served to further blur the already confusing lines of command and control for the partisans, who were still operating without any clear mission statement.

CCRAK had been redesignated in September as the 8242d Army Unit and assumed operational control of FEC/LD (K), which was the immediate higher headquarters of the Guerrilla Division of the 8240th Army Unit.[5]

On December 10 the theater army, U.S. Army Forces, Far East (AFFE) became what was referred to as the "executive agent" for behind-the-lines activities, essentially taking control of partisan operations from FEC. AFFE had no operational control of the activities and served primarily as an operational overseer.

In addition, two more staff organizations were inserted between the actual operational level, where I worked, and the AFFE. The most significant of these was the Special Operations Division (SOD) within AFFE G-2. The Far East Command/Liaison Group, Korea (FEC/LG [K]), 8240th Army Unit, through which CCRAK had liaison with AFFE G-2, was redesignated the Support Group, 8240th Army Unit.[6] Although we remained under operational control of G-2, there was still no command authority and we now had two additional staff organizations to go through to reach the top. The army, as it frequently does, had put together a top-heavy, complex structure without any clear lines of command and control and no clear mission for the partisans it controlled.

The reorganization did nothing to enhance the capabilities of the partisans. If anything, all the name changes and organizational restructuring over the last two years had actually set up bureaucratic impediments to partisan operations that, as originally conceived by Col. John McGee in early 1951, had been relatively simple and easy to manage. Under McGee, the partisan fighters had been the primary focus. Now, it seemed the organization was the most important thing.

I could sense the concern of Mr. Pak and the men of Donkey-4 as I prepared to end my tour in Korea and return home. Although many of my colleagues had found working with the partisans to be frustrating and, in the words of some, "a waste of time," my views were quite different. It had been an eminently challenging assignment and an immensely rewarding one. I had learned a great deal about myself, about my capabilities as an infantry officer, about my ability to handle myself and lead other men under fire, and about how to work with people in a culture I knew nothing about until I was thrown into the middle of it.

My year of working with the partisans had been frustrating only in the sense that I never thought their abilities were fully utilized. The nightmare that was our logistics system played a major role in that. The reluctance of the upper echelons of the army to find merit in unconventional warfare also contributed to that sense of frustration.

As I was preparing to leave Leopard Base the North Koreans threw a surprise party for me. At least I at first thought it was for me. I later learned that President-elect Dwight Eisenhower was visiting Korea the first week in December, and the North Koreans might have simply wanted to get his attention.

On December 7 we had just finished the evening meal and returned to our billets before lights-out. It was a beautiful night with a bright moon and the temperature a crisp ten degrees. Suddenly, we heard the sound of propeller-driven aircraft approaching from the south. It was so unusual and so surprising to have aircraft approaching the compound at that hour and from that direction that we all froze in place.

A large explosion shook our Quonset hut and rattled the walls as dirt and debris rained down on the roof. Everyone dived for the floor and we all covered our heads waiting for the next blast.

But we could hear the explosions trailing off to the north so we grabbed our boots and rushed outside. Silhouetted against the sky were the dark shapes of about a dozen North Korean aircraft. The antiaircraft batteries on surrounding hills opened up as the planes turned out over the Yellow Sea. We jumped into the bunkers we had prepared for just such an attack and waited for the next bombing run.

And we waited. And waited. And waited.

The second attack never came. After about thirty minutes of crouching in the bunkers we were convinced that the attackers would not return and we emerged to inspect the damage. It was obvious the aircraft had targeted only the Leopard Base compound. One of the NKPA's informants on the islands must have told them exactly where we were so the planes could zero in on us. The U.S. Marines and the air force radar station had not been touched in the brief raid.

Fortunately, the aim of the NKPA pilots was no better than that of North Korean artillerymen. The only damage was to our well. The first bomb destroyed the wooden structure we had built to protect it. The remainder of the bombs exploded harmlessly in the rice paddies outside our compound.

Officials in Seoul were as surprised by the raid as those of us on Leopard Base. They said it was the largest night attack of the war by the NKPA's air forces and thought it might have something to do with the fact that Eisenhower, on a tour of Korea after winning the 1952 presidential election, was taking off from an air base near Seoul on his return flight home when the attackers hit. Whatever the real target, the Fifth Air Force had scrambled jets to intercept the intruders and sent them scurrying back into North Korea before any real damage could be done.

News reports of the raid said it had taken place "at an unidentified point" against "United Nations installations from which the jet interceptors were being directed."[7]

That, of course, was us. But due to the secrecy of the operation it could not be revealed that the raid had actually been 125 miles behind North Korean lines.

After the initial surprise of the raid had worn off, I looked on it as something of a going-away present from the North Koreans.

By December 13 my replacement had arrived at Leopard Base. The Korean winter was upon us and operations were at a virtual standstill, so I had plenty of time to go through the numerous administrative procedures that included turning in my weapons, heavy clothing, and sleeping bag. It also gave me time to say my good-byes to Mr. Pak and the men of Donkey-4.

On December 15 Mr. Pak and his staff arrived at Leopard Base and escorted me to the local village, where I was the guest of honor at a farewell luncheon. There were the usual mounds of rice, kimchi, octopus, seaweed, eel, and rice bread spread out on the tables before us. There were also numerous bottles of rice wine.

Each of Mr. Pak's staff members rose to salute me, offer a rice wine toast, and give a brief speech about what he thought I had done for the Donkey-4 partisans.

We had accomplished a great deal since I arrived ten months earlier simply because of the trust Mr. Pak and I had developed in one another. Mr. Pak had gone from being the partisan leader whose loyalty was most seriously questioned by American officials to the most trusted. His Donkey-4 unit had grown from 565 dedicated but untrained partisans in January 1952 to 826 tough and disciplined fighters who could conduct any kind of operation from a one-man infiltration up through a company-size operation as effectively and efficiently as any American unit.

We had conducted dozens of operations and inflicted hundreds of casualties on the NKPA and CCF, yet had suffered very few casualties of our own. We made the enemy take notice of us by our persistence and our unpredictability. We forced him to allocate additional resources to our area to combat us at a time when our own higher headquarters continued to question our effectiveness.

We did not accomplish all we had hoped. We did not sever the north-south rail lines running along the west coast that might have had significant impact of what was happening at the front. We did not exploit the partisan-controlled area on Changsan-got. But neither were we forced to relinquish it.

Despite the smiles and the pleasantries being exchanged at the luncheon, I could sense an underlying concern among the members of Mr. Pak's staff. Donkey-4 was changing as a unit and would not be the same as it had been through much of 1952. No American adviser would be assigned to the unit once I left. My replacement would work strictly as the S-2 at Leopard Base. The quality of men being assigned to the unit was not being maintained because of the new recruits. And now there was concern that an unwelcome peace agreement would be forced on them and there would be no reinvasion of the North, no new offensive, no return in force by the North Koreans to their homeland.

Rumors also were circulating that once the truce was signed there would be efforts to integrate the partisans into the ROK Army. I knew Mr. Pak and his men would never agree to that. Nor would they consent to move to South Korea. Their families were in North Korea. Their homes were in North Korea. Their hearts were in North Korea.

As I listened to the speeches I felt almost as if I were abandoning these men of Donkey-4 to an uncertain fate, although I knew I could do nothing to change the plans the U.S. Army and the ROK government had for them or for me. Finally, it was Mr. Pak's turn to speak. He reiterated many of our accomplishments that year, especially the successful raid on the 76mm gun and the recruiting trips. He thanked me for my loyalty and for my efforts, then asked me to stand.

As I did he reached into his pocket and pulled out a small silver knife in a silver sheath and held it in front of him.

"I want to give you something that will show my appreciation for your help," he said, his voice thick with emotion.

"Until you arrived D-4 was not very well thought of. No one thought we had a safe area on the mainland. I received very little support for my raids. Now, I am respected. My men are well trained.

"This special knife I present to you is over two hundred years old. It was of great historical value in my hometown on the mainland. It was kept in a special place in City Hall. A small team of my people hit the police station and City Hall last week and brought it back.

"I want you to keep this knife and remember the freedom fighters of North Korea. Some day we will return to our homes. When we do, we will take back with us all these historical items that mean so much to us and return them to their proper place."

Mr. Pak handed me the knife. Then, in one of the few displays of affection I had ever seen from him, he wrapped his arms around me and hugged me as if I were his brother.

The next morning I was on the resupply flight back to Seoul. As the C-47 lifted off from the beach, Paengnyong-do slipped beneath the wings and was gone. Out the left side of the plane Wollae-do was a small brown speck that was quickly swallowed up by the Yellow Sea as the plane gained altitude. Changsan-got and the North Korean mainland became a blue-green blur and eventually disappeared under the clouds.

I took out the knife Mr. Pak had given me the previous day and turned it over in my hands, admiring the craftsmanship that had gone into its design. I thought of Mr. Pak and wondered if I would ever see him again. I wondered what would become of him and his partisans. I wondered if I would ever be able to return that knife to him and his hometown to honor all the courageous partisans of Donkey-4 who had fought with me and would continue to fight long after I was gone.

15

Disbanding the Partisans

As the war wound down in early 1953 the legal status of the partisans and what would be done with them when the fighting ended was becoming a sticky issue for AFFE and the ROK government. The partisans loomed as a major impediment to any peace settlement at the same time that they were being used as a bargaining chip. It had been decided that the partisans would continue to operate as long as the North Koreans did not adequately address the issue of prisoner of war repatriation in the truce talks.

The North Koreans wanted the partisans disarmed and disbanded as soon as the truce was signed. The South Koreans were fearful that partisans opposed to any settlement might be recruited by North Korea to conduct guerrilla operations against them if they were not somehow accommodated by the ROK government. Little note was taken of what the partisans wanted, but I knew from my experiences with them that they were not likely to go away quietly. Their primary goal, the liberation of their homeland, had not been achieved and now they finally were about to be told it would not happen—although many of them had suspected as much for a long time.

No effort had been made by either the ROK government or American officials to address the legal status of the partisans before it became a problem. This was particularly significant in this conflict where political considerations played a major role in military strategies and tactics during the war and became the overriding factor in the talks to end the war.

At the end of World War II the partisan/guerrilla issue was resolved primarily by the individual countries who were party to the Allied

victory. Political concerns of Germany and Japan were not a consideration because most of the partisan and guerrilla activity had taken place
outside their borders. There was no need to integrate these fighters into
any police force or armed services of the defeated and subsequently
occupied countries. In France, Russia, Yugoslavia, Burma, and the
Philippines, all parties to the Allied victory, most of the partisans simply
returned to their civilian lives.

Korea, the first Cold War conflict, was unique because there was no
battlefield victory. The political concerns of the other side had to be taken
into consideration while the treaty was being negotiated and thus the
issue of partisan status had to be addressed from a political perspective.

The ROK government had had little say initially in the formation of
the partisans. Although the ROK Navy came to the rescue of partisan
groups in January 1951, the U.S. Eighth Army quickly took over the
operation and claimed it for its own. But good sense and army doctrine
regarding use of such partisan fighters, which was still being written and
eventually emerged as FM 31-21, "Organization and Conduct of
Guerrilla Warfare," were ignored.

The partisans were sworn into no army. They had no identification
cards. They wore no standard-issue uniform. No records were kept of
their individual accomplishments. And no effort was made to form
them into regular fighting units until November 1952, when UNPFK
was created. But UNPFK had been little more than a cosmetic name
change through which AFFE and FEC could deal with the partisan regiments. At the tactical level there was never any real sense that these
irregular troops were an extension of either the U.S./U.N. forces or the
ROK Army. To the U.S. Army, the partisans were little more than
refugees who had taken up arms to fight as irregular troops on our side.
They had become wards of the U.S. government.

The ROK government eventually agreed to recognize the partisans as
part of a special U.S. Army combat force. ROK officers were given
some administrative control over the partisans but had no say in what
operations they conducted. And there was still no clearly defined effort
to provide the partisans with some sense of their future. They were
unwanted by the North, unwanted by the South, unwanted by their
U.S. Army protectors.

In these circumstances any normal soldier might throw up his hands
and go home. But the partisans had no place to go. Without hope of victory, without hope of being welcomed by either side, the partisans
seemed to have no motivation to continue fighting. Yet fight they did.

In a major study of partisan operations done after the war much was
made of the reasons the partisans continued to fight when there seemed
to be no apparent reason to do so. Their motivation has been cynically
and wrongly attributed to "the prospect of material reward."[1] Partisans

who continued to fight in the latter stages of the war have been portrayed as freebooters for whom plunder from either North Korea or the U.S. government was the primary motivation. The possibility that it was patriotism and loyalty to their country that motivated them was never addressed.

No doubt there were among the partisans a few pirates and brigands for whom the war was largely a means of getting rich. But I know from my experiences with Mr. Pak and Donkey-4 that most of them fought for one reason: freedom. They fought to liberate their country and to free their families and homeland from the tyranny of communism and Kim Il Sung. To ascribe mercenary motives to the partisans does them a great disservice as soldiers and patriots.

The percentage of true soldiers and patriots within the ranks of the partisans was being diluted, however, through late 1952 and early 1953 as a result of the recruiting drive. By January 1953 the number of partisan fighters had increased to 18,395.[2] The objective was to have 20,000 partisans by the middle of March and a total of 40,000 by the middle of July 1953.[3]

These numbers were a reflection of three plans proposed for partisan activity in 1953. The plans were virtually identical and did little to redefine or clarify the mission of the partisans. They were, in fact, virtual carbon copies of Operational Plan One, which Col. John McGee had written two years earlier when the partisans were first formed.

Plan Phase I, which covered operations from January 28 to March 15, placed a priority on operations in Hwanghae Province and included "harassment of enemy through normal operations . . . attacks by interior units particularly aimed at disruption of military units . . . (to) contain maximum enemy troops in coastal areas. . . . Direct maximum effort at destruction of bridges and tunnels. . . . Employ normal guerrilla and partisan tactics directed at support of EUSAK (Eighth U.S. Army, Korea)."[4]

When AFFE became concerned that the NKPA and CCF might launch a spring offensive, CCRAK issued Annex II to Plan Phase I calling on partisan units to increase their reconnaissance of enemy troop movements.[5]

Plan Phase IIA for the period March 15 to September 15 repeated these objectives and included an expansion north of Wonsan of the territory in which the east coast operations would be conducted. Plan Phase IIB, which presumed a late-summer U.N. offensive, repeated the previous plans and gave the partisans no additional responsibilities or missions.[6]

There was nothing particularly innovative about any of these plans. They reflected the thinking of McGee and, to some extent, codified the conduct of partisan operations that had evolved over the last two years.

There had been no clear-cut mission statement regarding partisan activities in the beginning and now CCRAK and AFFE were giving their stamp of approval to what we had been doing during that time.

These plans for 1953 operations once again demonstrated that within the upper echelons of the army there was little knowledge of or appreciation for the use of unconventional warfare in a conventional theater. The regular army types simply did not know what to do with the partisans. So they let them do what they had been doing all along.

While these plans were being formulated it became obvious that the increased manpower of the partisans made it necessary to assign additional American advisers to the units. The first soldiers from the newly formed U.S. Army Special Forces began arriving in March 1953 to work with the partisans. The addition of these sixty officers and fifteen enlisted men was the appropriate response to the difficult task of training partisans, but the program was flawed.

First, there were not enough advisers. Plans called for 193 officers and 448 enlisted men to be assigned to the partisans. But by May 1953 only 66 officers and 134 enlisted men, less than half the assigned total, were overseeing more than 22,000 partisans.[7]

Second, the Special Forces personnel were insufficiently trained for Korea. Their training focus had been primarily on Europe, not on the Far East.

Third, and perhaps most important, the SF personnel were sent to Korea as individual replacements—they did not come as members of their twelve-man "A teams"—thereby reducing their effectiveness. They were as lost in this environment as were those of us who had been plucked out of regular combat assignments and sent to the 8240th Army Unit in the previous years. (A more detailed discussion of the use Special Forces in Korea can be found in Chapter 16.)

During this time of uncertainty enemy strength in the partisan areas of operations fluctuated greatly. From a high of 160,300 in October 1952, NKPA and CCF forces were cut to 146,300 by March 1953. Following that, however, reinforcements were sent back into the partisan areas and by June 1953 they totaled 203,900.[8]

Despite the increase in the number of partisans and the strength of enemy forces opposing them, thus providing more targets of opportunity, the average number of partisan operations declined in the spring and summer of 1953. The previous year the partisans had conducted an average of 220 operations per month. Now, in 1953, with three times more partisans, the number of operations was down to an average of 160 per month. Enemy strength and the declining morale of the partisans and their American advisers were cited as contributing factors.[9]

These were not good times for the partisan operations. What had begun so nobly little more than two years earlier had degenerated into an operation that seemed to be running strictly on its own momentum. It had no backing from the ROK government and little from the U.S. government. Bureaucratic infighting among the services, ROK government suspicions about the intentions of the partisans, and sagging morale among American advisers and the partisans seemed to be increasing.

The 8240th Army Unit was under attack from within the army by those opposed to unconventional warfare. The Eighth Army's representative to CCRAK, a lieutenant colonel working in G-2, let it be known in no uncertain terms that he disliked unconventional warfare in general and the partisan operations in particular.

"I fear that we may have created a Frankenstein's monster," he told one interviewer. "We have introduced [the partisans] to these methods and motivated them to go in and shoot and steal. I am sure that wanton murders have been committed by those people. . . . I am convinced that the reports submitted by the partisans on their operations are grossly exaggerated. If you totaled up the figures you would find that most of the people in North Korea have been killed. Furthermore the strength and dispositions of enemy troops in the area does not indicate that they are influenced by concern about the guerrillas. What they do indicate is purely the defense of the coast. . . .

"Very bad types were selected for or gravitated to the 8240th Army Unit and the partisan headquarters. I cannot think of one that I know of who went there for the sake of the organization and the job. This appears not only in the conduct of these men, but also in the motives revealed by men asking to be transferred to the organization."[10]

The lieutenant colonel went on to charge that within the 8240th "there were many deficiencies in conduct, from wearing unauthorized decorations to laxity of administration, failure to report, and drunkenness on duty."[11]

Those statements left little doubt about what the Eighth Army and the regular army types who populated higher headquarters thought of the partisan operations. The Eighth Army had grown tired of the partisan operations, as had the ROK government. But what to do about them? There were no plans for dealing with the partisans at the end of the war, even though terms of the truce agreement being drafted called for them to be evacuated within five days of the cease-fire from west coast islands north and west of Hwanghae Province, with the exception of five islands, one of which was Paengnyong-do.

On April 16 an order was issued to stop recruiting partisans and to begin going through the ranks to get rid of those who could not or would not fight. The expansion did not cease immediately because of those recruits already in the pipeline. Partisan strength finally peaked in May 1953 at 22,227.[12]

Cutting off partisan forces at that number called for a revision of the plans that had been drawn up in February, since those plans presumed there would be forty thousand partisans by the middle of July. A revised Plan Phase IIA was published in mid-May. But the only minor modification to the original plan was the inclusion of the responsibility of protecting the left flank of the Eighth Army. This meant defending Kanghwa-do and Kyodong-do, two large islands in the Han River estuary on the western terminus of what would become the DMZ. Again, this was not new or innovative thinking. Flank protection for the Eighth Army had been part of McGee's original plans for the partisans developed more than two years earlier.

In addition to these general operations plans, two covert "stay-behind" missions were developed. One was code-named Beehive, the other Camel. They called for separate groups of 124 partisans each from the 2nd PIR to be sent into North Korea prior to the cease-fire and to remain dormant until after the truce agreement was signed. Then they were to infiltrate military and civilian offices, develop an underground network of agents, and be prepared when called on to implement plans to disrupt government functions.

Operation Beehive began on May 26. Before it was terminated in February 1954 the 102 partisans sent into North Korea reported back that they had recruited 674 additional members of the underground.[13] Operation Camel, with 82 partisans, was launched on July 27, the day the cease-fire began. It too reported "satisfactory" success before being disbanded in February 1954.[14]

The plan to withdraw the partisans from the islands and begin the demobilization process was known as Operation Plan PAPPY. It called for CCRAK and the Guerrilla Division of the 8240th Army Unit to pull all partisans off the mainland and the islands north of the 38th parallel (except those five specifically allowed by the truce agreement) twenty-four hours before the truce was signed to prevent fights with North Koreans trying to reclaim the islands.[15]

The order to execute PAPPY was issued on June 12. The partisans began withdrawing from the islands as ordered. But the next morning, FEC's G-2 called CCRAK's G-3 and told him to retake the islands. The truce was not going to be signed that day as planned. The partisans tried to fight their way back onto the islands they had just vacated, but in many instances they were not successful and suffered a number of casualties.[16]

Convincing the partisans to withdraw from the islands was not always an easy task. The partisans basically were given two choices: (1) withdraw and continue to receive logistical support from the U.S. Army while waiting to come under ROK Army control, or (2) stay on the islands, have your support cut off, and become stateless refugees.

It was not much of a choice.

There were, of course, a number of partisans who wanted to stay and fight, no matter what the consequences. The Americans left the decisions up to the individual partisan commanders, who were not always in agreement. One incident in the former Wolfpack area of operations is illustrative of how the partisans dealt with the decision-making process.

Several partisan commanders were sitting in a tent arguing the pros and cons of withdrawing while an American adviser listened and answered their questions. One partisan was adamantly opposed to leaving. The others were trying to talk him into it. After some time had passed, several of the partisans asked the American to leave the tent. Shortly after he did there were sounds of a scuffle from inside and a single gunshot. When the American was invited to return, the man who had been opposed to the withdrawal was gone. "We are now unanimous. We will withdraw," the partisans said.[17]

Evacuating the partisans, their families, tons of equipment, and thousands of refugees from the islands to which they had fled was no small task. FEC planners estimated that there were nearly ten thousand partisans (about three thousand of whom had their families with them), fifteen thousand refugees and other inhabitants, and more than eleven hundred tons of equipment to be removed from sixteen islands.[18]

The withdrawal in late July 1953 was done in stages. The first stage moved people back from the smaller islands to consolidation points on larger islands. From there the withdrawal proceeded to the five islands the truce agreement permitted the partisans to occupy: Paengnyong-do, Taechong-do, Sochong-do, Yonpyong-do, and U-do. The movement required dozens of LSTs, fishing junks, and any other vessel available to assist in uprooting these people from the homes in which many of them had lived for more than two years.

The legal status of the partisans remained a sensitive issue. Not until the truce was signed on July 27 did the ROK government finally address it. On August 16 the minister of national defense reached agreement with CCRAK that a provisional unit, designated the 8250th ROK Army Unit, would be formed to deal with some of the administrative burdens of the partisan operations. The new unit would handle personnel policy, determine rank for the partisan fighters, and grant the same benefits to the families of partisans killed in fighting as were given to ROK Army personnel. The U.S. Army's 8240th Army Unit would continue to handle operations, logistics, and training for the partisans since the 8250th ROK Army Unit was actually under control of the civilian arm of the government, not the military.[19]

The U.S. Army's organizational structure for handling the partisans continued to go through changes after the cease-fire much as it had during the war. In September 1953 FEC/LD (K) was reorganized and its Guerrilla Division was redesignated United Nations Partisan Infantry, Korea

(UNPIK). CCRAK was pulled out of Korea, sent to Japan, and became the Combined Command, Reconnaissance Activities Far East (CCRAFE), 8177th Army Unit. The AFFE Coordinating Detachment, 8078th Army Unit, was formed and became CCRAFE's representative in Korea.

Throughout the fall of 1953 and on into the winter, the partisans continued to be charged with the mission of defending the left flank of the Eighth Army from the islands of Kanghwa-do and Kyodong-do, remaining combat effective, and preparing to initiate unconventional warfare against North Korean targets. One other mission, far down the list, was "Be prepared to evacuate in the event it becomes necessary."[20]

There is no record of what the partisans thought about the various plans, missions, and organizational changes that left them dangling like a piece of unwanted bait at the end of a long line held jointly by the ROK government and AFFE. My efforts to remain in touch with Mr. Pak were thwarted by his reluctance to correspond in English and the press of events in my own life.

But it is clear from what transpired in January 1954 that the partisans were not pleased with the manner in which their contributions to the war effort were being rewarded. Early that month, the ROK government transferred the 8250th ROK Army Unit, which had been oversee-ing administrative matters relating to the partisans, from control of the civilian Ministry of National Defense to the ROK Army. That brought an end to the agreement with CCRAK (now CCRAFE), made the pre-vious August. Now the partisans were part of the ROK Army.

The deadline for integration of the partisans into ROK units was February 24, 1954. The plan, known as Quicksilver, made note of the special skills in unconventional warfare the partisans possessed and informed commanders of the potential risks they faced from partisans within their ranks. The ROK Army was so concerned that the partisans would disrupt army units that it ordered commanders to place no more than seven partisans in any ROK Army company and said that they had to be from different partisan units. The order also urged commanders to keep partisans away from "the rear areas where it would be easy to desert and join bandit groups."[21]

The unconventional warfare skills of the partisans were largely ignored. Here was a group of fighters who possessed the combat skills, the dedication, and the knowledge necessary to form the nucleus of a superb special operations unit. But they were to be broken up and scat-tered throughout the army because of ROK suspicions about their motives.

Quicksilver called for those partisans with at least two years of ser-vice to be honorably discharged and given their uniforms, mess gear, four blankets, two hundred pounds of rice, and transportation to any city of their choice in South Korea. Those partisans who agreed to enlist in the ROK army for at least two years were offered the same incentives, except for transportation home. In its place they were given an additional one hundred pounds of rice.[22]

The only thing the U.S. Army required of the partisans before their transfer to the ROK Army was that they turn in their weapons and, for some unexplained reason, their canteen cups.

There was great concern within the U.S. and ROK armies about how the partisans would react to Quicksilver. No one was sure whether there would be mutinies, wholesale desertions, or efforts to upset the truce. There was, in fact, a little of each.

As Quicksilver was being implemented two companies of partisans on Kanghwa-do decided to have one last shot at the North Koreans dug in across the Han River from them. They started firing mortars and artillery. Concerned that this might disrupt the armistice, Eighth Army commanders sent an urgent message to Lt. Col. Glenn Muggelberg, then commanding officer of UNPIK, to get the shooting stopped. Muggelberg hurriedly flew to the island on a helicopter and talked the partisan leaders into a cease-fire before the ROK Army sent in troops that he feared would precipitate a firefight worse than anything they got into with the NKPA.[23]

The desertion rate among the partisans was a good indicator of what they thought of Quicksilver and plans to make them part of the ROK Army. From a high of more than 22,000 the previous May, the partisan numbers had dwindled dramatically through discharges, desertions, and a general weeding out process. By February 1954 there were only 11,832 partisans. More than 2,000 deserted between the time they learned about Quicksilver in early February and when it was finally completed in early March 1954.[24]

Of those 22,000 partisans under arms in May 1953, fewer than 10,000 actually were transferred into the ROK Army. That means more than 12,000 partisans, over half the partisan force, disappeared between May 1953 and March 1954.[25]

Where did they go?

Undoubtedly, many of the South Koreans who had been recruited in the previous year deserted or were discharged and returned to their homes and families south of the DMZ. As for the North Koreans, I believe many went back to North Korea and tried as best they could to blend back into the society. Some went into the mountains and continued fighting. Radio traffic seeking assistance continued well after the armistice was signed. But the Americans had been instructed to break all contact with those units, some of which were true partisan operations, some of which probably had been doubled.[26]

By March 1954, the U.S. Army's role in the partisan operations in Korea had ended. It had lasted little more than three years, about two of which involved combat, with 1952 the most productive period.

So what did the partisans accomplish?

Records show that between May 1951 and the signing of the truce in July 1953 the partisans claimed to have conducted 4,445 actions throughout North Korea in which 69,000 casualties (dead and wounded) were inflicted, 950 prisoners and 5,000 weapons were captured, 2,700 vehicles and 80 bridges were destroyed, and 3,800 tons of food were destroyed or liberated from the North Koreans.[27]

The total cost to the U.S. government: roughly $100 million.[28]

There were many arguments during and after the war about the validity of the casualty claims by the partisans. Some reports on the effectiveness of partisan operations implied that if it could be shown the partisans lied about the number of casualties they had inflicted it would call into question their usefulness and the usefulness of unconventional warfare in a limited war.

But partisan claims of success were probably no more inflated than those of many American line officers in Korea and later in Vietnam. There is in any military operation the tendency to exaggerate one's successes—not only to justify what has just been done but to better one's position with his superiors. To a numbers-driven army, that was a way of business. Body counts were part of the fabric of Korea, even more so in Vietnam. Higher body counts meant faster promotions and more medals, even though they painted an unrealistic picture of the progress of the war.

In Korea, who could blame the partisans for exaggerating their successes when doing so meant more food, clothing, and shelter for the men to whom they were responsible? And obtaining accurate numbers in any partisan/guerrilla operation is extremely difficult because many of the actions are conducted at night or just before dawn and are of the hit-and-run variety. Partisan and guerrilla commanders seldom have the luxury after a mission to casually stroll around the battlefield counting the dead and wounded.

As was later demonstrated in Vietnam, the true worth of a partisan/guerrilla operation is not measured in hard numbers. It is best evaluated in those things that are difficult to measure, such as the morale of the enemy and the erosion of their will to fight as a result of a continuing campaign of unexpected partisan/guerrilla actions against what are considered safe targets.

In that respect the partisans were never properly utilized during Korea. Partisans are successful only if they are used in conjunction with regular forces and are allowed to operate on the fringes of the battle areas where the enemy least expects them. Operating alone, the partisans are doomed to carry out raids that may be of short-term tactical value but usually are of questionable strategic value.

In Korea, the lack of understanding about the true role of partisans in a major conflict, even in a limited war as this one was, and the dislike for unconventional warfare that permeated the army at that time prevented the partisans from being used to their maximum effectiveness. Then, when the decision was made to negotiate an end to the war rather than win it on the battlefield, the partisans were employed primarily as a diversion and later as a bargaining chip.

The partisans were not handled well from beginning to end. The U.S. Army first created an awkward and top-heavy organization with no clear lines of command and control and no clear mission statement to oversee the partisans. Then it refused to acknowledge the benefits of unconventional warfare and failed to provide the partisans with advisers specially trained to assist them. Those of us sent to advise the partisans had no special training or skills to bring to the job. For those unable or unwilling to adapt, it became an incredibly frustrating assignment.

It was clear from our experiences in Korea that the army had to address the issue of unconventional warfare and how to deal with it in future wars. It could not continue to treat it with disdain, as it had in Korea. It could not continue to throw untrained and unskilled advisers at it on an ad hoc basis.

Although I did not know it at the time I was serving in Korea, some of the more insightful senior officers in the army with backgrounds in unconventional warfare during World War II were fighting diligently through the bureaucracy arrayed against them to address this shortcoming within our ranks.

16

The Missing Link

The question of how the army would deal with unconventional warfare, partisan operations, and the training of indigenous paramilitary groups in future conflicts was not one about which those of us involved in the day-to-day planning and training at Leopard Base gave much thought. The daily grind left little time for pondering the great unknowns. We would start before dawn each day, do a dozen different things, chow down at night, then disappear into the blessed blackness of sleep. Worrying about what would become of us and the jobs we were doing was not part of the mission so we did not bother with it.

But a handful of visionaries had taken notice of what we were doing and used our operations as another lever in their ongoing battle to incorporate some semblance of special operations or unconventional warfare units into the basic structure of the army.

The first realization I had of that came one day in September 1952 while I was working on Wollae-do with Mr. Pak and the Donkey-4 partisans. I received an urgent radio message to return to Paengnyong-do immediately. Not knowing who or what was so important as to take me away from my work, I asked Mr. Pak to have his boat crew ferry me back to the main island as fast as the fishing junk's little four-horsepower diesel engine could carry us.

When I arrived at Leopard Base several hours later I found an army major waiting for me in Maj. Tom Dye's office. He introduced himself and explained that he was from Fort Bragg, North Carolina, on a tour of the partisan operations in Korea. He said he represented a new army program that specialized in unconventional warfare and asked me to brief him about my experiences with the partisans.

I spent the next two hours talking about Donkey-4's numerous raids into North Korea, my methods for training the partisans, the types of skills advisers needed to better assist the units with which they worked, and the shortcomings in how the army was dealing with the partisans and unconventional warfare.

The major seemed sympathetic to the fact that I was the lone trainer/ adviser for nearly eight hundred partisan fighters. He had heard the same story at many of his other stops. The new program would address that, he said. The army was finally beginning to understand its post–World War II shortcomings in unconventional warfare and special operations.

This new program was called Special Forces. It was designed to utilize small, highly skilled groups of soldiers (originally fifteen, later reduced to twelve-man A-teams) to train with partisan and indigenous fighters behind enemy lines. The heart of Special Forces was the team concept, he said. If Special Forces were properly utilized, no longer would individual soldiers with little training be sent into situations such as the one I and about two hundred other American advisers to the partisans in Korea found ourselves in.

The idea had great appeal to me. Too many times in Korea I found myself trying to do a dozen different things at the same time. My year of working in basic training at Fort Knox prior to Korea had enabled me to become proficient in a number of different skills that I found particularly useful while working with the partisans. But when it came to specialized skills in communications, demolitions, weapons, or medicine, I had to teach myself before I could teach them. I spent a great deal of time reading army manuals to stay a step or two ahead of the partisans. Having skilled Special Forces A-teams would eliminate that. Different skills could be taught to different groups of fighters at the same time. Training could be done more quickly and more efficiently, thus making partisan operations more effective.

Unfortunately, said the major, the first Special Forces personnel would not begin arriving in Korea until the following spring, long after I was gone.

"But we'd like you to come to Fort Bragg as a trainer," he said. "Here's my telephone number. Call me when you get back to the States, let me know when you're available, and we'll have you assigned to Fort Bragg as an instructor."

After the major departed there was a brief flurry of excitement around Leopard Base about the Special Forces concept. It led us to believe that the army brass had been convinced that unconventional warfare was an integral part of the combat arms package, worthy of equal billing with infantry, armor, and artillery branches.

I heard about the Special Forces again, but only in passing, during my lengthy debriefing in Seoul in December 1952. Despite the obvious benefits that could be derived from Special Forces, there seemed to be no sense of urgency at Guerrilla Division Headquarters of the 8240th Army Unit to get these men into the field where they were needed.

When I returned to the United States I discussed the possibility of getting into Special Forces with my infantry branch assignment officer. He told me I could go if I wanted. But, he said, if I had any desire to stay in the army I needed to get my career back on track. Many of my infantry contemporaries with whom I would be competing for promotions in later years had returned from Korea with the requisite platoon commands reflected in their records.

My records indicated I had been a "Special Forces commander" in Korea. Serving consecutive tours in Special Forces would not be conducive to an army career, I was told. I had to get my ticket punched in all the right ways to reflect regular army thinking. I needed the experience of commanding a company and it was important for my records to reflect that.

I had mixed emotions. I had decided to make the army a career and was holding orders to command a basic training company at Fort Gordon, Georgia, only seventy miles from my home. Although I found a Special Forces assignment to be quite appealing, I had no desire at that point in my career to buck the army bureaucracy. I opted to return to the traditional infantry career track. Basic training at Fort Gordon, rather than Special Forces at Fort Bragg, became my first duty station after Korea.

It would be another ten years until I saw the Special Forces in action. By then they had progressed from their tentative formation during the Korean War to the fabled Green Berets who were a favorite of President John F. Kennedy.

The Special Forces were largely the creation of Col. Aaron Bank, a short, wiry veteran of the OSS during World War II. Bank was one of the original Jedburghs, who parachuted into France prior to the Normandy landing to work with the French underground and conduct unconventional warfare against the Germans.

The OSS Jedburghs, along with the likes of McGee and Vanderpool in the Philippines and the little-known multinational V-Force in Burma, helped set the standard for special operations and unconventional warfare at a time when there was no literature on the subject and few trained experts. Unfortunately, conventional army thinking after the war did not permit these men to become the nucleus of a unit that specialized in such missions and the OSS was disbanded. The knowledge possessed by the veterans of the unit was lost or scattered throughout the army or other federal agencies.

Bank was one of a handful of officers who recognized the potential this type of warfare would have in the future. He realized that wars in the Cold War era were likely to be fought on a smaller scale than had World War II, making special operations and unconventional warfare key strategic concerns.

"What concerned me," he later wrote, "was whether or not the vacuum left by blindly dismantling an organization that had proved itself so indispensable as an essential component of total warfare would be properly filled."[1]

While staff studies were done and position papers were written about what role the army should play in unconventional warfare, it was not until the CIA was formed in 1947 that the issue of retaining this capability within the uniformed services began to be seriously studied. The CIA was unilaterally assuming unconventional warfare roles that previously had been the military's private province, and the Pentagon found that totally unacceptable.

By the time the Korean War broke out the CIA had established its Office of Policy Coordination (OPC) to conduct unconventional warfare missions. The army was still trying to decide how to deal with the issue and went into Korea without a clear plan. Those of us who were thrown into the unconventional warfare jobs in Korea on an ad hoc basis had to relearn the lessons our World War II predecessors had learned just a few years earlier. Despite that cadre of experts who had been trained and blooded during World War II, the army utilized only a few of them in Korea. Bank, for example, was assigned to the 187th Regimental Combat Team (Airborne) in Korea rather than the 8240th Army Unit, which could have utilized his expertise.

The course of events in Korea demonstrated the need for an unconventional warfare capability within the army. Plucking infantry officers out of the ranks and telling them to go train and advise partisan groups without any special training of their own was an incredibly poor way to address the problem. It also was a terrible use of manpower and resources. Bank continued to push for creation of a unit that would train soldiers to train partisan and indigenous fighters who could then operate in small groups behind the lines. But the overall impact of these special operations groups against enemy forces would be much like a larger paramilitary army.[2]

Realizing the command-and-control problems that unconventional warfare units often found themselves tangled up in, Bank wanted to ensure that if the army gave approval for such a unit it would have a separate theater command, rather than be controlled at field army level. That would put the unit out of the reach of corps and division commanders who might attempt to use it for short-term tactical missions rather than the strategic purposes for which Bank thought it better suited.[3]

Despite objections from the CIA and army purists who thought unconventional warfare was not a proper mission, Bank won army approval for his idea. In April 1952 he opened the Psychological Warfare Center at Fort Bragg, and in June that year the 10th Special Forces Group, with two officers and eight enlisted men, was activated.

The war was still going on in Korea but the initial focus for Special Forces was Europe. Army personnel with skills in European languages were sought in the initial calls for volunteers.[4] The overall strategic threat in Europe was perhaps greater than the threat in Korea. But it was also easier to train for Europe than Korea. The languages were not as difficult. Senior officers such as Bank had extensive experience in Europe and little in Korea. Most important, it was far easier for Special Forces personnel to blend in with the European population that it was with the Korean population.

In the fall of 1952 the Department of the Army ordered Special Forces to begin supporting the partisans in Korea. The September visit by the Special Forces major to Leopard Base and other partisan facilities was a scouting mission to see what his soldiers would be dealing with when they arrived. The initial request for Special Forces personnel was for sixty officers and fifteen enlisted men. The officers were to include five majors, the remainder captains and lieutenants. The enlisted men were to be of ranks between E-4 and E-7. All were to arrive during the spring of 1953.[5]

An intelligence course developed by FEC G-2 was given to new advisers on their way to Korea. The "Advanced Intelligence Course for Officers and Enlisted Men" was, according to its outline, a detailed study of such issues as espionage, escape and evasion, sabotage and demolitions, unconventional warfare, order of battle, intelligence gathering, interrogation, map reading, and the history of the NKPA.[6]

The course turned out to be largely a study of theory. It provided the new Special Forces personnel with little practical knowledge of the situation they would be facing in their assignments in Korea because the courses were largely taught by those who had no firsthand experience.[7]

In addition, the new advisers were given no special training in the language, culture, or history of Korea either at Fort Bragg or at Camp Drake, Japan, where the intelligence course was taught. A missionary who had served in Korea was brought in to talk about the people and the culture, but the Special Forces personnel did not take him or what he had to say seriously.[8]

When the Special Forces soldiers were finally sent to Korea the A-team structure was disregarded. CCRAFE believed the twelve-man cells would not work. The teams were broken up and individual members were scattered among partisan units. As a result, unit integrity of the A-teams was lost and the special skills of individuals were so diffused that the soldiers had little positive impact in the units to which they were assigned.[9]

It did not help that Special Forces personnel were sent to the theater so late in the war, when the lines were relatively static and partisan operations were tailing off. Had they arrived in early 1952, when the partisans' operational tempo and morale were at their peak, they might have made more of a difference. But by the spring of 1953 the partisan ranks had been bloated by many recruits of questionable motivation and the morale of the veterans was sagging as a result of the realization that the war would end without a new offensive against North Korea.

Although American advisers who worked with the partisans generally welcomed the idea of having Special Forces working with the units, the execution of the plan was not good. Language skills were a major problem, as they were for all American advisers to the partisans. Special Forces personnel were critical of the accounting procedures of the partisans, of their morale, and of the cumbersome command-and-control structure of the 8240th Army Unit. They also were generally disappointed that they were not on jump status. Many had been led to believe they would be conducting amphibious and airborne raids behind enemy lines, only to learn otherwise when they arrived in Korea.[10]

A number of valuable lessons were learned from this initial Special Forces deployment, though. First and foremost was that greater care should be given to who was assigned to work with indigenous personnel. It was generally found that the older or more mature the individual, the better he adapted to the uncertainties of partisan and guerrilla warfare and working with people from a culture about which he knew little.[11] More training should be given in language, customs, culture, and the history of the people with whom Special Forces would work.[12] It was even suggested that the army maintain a cadre of guerrilla warfare specialists who were experts in particular foreign cultures and languages and who had practical experience in those areas to which they might be deployed.[13]

It took several decades for the last suggestion to take root, but Special Forces now has specialists in any number of languages and cultures who can easily move into their regions of expertise and feel perfectly comfortable.

Had they been given more time, better training, more incentive, and a command-and-control structure that maintained unit integrity, the Special Forces could have worked in Korea. They just came too few, too late, and too unprepared for the realities of what the partisan operations had been, or could have been.

There was little question in my mind that Special Forces were the appropriate way to deal with partisans, guerrillas, and indigenous paramilitary groups in a limited war. It was the logical extension of the OSS. It was the link necessary to carry unconventional warfare operations from what they had been in World War II into an era in which the superpowers fought limited wars by proxy.

But what of those of us who held the line for unconventional warfare in Korea? What of John McGee and Jay Vanderpool? What of Leo

McKean and Tom Dye? What of Jim Mapp, Don Seibert, myself, and the other two hundred American personnel plucked from infantry and armor and artillery units and told to be advisers to the partisans?

We had, as best we could with the limited resources available to us, provided a semblance of continuity within the army for unconventional warfare operations. We learned the hard way: on the job. Yet when the war was over the knowledge and expertise we had gained working with the partisans was either ignored or overlooked. We were sent back to our regular branches and told that if we wanted to make a career of the army we had best begin conforming to the army program for promotions.

The lessons we had learned in Korea about the implementation and utilization of unconventional warfare in a limited war, the skills we had acquired while working with a people in a culture that was totally alien to us, and the knowledge we had gained of how partisan and guerrilla operations can affect the morale and will to fight of the enemy were largely disregarded after Korea by a bureaucracy that still had little use for unconventional warfare.

A new generation of unconventional warriors, these specifically tasked for the job, would have to learn all those lessons all over again. The repository of knowledge that those of us who had worked with the partisans in Korea possessed was never tapped. The lessons learned in Korea about unconventional warfare were learned by a select few. The army itself chose not to learn them.

So it was not surprising when I was in Vietnam twelve years later and discovered that another new generation of soldiers was having to relearn the lessons of unconventional warfare that had been learned by the likes of Bank, McGee, and Vanderpool in World War II, and by myself and others in Korea.

Only this time we were looking at unconventional warfare from the other side. Instead of being the hunters, we were now the hunted.

17

Lessons Not Learned

The road between the town of Ban Me Thuot in South Vietnam's central highlands and the airstrip that served it was about a three-mile, one-lane, winding dirt track with several blind curves and heavy foliage on both sides. It was made to order for ambushes.

The first time I saw that road I knew I did not like it. All the old instincts I had felt going into combat in Korea came rushing back: the heightened awareness, the rush of adrenaline, the sense that I had to move quickly and decisively. Only this time I felt as if I were looking down the wrong end of a gun barrel.

The day was miserably hot when I arrived in Ban Me Thuot, the provincial capital of Darlac Province, which had Cambodia on its western border. I had been assigned as an adviser to the 23rd Division of the Army of the Republic of Vietnam (ARVN), headquartered there.

A lone American soldier armed only with a carbine was sent to meet my flight from Pleiku, retrieve me, and ferry me back to the American compound that had once been a hunting lodge for former emperor Bao Dai. No sooner had I tossed my gear into the back of the jeep than the driver slammed it into first gear, popped the clutch, and tore off down the road at high speed, the wheels churning up billowing clouds of red dust.

"Any problems with the guerrillas around here?" I shouted above the noise of the jeep's motor, hanging on to my seat as we bounced through the ruts.

"They're hitting all around us," the driver said curtly, never taking his eyes off the road or the foliage on either side.

"What about security along this road?"

"We've been hit along here before," he said grimly.

It was obvious the driver liked this road as little as I did. He was eager to get back to the American compound and some semblance of security as quickly as possible. I found myself agreeing with him. But as we sped down the road I could not help but look at the surrounding terrain as I might have twelve years earlier in Korea.

Where were the likely ambush spots with the best fields of fire? Where could the guerrillas block the road and prevent us from turning around? Where would a single vehicle be most vulnerable? What about a convoy? Where were the avenues of withdrawal that would offer the best cover and concealment?

I made a note to myself never to travel that road unarmed or unescorted again. A single vehicle made an inviting target. An officer in a single vehicle was a magnet for ambush.

I was one of about ten officers and fifteen enlisted men who made up the U.S. Army's advisory team to the ARVN 23rd Division. The senior adviser was a full colonel. He had a lieutenant colonel as a deputy and four majors to advise the ARVN G-1, G-2, G-3, and G-4 sections. The remaining American officers were captains who served in a variety of capacities.

Despite my combat experience in Korea and my knowledge of unconventional warfare and guerrilla tactics, I was assigned to assist the 23rd Division's G-1. Casualties, absences without leave (AWOL), and desertions among the division's troops were rising. It was my job to work with the G-1 on his personnel requisitions and his casualty reports, and to find out for Vietnamese and American officials why the desertion rate was so high.

To get a better sense of why this was happening I began accompanying the G-1 on trips to remote hamlets and ambush sites to talk to ARVN soldiers. Since our air assets were rather limited we usually traveled by jeep or truck. But knowing the tactics of the guerrillas and our vulnerability on the roads, I made it a point to travel in strength. Before each trip I studied aerial photographs of our route, looking for possible ambush sites and areas where mines might be planted in the road. Then I insisted we travel in convoys with at least three vehicles, preferably five, with machine guns mounted front and rear. When we came to likely ambush spots we would dismount and approach on foot. I had no desire to contribute my name to a Viet Cong (VC) commander's kill list.

I'm not sure whether it was through luck or preparation, but aside from a few isolated sniping incidents, none of the convoys in which I traveled was ever ambushed.

My initial impression of the ARVN soldiers was not good. The Korean partisans I had worked with a decade earlier had been much more impressive fighters. They had a mission to free their families and reclaim their homeland. They were fighting for a cause. The ARVN did not demonstrate the same eagerness for combat. Many were draftees more concerned about their personal problems than their country. There was little unit pride among 23rd Division soldiers, unlike the Korean partisans, who had felt it was a great honor to serve with Donkey-4 and Mr. Pak.

We were also in a very unsettled political period following the assassination the previous year of John F. Kennedy in the United States and Ngo Dinh Diem in South Vietnam. Morale was dropping dangerously low among the ARVN troops because of problems in the government. As it did, the desertion rate climbed and the desire to get out and fight the guerrillas waned. The ARVN seemed to prefer to sit in their sandbagged bunkers and wait for the guerrillas to come to them.

But that was no way to fight a guerrilla war. That merely provided the guerrillas with easy targets. The ARVN had to go out and fight the guerrillas where they lived. They had to learn where the enemy was coming from and where he was getting his resources and attack him there. They had to get soldiers out on the trails and in the villages to monitor guerrilla movements and ambush the ambushers. Unless they did that, the VC would do the same thing the Korean partisans had done to the NKPA. The ARVN were thinking defensively, not offensively. The VC were hunting them, not vice versa. And because we were allied with the ARVN, we were among the hunted.

Prior to going to Vietnam I had received some training relating to the Communist insurgency there. At the Command and General Staff College at Fort Leavenworth in 1962 I learned about the French experiences in Vietnam. At the army's infantry center at Fort Benning, Georgia, where I served as the S-3 of the 2nd Infantry Division's 2nd Brigade, Vietnam and the guerrilla tactics of the VC were all the talk of the young officers eager to serve their time in a combat zone.

But there had been no formal training in unconventional warfare or guerrilla tactics and how to counter them. Not a word was mentioned of what the American-backed partisans had done in Korea and what the NKPA had done to counter us. If lessons had been learned in Korea, they were lessons now lost.

During discussions with my fellow American advisers at Ban Me Thuot I learned that they also had received only a minimal amount of training in unconventional warfare and guerrilla tactics. Most of the advisers had been trained in traditional line companies and were adhering to those principles while trying to teach the ARVN how to fight a counterguerrilla war. It was disheartening to realize that much of what we had learned in Korea about unconventional warfare was not being passed on to those sent to Vietnam. A whole new generation of soldiers was being forced to relearn the lessons the OSS had learned in World War II and the Guerrilla Division of the 8240th Army Unit had learned in Korea.

It did not appear that either the Vietnamese or Americans at levels above division fully understood the concept of guerrilla and unconventional warfare in those early years. They were concerned about why jeeps were being blown up, why we were taking casualties that were slowly diminishing morale and combat effectiveness, and why the VC had free access to the countryside and we did not. But there appeared to be little understanding of how it was happening.

In Korea, we had safe areas on the islands that permitted us to rest and plan strikes against the NKPA when they least expected them. Had we been forced off those islands and kept on the run, we would have lost much of our effectiveness. The VC had their safe areas deep in the jungles and in the mountains. They also controlled the villages at night. The ARVN were permitting the VC to use those sanctuaries to strike when and where it best suited them and least suited us.

To effectively combat the VC their safe areas had to be eliminated and they had to be fought on their terms. Small patrols, killer teams that knew how to live in the jungle, had to seek the VC out where they lived and do to them what they were doing to us. We had to take the battle to them, and it was not being done. Instead, the Americans and ARVN were defending small hamlets and building secure bases from which they were trying to fight a more conventional war. The only Americans I saw who had a real understanding of what the VC were doing and how to counter them were the U.S. Army's Special Forces teams.

Special Forces had been active in the Ban Me Thuot area for about eighteen months when I arrived. Unlike what had happened in Korea, they had been sent to Vietnam with their twelve-man A-teams intact. One of their first missions was to train Rhade tribesmen in villages near Ban Me Thuot. The plan was eventually to ring the provincial capital with well-defended villages to deter the VC. But once that was accomplished the Special Forces began pushing the villagers into conducting small unit operations against the VC.[1]

I visited a number of the villages where Special Forces personnel were working and was quite impressed with the quality and dedication of the soldiers and with their knowledge of unconventional warfare tactics and how to counter them. I felt far more comfortable with them and the villagers they had trained than I did with the 23rd Division.

It made me wonder what I might have been able to do in Vietnam had I decided to follow my heart instead of my head and go straight into Special Forces after Korea rather than follow the traditional army career track. I had certain knowledge about unconventional warfare and its applications that the army had no interest in tapping. I do not know if the army's lack of interest was due to the fact that it considered our work in Korea less than satisfactory or if it was because the situation remained so unsettled that it was considered unwise to open the files on special operations there. Whatever the reason, it was terribly frustrating to not be able to pass along the knowledge I had about the type of war we were fighting in Vietnam.

My influence on tactics within my own advisory group and the 23rd Division was minimal. As adviser to the G-1, my views of unconventional warfare were neither sought nor welcomed by the G-3. As a major I was in no position to rewrite our strategy or influence tactics, but it was obvious to me that the war was not being fought correctly if the intent was to suppress the guerrillas and establish a stable government in South Vietnam. The thinking was conventional and the tactics were conventional. But the enemy was totally unconventional.

The VC had learned the tactics of guerrilla warfare quite well. What they were doing to the ARVN and the Americans was much the same thing the OSS did to the Germans and Japanese, Mao Tse-tung's guerrilla army did to the Nationalists of Chiang Kai-shek, and the partisans of the 8240th Army Unit's Guerrilla Division did to the North Koreans and Chinese.

One of the primary concerns of the Americans and the ARVN soldiers was how to differentiate a VC from a peaceful Vietnamese. They spent many long hours discussing it. Truth be told, it is quite impossible to do so. That was the same problem we had tried to give the North Koreans. We were successful there in infiltrating our people by providing them with various forms of identification. Now the VC were doing the same thing to us. The only way to successfully counter it was through martial law and total suppression of human and civil rights, as the North Koreans had done in their villages.

Fear and intimidation of the civilian population are two of the primary devices for shutting down an insurgency. That is why the totalitarian regimes are much more successful in rooting out insurgencies in their midst than are free-world countries. They have no second thoughts about total suppression of human and civil rights. Americans were not willing to go that far in Vietnam, and rightly so. It would have sent the wrong message to the government of Vietnam. The way to deal with the problem correctly under those circumstances was a complex procedure that should have involved winning the confidence of the people by making the villages secure from threats, intimidation, and assassinations by the insurgents. The ARVN and the government of Vietnam were never able to do that.

Vietnam was an uncomfortable assignment for me in many respects. I could see what was happening but could do nothing to influence changes. And I much preferred to be on the attacking side of any operation. I was not comfortable in a fight where I did not have some control over the situation and was put on the defensive.

I had been very comfortable in Korea because I knew everything about the enemy I needed, based on intelligence provided by our partisan agents, to make good tactical decisions. In Vietnam, I knew virtually nothing about the enemy. We never got a good handle on the VC to analyze where they lived, what they were doing at any particular moment, where they got their supplies, and what routes they used to attack us. But the VC seemed to know everything about us.

In Korea we utilized our own network of agents to gather what intelligence we needed for our missions before sending it up the line. The problem there was, as I have mentioned previously, that little information of any strategic value to us came back down the line. The information flow went one way.

It was the same in Vietnam. Seldom, if ever, did any of the information the 23rd Division collected come back with a larger overview of the enemy situation and what we were facing. Even the Special Forces troops said they were collecting a great deal of intelligence and passing it on to higher headquarters but were receiving very little useful information in return. The problem here, at least from my perspective, was that we did not have the same in-depth network of agents among the VC as we had had in Korea.

In Vietnam, as in Korea, it was as if information was being collected solely for the intelligence community and those echelons above division, where it was of little practical value. By the time any of the heavily sanitized information made its way back down the chain it was too dated or too diluted to be of any use to the people who had the most need of it.

My job, though, was in neither intelligence nor operations, and I had little influence in how those things were done. My job was to find out why the desertion rate among the ARVN was so high. There were thousands of soldiers languishing in prison charged with desertion.

In late November 1964 I was ordered to prepare a briefing for the J-1 of Military Assistance Command, Vietnam (MACV) on the reasons for the desertions and what we were doing about it. Although I did not have access to imprisoned deserters and those who had gone AWOL from the 23rd Division, I talked with members of their units and found that family problems and the inability of soldiers to get leave to take care of the problems had resulted in many of the desertions.

Many times there were legitimate reasons for going home: a death in the family or a home that had been burned by the VC because the owner was in the army. But the ARVN leave policy was so inflexible that it was difficult for soldiers to get away from their units even for short periods of time to deal with a crisis. So they simply deserted, only to be picked up a short time later and thrown into prison. Many were good soldiers. But they were useless to the war effort in prison. Somehow they had to be recycled.

I tried to convince the ARVN officers that they had to be more flexible and understanding of the personal problems of their soldiers. A soldier who worries constantly about his family is not a good soldier. Unless that soldier believes his family is safe and is being taken care of in his absence, he will not be able to concentrate on the mission at hand.

I briefed the J-1, Maj. Gen. Ben Sternberg, and he thanked me and asked about my background. I told him I had served in a special operations unit in Korea and had seen combat there.

"I want you on my staff," he said. "I don't have anybody else who has ever been shot at and I need somebody who can go out into the field and give me some accurate reports about what's going on out there."

Within a few days I found myself sitting in an office in the MACV headquarters in Saigon, working as a plans and programs officer in a subsection of J-1 known as J-14, under the direction of Lt. Col. Lewis J. Ashley, the staff director of J-14. My job was to work with the ARVN on their personnel requirements.

Over the next few months I spent a great deal of time in prisons interviewing deserters. Some days I would interview two dozen or more, asking them why they had deserted and what could be done to rectify the situation. The answers were much the same as I had heard while with the 23rd Division. Most had not deserted because they did not want to fight. They simply were concerned about some family matter and were not granted leave to attend to it. After interviewing more than two hundred deserters I wrote another report, in which I again stressed that if ARVN officers wanted to command good soldiers they must first be good commanders themselves and look after the welfare of their men and their families.

But the job for which Sternberg had specifically tasked me was to get out into the field whenever possible and get a close look at the situation there. I had access to his helicopter and was able to fly into hot spots to check on casualties and determine personnel needs, often while the fighting was still going on. By getting on the scene early we were able to do a much better job of helping the ARVN keep its units up to strength. We bypassed much of the Vietnamese and American bureaucracy and cut the personnel replacement time from weeks to days. The forays also helped me better understand how the VC were fighting the war and how similar their tactics were to those we had used in Korea.

On one occasion I flew into a hamlet about fifty miles northeast of Saigon not long after the fighting had supposedly stopped. It was late afternoon and I planned to talk to the province chief and the military commander, then fly back to Saigon before dark. Just as we sat down in the province chief's office to discuss what had happened earlier in the day a tremendous explosion shook the building and sent all of us sprawling on the floor. I quickly jumped up and looked out the window. About five hundred yards down the road the VC had sprung an ambush on a ten-vehicle convoy coming into the hamlet. Command-detonated mines and automatic weapons were taking a toll of the vehicles and soldiers.

I had only a .45-caliber pistol with me, but we rushed out of the hut and jumped into nearby bunkers and trenches, ready to defend the village. Just as we got there several badly wounded ARVN soldiers were brought into the province chief's compound. They needed immediate evacuation and medical attention. I told the pilot of my chopper to take as many as he could to Saigon, then come back for me. Within minutes the chopper was loaded and headed for Saigon.

Even before the chopper got off the ground the shooting around the ambush site had stopped except for a few random shots from frustrated ARVN soldiers. The VC were gone. They had destroyed four vehicles, killed at least six soldiers, and wounded a dozen more before vanishing. We sent out search teams but found no blood trails and no traces of the attackers other than spent shell casings.

I could not help but admire the skill with which the VC had done their job. They hit with surprise, speed, and overwhelming violence, inflicting casualties, creating confusion, and sowing fear that they were everywhere and could strike at will. Then, before the ARVN could recover and call in artillery or air strikes, the VC faded into the jungle.

The VC tactics were working. They created fear and uncertainty. They made us believe they were everywhere and could attack anything at any time. Not knowing how or when the VC would strike and the anxiety of waiting for attacks to happen were part of their campaign to erode our confidence and morale. It was exactly the same thing we had done in Korea.

The VC had focused much of their energy and attacks on outlying regions in those early years, sparing Saigon. The city was something of an island in the midst of the fighting going on in the jungles around it. It was an incredibly bizarre experience to be able to put on civilian clothes, walk down to the Brink Hotel, order a steak and a beer, and watch a firefight going on five miles away. Colored tracers would streak through the black night sky and balls of orange flame would explode out of the darkness as helicopters, jets, and ground troops fought it out with the VC.

Then came Christmas Eve 1964, when the VC brought the war to the city.

I was on my way to the Brink Hotel that afternoon for lunch. The Brink served as the quarters for many officers assigned to MACV and was a favorite dining place for Americans in Saigon. I was two blocks from the hotel when I was knocked backward by an incredible explosion. I looked up to see smoke rising from the direction of the hotel. I raced down the street and found stunned and bloodied survivors of a truck bomb attack streaming out of the hotel. I did what I could to help, but all the while I was doing it I marveled at the ease with which the VC had struck at the heart of Saigon.

Only later did I learn that somehow only two people had been killed, one of them an American naval officer. More than one hundred were wounded. But the intended targets of the attack, entertainer Bob Hope and his troupe, had escaped unscathed. They had been delayed at the Tan Son Nhut airport unloading equipment for their Christmas show. The VC sapper had detonated the bomb prematurely.[2]

More attacks on what were thought to be secure American installations quickly followed. On February 7, 1965, the VC attacked Camp Holloway, a facility for American advisers near the provincial capital of Pleiku in the central highlands. Eight Americans were killed, more than one hundred were wounded, and ten U.S. aircraft were destroyed. The VC escaped virtually untouched.[3]

A retaliatory air strike later that afternoon against targets in North Vietnam failed to impress the VC. Three days later they bombed a barracks for American enlisted men in the coastal city of Qui Nhon, killing twenty-three and wounding twenty-one.[4]

The arrival of the 9th Marine Expeditionary Brigade at Da Nang's Red Beach on March 8, 1965, represented a major escalation of the war from which there was no turning back. Now we were looking at conventional forces trying to fight an unconventional war. The sense was that if we threw enough troops at the problem it would somehow be solved. But it seemed the more troops we sent to Vietnam, the worse it got.

By the time I returned to the United States in September 1965, the transition from guerrilla insurgency to full-scale war had been completed. American troops were flowing into the country by the thousands. North Vietnamese Army regulars were becoming more involved in the fighting. The opportunity to win the peace by countering the guerrilla insurgency and winning the people had passed. Unconventional warfare and special operations would now have to be employed in a different manner, as a smaller part of a wider war in which more conventional units and tactics were also being employed.

During my time in Vietnam I saw no indication, other than among the Special Forces personnel, that any of the knowledge we had gained about special operations and unconventional warfare in Korea had been passed along. The army had decided to keep the history and lessons learned by those of us who had served with the Guerrilla Division of the 8240th Army Unit classified. Line officers being sent to Vietnam had no access to a large source of material and experienced personnel who could have helped them better understand what they were facing.

Instead, the lessons of unconventional warfare and special operations and how to deal with them were learned in Vietnam as they had been in Korea and during World War II—the hard way, one unit at a time, one soldier at a time.

It made no sense then. It makes no sense now.

Epilogue

The army bureaucracy's efforts to downplay what those who served in special operations and unconventional warfare jobs in Korea had done was apparent in the manner with which it dealt with the issue of who was authorized to wear the Combat Infantryman's Badge (CIB).

The CIB is sometimes referred to as the Blue Badge of Courage. It is one of the army's most distinctive and coveted awards. It is worn above all other badges and decorations on the uniform, signifying that the wearer is an infantry soldier who has served his country in ground combat against the enemy.

Army regulations governing who can wear the CIB are quite restrictive, and rightly so. It would cheapen the award and the honor of those who have earned it with their blood for the regulations to be any less rigid.

In Korea, those who served with the Guerrilla Division of the 8240th Army Unit were told that while most of us were infantry officers leading infantry troops into combat against the enemy, we were not authorized to wear the CIB. Special operations combat was not considered real combat. I'm not sure what differences there were in getting shot at while serving with an infantry unit and getting shot at while serving with a special operations unit, but someone within the army bureaucracy had made that distinction in World War II and was continuing the tradition in Korea.

It did not matter that I was one of only a handful of American soldiers to go on extended missions behind enemy lines with partisan infantry forces.

It did not matter that I had participated in raids against North Korean and Chinese soldiers on their turf.

It did not matter that on numerous occasions I had been closer to the enemy, including engaging in hand-to-hand combat, than had many line officers who had been forced to sit in trenches along the front during the last two years of the war and never got to within several hundred yards of the enemy.

My job title in Korea was Special Forces Commander, and that was enough to disqualify me from wearing the CIB.

Some of my colleagues found the ruling just another item on a long list of frustrations that went with the job of working with the partisans. I took it as a personal insult and decided to do something about it. On July 29, 1953, I launched my own one-man battle against the entrenched army bureaucracy to win approval to wear the CIB. It was a campaign that would drag out for nearly twelve years. The army resisted me at every turn and rejected every argument I proposed. But I was patiently, if not obstinately, persistent.

Although I was fighting for myself, I was also fighting for every other infantry soldier who had served with the partisans. If I broke through the bureaucratic mind-set regarding the CIB and special operations forces, it would open the door for others who had served with me.

In addition to being denied the CIB, I and other members of the 8240th Army Unit were denied a combat patch. Neither the 8240th nor UNPIK had an officially recognized combat patch. But a patch design had been drawn by someone at Guerrilla Division Headquarters in Seoul during the early years of the war, and I had gone so far as to have a few cloth patches actually made while I was on R&R in Tokyo in 1952. The patch had a white parachute on a field of blue, flanked by a flaming torch and a red sword, descending on a green mountain. Above it, "UNPIK" was in black letters on a field of red. But the army never officially recognized it for wear.

Without the CIB or a combat patch on my uniform, I was often put in the awkward position of having to explain why I was wearing a Silver Star. That particular award is not given for meritorious service. It can be won only in direct combat with the enemy. How, I was frequently asked, could an infantry officer win a Silver Star without earning a CIB or a combat patch?

It was an uncomfortable and occasionally embarrassing situation. I tried to talk around the issue as much as possible, explaining only that I had been with a special unit during the war. For years I felt compelled to remain silent about the partisan operations and my role in them. The unit's records remained classified, and since we had only a truce agreement with the North Koreans, not a true peace, I did not know if I might jeopardize any ongoing partisan operations by talking about the 8240th.

In my initial request to the army's adjutant general about the CIB I pointed out that I was an infantry officer who had served in Korea with a partisan infantry battalion, that I had received ten months of combat pay, and that I had been awarded the Silver Star and the Bronze Star for my combat service. The rejection came flying back from Washington in little more than two weeks, something of a record considering the levels of bureaucracy these things normally have to go through.

The two-paragraph letter set out the criteria for being authorized to wear the CIB, then stated: "Since no record can be found to show that you were assigned to an infantry unit of regimental or smaller size in combat, your request for the Combat Infantryman Badge cannot receive favorable consideration."

The U.S. Army did not consider the partisan units to be true infantry units, or what we did against the NKPA to be true combat.

Subsequent rejections over the years simply expanded on that argument. The army simply did not recognize special operations missions as combat, whether they had occurred in World War II or Korea. The concept that special operations advisers had been in combat was totally foreign to the army bureaucracy. Combat was thought of in the traditional sense, with large units and massed formations. Unconventional warfare and special operations were not combat in the traditional army thinking. It was not until the Special Forces troops who served in Vietnam began to be recognized as combat soldiers as well as advisers that the army's thinking began to change.

Still, it was July 28, 1965, nearly twelve years to the day since I had started what to some of my colleagues seemed a Quixotic quest, that I received authorization from the Department of the Army to wear a CIB. That night I proudly pinned the blue-and-silver badge on my uniform, content that I had beaten the bureaucracy, relieved that I no longer would have to answer embarrassing questions about my awards.

After my tour in Vietnam I went through an assortment of key officer assignments. I was a battalion commander and G-3 with the 82nd Airborne Division, attended the Air War College, and then, as a colonel, was selected for helicopter pilot training.

But no matter where I went or what I did, thoughts of Korea and the partisan fighters of Donkey-4 were never far from my mind. The partisans had helped mold much of my thinking about the military, special operations, and unconventional warfare even though their efforts were unrecognized by many veterans of the Korean War.

When I returned to Korea in September 1972 to command the 2nd Infantry Division's 2nd Brigade I found the partisan legacy was as unknown there as it was in the U.S. Army. All of South Korea had gone through an incredible transformation over the last twenty years. I was stunned by what I saw as I flew into Kimpo International Airport. The only thing I recognized was the Han River.

The rubble of war and shells of buildings that had made up so much of Seoul in 1952 were long gone, replaced by sleek high-rise office buildings and apartments. The shell-pocked streets and roads had been paved over and widened into expressways. The refugees and orphans begging on street corners had given way to an industrious and energetic people who had transformed Seoul into the economic rival of Tokyo and Hong Kong. Only outside the city were there some vestiges of the Korea I had known: the neatly manicured rice paddies and mud houses with thatched roofs.

The American military presence had been reduced considerably since the end of the war, but at least 20,000 soldiers remained in the 2nd

Division and its supporting units to serve as a deterrent to the North Koreans. The ROK Army had made considerable strides over the last two decades, assuming much of the responsibility for defense of the DMZ and of South Korea. It had been outfitted with better equipment and given first-class training that had instilled in its members a great sense of duty to their country.

My brigade was headquartered at Camp Hovey, near the town of Tongduchon, north of Seoul. Between us and the DMZ were about ten miles of rugged mountains that I knew would not deter the NKPA in the least little bit. If the North Koreans attacked, my unit would be sent to plug whatever leaks there were in the line, so we had to maintain combat readiness at all times. In order to do that I relied greatly on the experience and expertise of the three top-notch battalion commanders, all lieutenant colonels and good soldiers, who served with me over much of the next year: Bob Bass (retired as a colonel), Jim Hall (retired as a lieutenant general), and Pete Dawkins (retired as a brigadier general), the latter a Rhodes Scholar and football player of some note during his undergraduate days at West Point.

My brigade also had the responsibility of defending antiaircraft missile sites throughout South Korea. I had companies and platoons scattered all over the peninsula. The fact that I was now a helicopter pilot made it much easier to grab a chopper and fly out to inspect one of my far-flung units without having to scrounge around for a pilot. Many times I flew myself on these inspection trips. When I was burdened with paperwork, I got someone else to fly while I worked.

Over the next year my numerous inspection flights enabled me to see much of Korea that I had not gotten an opportunity to see twenty years earlier. These trips also gave me a much better sense of the state of readiness of the country and its armed forces, particularly along the DMZ, where I flew occasional inspections. When I flew up around the DMZ I was always a passenger in a helicopter piloted by someone experienced flying in the area because of the risks of straying into forbidden airspace.

On those occasions when I made closer inspection tours of our positions on the south side of the DMZ, I often found myself peering through a pair of field glasses at a North Korean soldier looking back at me. It was the first time in twenty years I had seen a North Korean that close. Back then we would have shot it out. But in 1972 all we did was stare at each other.

Things were always tense around the DMZ. But I did not realize how tense they were in the rest of the country until I triggered a full-scale alert at a secret ROK jet fighter base. The incident occurred as I was being flown back to Camp Hovey from an inspection trip to one of our missile sites near Pusan. I was a passenger at the time, going over some paperwork, when the pilot informed me that bad weather and darkness were about to force us down far short of our destination.

The pilot began looking for a small civilian airport near Osan, south of Seoul. Through the thickening clouds and darkness he spotted what he thought was the airport. He quickly radioed for permission to land and received it. But no sooner had the Huey's skids hit the tarmac than we were surrounded by grim-faced ROK military guards in jeeps mounted with .50-caliber machine guns pointed right at us. Although the pilot had been talking to the tower at the nearby civilian airport, he had actually landed at a high-security air force installation. We had breached security, and the ROK guards were in no mood for explanations.

Fortunately, a U.S. Air Force colonel arrived on the scene within minutes and I was able to explain our mistake. He said we were about ten miles too far north and suggested we leave as soon as we could. The pilot got the Huey cranked up and off the ground in record time and headed south for the civilian airport, which we finally found at around midnight.

One of my missile site defense units was on the Yellow Sea northwest of Seoul. Flying up there I could see some of the offshore islands that had been in Wolfpack's area of operations during the Korean War. Just seeing those islands and the Yellow Sea evoked a great sense of nostalgia about what had happened there two decades earlier and spurred me to make more of an effort to learn what had become of Pak Choll and Lt. Cho Byung Chan, our ROK Army interpreter at Leopard Base.

My initial efforts had been sidetracked by my duties as a brigade commander. But once I settled into the job I began making additional inquiries, all through unofficial channels, with ROK military and government officials about the partisans and Paengnyong-do. Most of my questions were answered with blank stares and puzzled looks. Few knew about Paengnyong-do. Fewer still knew about the partisans.

I checked rosters of the ROK Army looking for Mr. Pak and Lieutenant Cho. I talked to individual ROK Army soldiers when we were on maneuvers. I talked to the ROK Army lieutenant colonel who served as an adviser to the 2nd Infantry Division. He was only vaguely familiar with the partisan operations. He knew some of them had been integrated into the army but had little additional information. Besides, I was told, finding any particular partisan would be extremely difficult because some had given false names when they became a part of the ROK Army in order to protect their families in North Korea. Even the intelligence people I talked to were of little help. They either did not know or were unwilling to tell me what had become of the partisans.

I tried to get back to Paengnyong-do, which was still in South Korean hands. I assumed it was now being used as a listening post, given its prime location. But the only way out to it was by boat, I was told. I could fly a helicopter out, but there were no assurances I would be able to refuel once I got there. And if I went unescorted, I ran the risk of provoking an incident with the North Koreans. It would not do much for international relations to have the commander of a U.S. Army infantry brigade shot down or taken hostage while on a personal quest.

A chartered boat would take several days to get to the island and back, and I could not take that much time off. I had to be able to respond to the division commander, Maj. Gen. Hank Emerson, within ten minutes any time of the day or night. I could not afford to be that far from my post for several days.

By the time I finished my second tour in Korea in August 1973, I had made absolutely no progress in finding Mr. Pak, Lieutenant Cho, or any of the other partisans with whom I had served. They, like thousands of other partisans, had vanished.

I do not know how many fought on after they were officially disbanded in 1953. Nor do I know how many are still out there, resigned to a life of anonymity in South Korea or a life of fear in North Korea. But I like to think that their spirit still lives in the people of Korea. And I like to think that if the circumstances ever called for it again, the spirit of the partisans would be rekindled among Koreans on both sides of the DMZ and they would take to the islands and the mountains to fight as they did in the early 1950s.

Only this time I would hope that the U.S. Army, having ignored the lessons of unconventional warfare and special operations learned in World War II and Korea, would this time take note of those unique qualities possessed by partisan fighters and exploit them to their fullest.

Appendix A

HEADQUARTERS
OPERATION LEOPARD
APO 301

20 JULY 1952

SUBJECT: Recommendation of Awarding Reward for Meritorious Service
1st Lt. Ben S. Malcom, Infantry, S-2, Operation Leopard

TO: Commanding Officer
8240th Army Unit
FEC/LD (K)
APO 301

1. We hereby unanimously recommend, with our sincere appreciation, that
1st Lt. Ben S. Malcom, who distinguished himself in action, deserves high
praise for his outstanding military merit displayed during a raid in which, as
below recorded, he took up command of whole operation, fought gallantly
in unruffled manner, called and adjusted tactical support of aircraft and
Navy, and knocked out two enemy positions by exploiting and managing
maximum capacities of ground troops, aircraft and Naval vessels.

a. Time of Raid: From 140400 I July to 140600 I July 1952. Period of
preparation: From 10 July to 13 July 1952.

b. Objective of Raid: Kujin-ni, Haean Myon, Changyon Gun, Hwang
Hae Do, Korea.

(1) Gun position XC 632197.

(2) Heavy machine gun position, XC 635205.

c. The enemy strength and equipment: One NKA Company with
about 150 troops and one anti-tank gun and one heavy machine gun.

d. Record of Raid:

(1) Lt. Malcom made a plan of operation, prepared most carefully. On the
10th of July 1952, in order to annihilate the enemy troops and capture or
destroy the enemy artillery piece and heavy machine gun at the above
mentioned locations, Lt. Malcom left Leopard Base by himself and arrived
at Wollae-do, a small solitary Island which was so close to the enemy

217

mainland as the enemy anti-tank guns had been pouring their shells on almost every day. After querying and examining enemy situations and terrain all around the objective known to the Intelligence Corps of D-4, he selected and sent three D-4 members in the vicinity of the objective in secret about 102400 I July so to be conversant with enemy situations in detail. He ordered one of the three D-4 agents to return at night of 12 July, after watching enemy movements and report what enemy developments he had learned of the spot. The rest were to stay there until landing of the main strength so as to look out continuously if any change of enemy strength or location would be made. At night of 12 July, the agent returned safely to Wollae-do after checking the enemy situation, and Lt. Malcom drew up a complete plan of operation in detail prepared most carefully, based on information the D-4 agent reported. Pre-arranging that we total 120 raiders would land on after receiving a safety signal from the two agents then at the beach so to guarantee our secret mass-landing in the face of enemies, we got everything ready for action, then went aboard our four sailjunks at 132000 I July, and left Wollae-do at 2030 hrs for the objective.

2. Preliminary conduct for Action:

(a) It was a dark night and the moon was not supposed to appear, so through the darkness sailed the four sailjunks. However, tide, wind and each different speed of the junks deformed the column not later than an hour after we departed. One was too far ahead, another too slow, and it seemed that we could never expect all of us to land at a time, if leaving the junks to sail as each one did. Then Lt. Malcom, who knew what was going on, ordered all junks to close in only 10 or 20 meters to one of the junks, which was neither so speedy nor so slow, in order to see each other even in darkness. Also, he ordered "no smoking and no talking." The junks that had been put in order again proceeded toward beach in silence. As soon as we approached the beach we received a safety signal from the two waiting agents. Silently we entered the water and waded ashore, carrying out our secret landing in the face of enemies whose positions were located only 500 meters away. At 140100 I July, we formed in three teams. One was to secure the gun position, another team to surprise the heavy machine gun platoon, and the last to surprise the enemy rifle men. Three teams, under command of Lt. Malcom, advanced quietly to each prearranged position for raid. It was 0205 hours when we started sinking ourselves in grave silence and impatient excitement to wait for the very time of the raid.

3. Contact with the enemy:

(a) Lt. Malcom stationed his combat command post on a small hill which was a very dangerous spot only 100 meters away from the enemy pill-box positions, he got radio contact with aircraft and Navy vessels to start bombing and bombardment on enemy positions at 0500 hours. Two men were assigned to cut enemy communications, telephone wires, at 0420 hours as a precautionary measure so the enemy troops would not be able to appeal to the others for reinforcement when attacked. He then crawled about 50 meters onward with all of us raiders, and ordered volley-firing and charge. Directed and encouraged by Lt. Malcom, we overran the gun position, killed all of the last seven enemies with hand grenades, blew the anti-tank gun position up, and to our great joy, secured the hill completely after a "hand to hand" battle.

(b) Right after we took the gun position, Lt. Malcom rushed with all of the victors from the gun position toward the machine gun that was in a fortified four room bunker with six circle-lines of barbed wire, and resisting desperately against us attackers. He took the lead charge through "rain" of enemy bullets, commanding and encouraging all of us raiders. Then we charged the enemy machine gun position while two brave Donkey-4 men jumped in the position with anti-tank mines and blew up the enemy maxim heavy machine gun destroying this position. When we were searching or chasing the disorganized enemies in hiding or runnin(g), an enemy Bn C.P., about 4 kilometers away, sent a flood of reinforcements, who rushed down from a hill then north of us through thic(k) woods, toward us while another group was pinning us down. We fought a new and hotter battle, but the situation seemed to have been reversed in their favor. We were facing a tense situation but Lt. Malcom refused to leave his position and continued to direct the aircraft onto the approaching enemy with many direct hits that killed or wounded most of the attacking force, causing the remaining enemy to retreat. Two of our command post men were killed, and our Chief of Staff was wounded. We then left this bloody battle field with much triumph, and returned by our sailjunks to Wollae-do.

5. Results of Raid: 63 NKA killed, 9 NKA wounded. Destroyed 76mm A.T. gun, 1 maxim HMG, 19 cases ammo, 170 hand grenades, 3 barracks, 1 mess hall, 2 underground fortifications 4 room each, 1 Russian type Radio, 100 ft. telephone line, burned 25 bags rice. Captured 1 PPSH 1952 model, 65 hand grenades, 43,000 NK Won, 5 oxen, many documents. Friendly losses: 6 KIA, 7 WIA. Air-strikes were controlled from hill XC 625202 on NKA re-inforcements moving up valley from XC 639238 with following results: 162 KIA, 18 WIA, destroyed Bn C.P., 2 mess halls, 8 barracks built in hill, commo equipment, 15 cases ammo.

6. We believe and recommend, as Lt. Malcom's conduct of the raid was of the highest order, that his brave and steady and clever leadership by which

we performed the great success, his skillful and unruffled control of the crisis and his valor to fight until the last minute behind enemy lines will
deserve the highest praise from higher headquarters.

> DONKEY 4 PARTISAN FORCE (WHITE TIGERS)
> LEOPARD, 8240TH A.U., FEC/LD (K)
> PAK CHOL(L), D-4 LEADER
> SON WON JAE, CHIEF OF STAFF
> OH CHONG SUK, S-3
> PAK CHANG HOON, 1ST BN COMMANDER
> LIM CHONG SHIL, 3D BN COMMANDER

Appendix B

HEADQUARTERS
FAR EAST COMMAND
APO 500

GENERAL ORDERS
NUMBER 171

12 December 1952

Silver Star—Award

Section
I

***   ***   ***

I. AWARD OF THE SILVER STAR. By direction of the President, under the provisions of the act of Congress approved 9 July 1918 (WD Bul 43, 1918), and pursuant to authority contained in AR 600-45, and message, Department of the Army, 902663, 5 March 1952, the Silver Star for gallantry in action is awarded to the following-named officer:

***   ***   ***

First Lieutenant BEN S. MALCOM, 063033, Infantry, United States Army, a member of the Far East Command Liaison Detachment, distinguished himself by gallantry in action against an armed enemy of the United Nations on 14 July 1952. Committed to effect a clandestine amphibious maneuver to destroy enemy gun positions and personnel, Lieutenant MALCOM, commanding a group of partisans, landed on a small island off the enemy mainland in the early morning hours. Confronted by a well-entrenched, numerically superior foe, he immediately radioed for direct naval gunfire and air strikes on hostile positions. During the ensuing bombardment, Lieutenant MALCOM deployed his force in three teams for flexibility of movement and, after the preparatory fire lifted, led his men in a daring assault, overrunning hostile positions and routing the foe. While reorganizing and consolidating the newly won positions, the unit was ruthlessly attacked by a reinforced enemy. Calling for additional air and naval support, Lieutenant MALCOM assigned and coordinated fields of fire and, under his inspirational guidance, the men fought with great courage and skill, inflicting

221

numerous casualties and forcing the enemy to retreat. Lieutenant MAL-COM'S aggressive leadership and intrepid actions reflect utmost credit upon himself and are in keeping with the esteemed traditions of the military service.

***   ***   ***

BY COMMAND OF GENERAL CLARK:

OFFICIAL: DOYLE O. HICKEY
                                  Lieutenant General, General Staff
                                          Chief of Staff

C.C.B. WARREN
Colonel, AGC
Adjutant General

Endnotes

2: THROUGH THE LOOKING GLASS

1. Vanderpool, Colonel Jay D., Senior Officers Oral History Program, Project 83-12, U.S. Army Military History Institute, pg. 136.

2. Appleman, Roy E., *South to the Naktong, North to the Yalu*, Office of the Chief of Military History (Washington, D.C.: 1961), pp. 1–6.

3. Although Vanderpool knew much of the history of the 8240th, details of Col. John McGee's role in the formation of the unit are contained in his letter of March 24, 1986, to Col. Rod Paschall, director of the U.S. Army Military History Institute, Carlisle, Pennsylvania (hereafter referred to as "McGee letter"), on file at the U.S. Army Military History Institute, Carlisle, Pennsylvania.

4. McGee letter, pg. 4.

5. U.S. Army Forces, Far East, 8086th Army Unit (AFFE Military History Detachment), "UN Partisan Forces in the Korean Conflict, 1951–52 (A Study of Their Characteristics and Operations)," Project MHD-3 (hereafter "Project MHD-3"), pp. 3–4.

6. Ibid., pg. 71.

7. Ibid., pg. 72.

8. Ibid., pg. 73.

9. Ibid., pp. 65–66.

10 Ibid., pg. 35.

11. Cleaver, Frederick, et al., "UN Partisan Warfare in Korea, 1951–1954," Study, Operations Research Office (hereafter "ORO Study"), pg. 32.

12. McGee letter, pp. 10–11.

13. Ibid., pg. 12.

14. Ibid., pg. 13.

15. ORO Study, pg. 41.

16. Ibid., pg. 36.

17. McGee letter, pg. 21.

18. Ibid.

19. Vanderpool, pg. 144.

20. ORO Study, pg. 51.

21. Ibid., pg. 64.

3: BEHIND THE LINES

1. Thayer, Charles W., *Guerrilla*, Harper and Row Publishers (New York: 1963), pg. 47.

2. Authors' interviews with James Fletcher of Austell, Georgia, former V-Force member, June 1990; and "Secret Jungle War," *Military History*, interview with James Fletcher, June 1993.

3. Vanderpool, pg. 101.

4. Hilsman, Roger, *American Guerrilla: My War Behind Japanese Lines*, Brassey's (U.S.) Inc. (McLean, Va.: 1990), pg. 200.

5. Ibid., pg. 254.

6. Ibid.

7. Paschall, Rod, *A Study in Command and Control: Special Operations in Korea, 1951–53*, U.S. Army Military History Institute, Carlisle, Pennsylvania, June 1988, pg. 14.

8. Department of the Army, FM 31-21, *Organization and Conduct of Guerrilla Warfare.*

5: WAR OF THE DONKEYS

1. ORO Study, pg. 62.

2. McGee letter, pp. 12–13.

3. Darragh, Shaun M., "Hwanghae-do: The War of the Donkeys," *Army*, November 1984, pg. 72.

4. Project MHD-3, pg. 81.

5. Ibid., pg. 76.

6. Ibid., pg. 109.

7. Ibid., pg. 49.

8. Ibid., pg. 79.

9. Ibid., pg. 62.

6: PARTISAN TRAINING

1. Project MHD-3, pg. 40.

2. Ibid.

3. Ibid., pg. 39.

4. ORO Study, pg. 15.

5. *Guerrilla Operations Outline, 1952*, Headquarters, Far East Command Liaison Detachment (Korea), 11 April 1952, pg. 4.

6. Ibid., pg. 2.

7. ORO Study, pg. 72.

8. See Hilsman's *American Guerrilla* for a more detailed discussion of the various applications of guerrilla units in the China-Burma-India theater.

8: THE LOGISTICS NIGHTMARE

1. "Guerrilla Operations Outline, 1952," pg. 1.

2. Project MHD-3, pg. 77.

3. Muggelberg, Brig. Gen. Glenn; Steinbeck, Col. Paul; and Matzko, Lt. Col. Michael A. (group interview), Senior Officers Oral History Program, Project 85-S, U.S. Army Military History Institute, pp. 22–23.

4. Matzko, Lt. Col. Michael A. (individual interview), Senior Officers Oral History Program, Project 85-S, pp. 5–6.

5. Project MHD-3, pg. 139.

6. Ibid., pp. 288–99.

7. ORO Study, pg. 18.

8. Ibid.

9: THE INTELLIGENCE WAR

1. Goulden, Joseph C., *Korea: The Untold Story of the War*, Times Books (New York: 1982), pp. 204–5; and Heinl, Robert Debs Jr., *Victory at High Tide: The Inchon-Seoul Campaign*, J. B. Lippincott Co. (New York: 1968), pp. 66–69.

2. Sams, Brig. Gen. Crawford F., *Medic*, unpublished manuscript on file at the U.S. Army Military History Institute, Carlisle, Pennsylvania, pp. 712–13; and *The New York Times*, "Plague Is Believed Raging Among Foe," June 19, 1951, pg. 5.

3. Singlaub, Maj. Gen. John K., with Malcolm McConnell, *Hazardous Duty: An American Soldier in the Twentieth Century*, Summit Books (New York: 1991), pg. 164.

4. Fondecaro, Steve A., "A Strategic Analysis of U.S. Special Operations during the Korean Conflict, 1950–1953," U.S. Army Command and General Staff College, Fort Leavenworth, Kansas, 1988, pg. 42.

5. Ibid., pg. 69.

6. Goulden, pp. 468–69.

7. Ibid., pp. 469–70.

8. Singlaub, pg. 184.

10: THE MIDDLE GROUND: BAKER SECTION AND THE LINE CROSSERS

1. ORO Study, pg. 93.

2. Schuetta, Lawrence V., *Guerrilla Warfare and Airpower in Korea, 1950–1953*, Aerospace Studies Institute, Maxwell Air Force Base, Alabama, January 1964, pg. 143.

3. Much of this information is contained in a letter dated September 6, 1951, from Capt. David C. Hearn to Col. John McGee, head of the Miscellaneous Division; the letter is contained in the McGee papers on file at the U.S. Army Military History Institute.

4. Ibid.

5. Ibid.

6. ORO Study, pg. 91.

7. Ibid.

8. Ibid.

9. Ibid.

10. Schuetta, pg. 148.

11. Muggelberg, group interview, pg. 15.

12. Ibid.

13. Ibid., pg. 16.

14. ORO Study, pg. 91; and Schuetta, pp. 148–49.

15. Authors' interview with John deJarnette, April 24, 1994, Atlanta, Georgia.

11: FLANKING MANEUVERS: KIRKLAND AND WOLFPACK

1. ORO Study, pp. 32, 41.

2. Ibid., pg. 72.

3. Ibid., pg. 114.

4. Johnston, Lt. Col. Archie B., undated miscellaneous personal papers on file at the U.S. Army Military History Institute, pg. 5.

5. Vanderpool, pp. 148–49.

6. ORO Study, pg. 72.

7. Johnston papers, pg. 2.

8. ORO Study, pp. 113–14.

13: SPECIAL MISSIONS

1. Project MHD-3, operational summaries, pg. 97.

2. Blair, Clay Jr., "Robinson Crusoe of Schinz-do," *Life*, July 28, 1952, pg. 107.

3. Project MHD-3, pg. 118.

4. Schuetta, pp. 151–52.

5. Seibert, Col. Donald A., *The Regulars*, unpublished manuscript on file at the U.S. Army Military History Institute, Carlisle, Pennsylvania, pp. 429–30.

6. Ibid.

7. Report of Operations, Headquarters, Guerrilla Division, Far East Command Liaison Detachment, 8240th Army Unit, 7 November 1952, pg. 4.

8. *Guerrilla Operations Outline, 1952*, Headquarters, Far East Command Liaison Detachment (Korea), 11 April 1952, pg. 1.

14: ON LEAVING KOREA

1. ORO Study, pg. 99.

2. Ibid., pg. 77.

3. Ibid., pg. 76.

4. Ibid.

5. Ibid., pg. 30.

6. Ibid., pg. 66.

7. " 'Largest' Red Air Raid Foiled," United Press, 7 December 1952.

15: DISBANDING THE PARTISANS

1. ORO Study, pg. 12.

2. Ibid., pg. 77.

3. Ibid., pg. 62.

4. Ibid., pg. 63.

5. Ibid.

6. Ibid., pp. 63–64.

7. Ibid., pp. 113, 114.

8. Ibid., pg. 132.

9. Ibid., pg. 121.

10. Project MHD-3, interview of Lt. Col. Francis R. Purcell, G-2 Section, Eighth Army, 13 May 1953, pp. 255–56.

11. Ibid.

12. ORO Study, pg. 116.

13. Ibid., pg. 129.

14. Ibid.

15. Muggelberg, group interview, pg. 12.

16. Ibid., pp. 13–14.

17. Ibid., pg. 15.

18. "Logistics Annex of FEC/LD (K) Evacuation Plan," Headquarters, FEC/LD (K), 12 June 1953.

19. ORO Study, pp. 143–44.

20. Ibid., pg. 141.

21. HQ, ROKA, Operations Instruction 482, 23 Feb 54, reprinted in ORO Study, pg. 144.

22. ORO Study, pg. 145.

23. Muggelberg, individual interview, pp. 8–9.

24. ORO Study, pg. 145.

25. Ibid.

26. Muggelberg, individual interview, pg. 13.

27. ORO Study, pp. 3–4.

28. Ibid.

16: THE MISSING LINK

1. Bank, Aaron, *From OSS to Green Berets: The Birth of Special Forces*, Presidio Press (Novato, Calif.: 1986), pg. 130.

2. Ibid., pg. 157.

3. Ibid., pg. 137.

4. Ibid., pg. 168.

5. ORO Study, pg. 73.

6. Ibid., pp. 192–99.

7. Ibid., pg. 74.

8. Norton, Col. Charles, Senior Officers Oral History Program, U.S. Army Military History Institute, Carlisle, Pennsylvania, 1988, pp. 4–5.

9. ORO Study, pg. 16.

10. "Debriefing US Personnel," Headquarters, United Nations Partisan Infantry Korea, 8240th Army Unit, 21 March 1954.

11. Ibid.

12. ORO Study, pg. 4.

13. Ibid., pg. 24.

17: LESSONS NOT LEARNED

1. Colby, William, with James McCargar, *Lost Victory*, Contemporary Books (Chicago: 1989), pg. 283.

2. Westmoreland, Gen. William C., *A Soldier Reports*, Doubleday and Company (Garden City, N.Y.: 1976), pp. 107–8.

3. Karnow, Stanley, *Vietnam: A History*, The Viking Press (New York: 1983), pg. 412.

4. Westmoreland, pg. 138.

Bibliography

BOOKS

Anderson, Ellery. *Banner over Pusan*. Evans Brothers Limited (London: 1960).

Appleman, Roy E. *South to the Naktong, North to the Yalu*. Office of the Chief of Military History (Washington, D.C.: 1961).

Bank, Aaron. *From OSS to Green Berets: The Birth of Special Forces*. Presidio Press (Novato, Calif.: 1986).

Cable, Larry E. *Conflict of Myths: The Development of American Counterinsurgency Doctrine and the Vietnam War*. New York University Press (New York: 1986).

Chaliand, Gerard, ed. *Guerrilla Strategies: An Historical Anthology from the Long March to Afghanistan*. University of California Press, Ltd. (Berkeley, Calif.: 1982).

Clark, General Mark W. *From the Danube to the Yalu*. TAB Books (Blue Ridge Summit, Pa.: 1988).

Colby, William, with James McCargar. *Lost Victory*. Contemporary Books (Chicago: 1989).

Doyle, Edward; Lipsman, Samuel; Weiss, Stephen; and the editors of Boston Publishing, Co. *The Vietnam Experience: Passing the Torch*. Boston Publishing Co. (Boston: 1981).

———. *The Vietnam Experience: The North*. Boston Publishing Co. (Boston: 1986).

Goulden, Joseph C. *Korea: The Untold Story of the War*. Times Books (New York: 1982).

Heilbrunn, Otto. *Partisan Warfare*. Frederick A. Praeger Publishers (New York: 1962).

Heinl, Robert Debs Jr. *Victory at High Tide: The Inchon-Seoul Campaign*. J. B. Lippincott Co. (New York: 1968).

Hilsman, Roger. *American Guerrilla: My War Behind Japanese Lines*. Brassey's (U.S.) Inc. (McLean, Va.: 1990).

Karnow, Stanley. *Vietnam: A History*. The Viking Press (New York: 1983).

Leary, William M. *Perilous Missions: Civil Air Transport and CIA Covert Operations in Asia*. The University of Alabama Press (Tuscaloosa, Ala.: 1984).

Paik, General Sun Yup. *From Pusan to Panmunjom*. Brassey's (U.S.) Inc. (McLean, Va.: 1992).

Prados, John. *Presidents' Secret Wars: CIA and Pentagon Covert Operations Since World War II*. William Morrow and Company, Inc. (New York: 1986).

Ridgway, Matthew B. *The Korean War*. Doubleday and Co., Inc. (Garden City, N.Y.: 1967).

Simpson, Charles M. III. *Inside the Green Berets: The First Thirty Years, A History of the U.S. Army Special Forces*. Presidio Press (Novato, Calif.: 1983).

Singlaub, Major General John K., with Malcolm McConnell. *Hazardous Duty: An American Soldier in the Twentieth Century*. Summit Books (New York: 1991).

Smith, R. Harris. *OSS: The Secret History of America's First Central Intelligence Agency*. University of California Press, Ltd. (Berkeley, Calif.: 1972).

Thayer, Charles W. *Guerrilla*. Harper and Row Publishers (New York: 1963).

Westmoreland, General William C. *A Soldier Reports*. Doubleday and Co. (Garden City, N.Y.: 1976).

GOVERNMENT DOCUMENTS AND PUBLICATIONS

Cleaver, Frederick, et al. "UN Partisan Warfare in Korea, 1951–1954," Study, Operations Research Office, Johns Hopkins University, 1956.

Department of the Army. FM 31-21, "Organization and Conduct of Guerrilla Warfare." U.S. Government Printing Office (Washington, D.C.: October 1951). (On file at the U.S. Army Military History Institute Doctrine Collection, Carlisle, Pennsylvania.)

Fondecaro, Steve A. "A Strategic Analysis of U.S. Special Operations during the Korean Conflict, 1950–1953." U.S. Army Command and General Staff College, Fort Leavenworth, Kansas, 1988.

Paschall, Rod. "A Study in Command and Control: Special Operations in Korea, 1951–53." U.S. Army Military History Institute, Carlisle, Pennsylvania, June 1988.

Schuetta, Lawrence V. "Guerrilla Warfare and Airpower in Korea, 1950–1953." Aerospace Studies Institute, Maxwell Air Force Base, Alabama, January 1964.

U.S. Army Forces, Far East, 8086 Army Unit (AFFE Military History Detachment). "UN Partisan Forces in the Korean Conflict, 1951–52 (A Study of Their Characteristics and Operations)." Project MHD-3, Tokyo, March 1954.

ORAL HISTORIES

Matzko, Lieutenant Colonel Michael A. Individual interview. Senior Officers Oral History Program, Project 85-S, U.S. Army Military History Institute, Carlisle, Pennsylvania, 1985.

Muggelberg, Brigadier General Glenn. Individual interview. Senior Officers Oral History Program, Project 85-S, U.S. Army Military History Institute, Carlisle, Pennsylvania, 1985.

Muggelberg, Brigadier General Glenn; Steinbeck, Colonel Paul; and Matzko, Lieutenant Colonel Michael A. Group interview. Senior Officers Oral History Program, Project 85-S, U.S. Army Military History Institute, Carlisle, Pennsylvania, 1985.

Norton, Colonel Charles. Senior Officers Oral History Program, U.S. Army Military History Institute, Carlisle, Pennsylvania, 1988.

Steinbeck, Colonel Paul. Individual interview. Senior Officers Oral History
    Program, Project 85-S, U.S. Army Military History Institute, Carlisle,
    Pennsylvania, 1985.
Vanderpool, Col. Jay D. Individual Interview. Senior Officers Oral History
    Program, Project 83-2, U.S. Army Military History Institute, Carlisle,
    Pennsylvania, 1983.
Yarborough, Lieutenant General William P. Senior Officers Debriefing
    Program, U.S. Army Military History Institute, Carlisle, Pennsylvania, 1975.

MAGAZINE ARTICLES

Blair, Clay Jr. "Robinson Crusoe of Schinz-do." *Life*, July 28, 1952.
Flanagan, Lieutenant General E. M. Jr. "Col. Aaron Bank: SF's 'Father'—Truly
    Something Special." *Army*, June 1993.
Paschall, Rod. "Korean Wolfpack." In *The Infantry*, in the series *The Elite*.
    National Historical Society (Harrisburg, Pa.: 1989).

MISCELLANEOUS DOCUMENTS AND PERSONAL PAPERS

Johnston, Lieutenant Colonel Archie B. Undated miscellaneous personal papers
    on file at the U.S. Army Military History Institute, Carlisle, Pennsylvania.
McGee, John Hugh. Letter of March 24, 1986, to Colonel Rod Paschall,
    director of the U.S. Army Military History Institute, Carlisle, Pennsylvania.
Sams, Brigadier General Crawford F. *Medic*. Unpublished manuscript on file at
    the U.S. Army Military History Institute, Carlisle, Pennsylvania.
Seibert, Colonel Donald A. *The Regulars*. Unpublished manuscript on file at the
    U.S. Military History Institute, Carlisle, Pennsylvania.

Index

advisers; in Vietnam, 40, 201, 203, 209;
morale of in Korea, 187, 199;
numbers of, 142, 144, 186; to North
Korean partisans, xi, xii, 2, 3, 46, 54,
55, 59, 114, 142, 144, 171, 186, 187,
198, 199
air-sea rescue, 44, 166
airborne operations, 133–37, 176–77;
Boxer I–IV, 136; Green Dragon,
136–37; Hurricane, 136; Jesse James
I–III, 135, 136; Mustang III–VIII,
135, 136; Rabbit I–II, 136
amphibious operations, 19, 28, 46, 47,
49, 122, 131, 133, 141, 142, 170, 199
Army Forces Far East (AFFE), 133,
134, 135, 141, 178, 183, 184, 185, 190
Army of the Republic of Vietnam
(ARVN), 201–8; 23rd Division,
201–7

Baker Section, 20, 21, 28, 121, 133–38,
139, 140, 177
Ban Me Thuot, 201, 203, 204
Bank, Aaron, 196–98, 200
Bao Dai, 201
Bass, Bob, 214
Brink Hotel, 208–9
British Navy, attack on fishing junks,
50–51; in support of partisan
operations, 37, 49, 76, 80, 84, 91–92,
96, 101, 103, 104, 166–68
Burke, William, 19, 22, 59
Burma, xii, 15, 18, 33, 34, 35, 37, 39,
72, 109, 114, 129, 184, 196
Burma Rifles, 72

Cambodia, 201
Camp Drake, 9, 11, 198
Camp Hovey, 214
Cardigan Bay, 166
Castro, Fidel, 38
Central Intelligence Agency (CIA), xi,
xii, 14, 18, 24, 39, 40, 44, 121, 126,
129–32, 142, 197; Office of Policy
Coordination, 197
Central Intelligence Group, 14
Chang Jae Hwa, 59, 60
Chang Sok Lin, 59
Changsan-got, 1–8, 37, 42, 47, 59, 63–65,
120, 124, 126, 147, 153, 161, 169–70,
181, 182; NKPA troops on, 6, 105,
147, 159, 159; partisan safe area, 3–8,
37, 63–64, 170, 181; terrain of, 1, 47,
63, 147; timber harvest on, 4, 64
Changyon, 147, 153, 154, 155, 160
Chetniks, 38
Chiang Kai-shek, 205
China, xi, xii, 16, 37, 59, 72, 129, 130
China-Burma-India theater, 72
Chindits, 72
Chinese Communist Forces (CCF), 16,
17, 19, 25, 26, 35, 109, 123, 131, 132,
134, 138, 139, 140, 141, 143, 145, 146,
171, 173, 174, 180, 185, 186; 40th Army,
145, 174; 42nd Army, 145, 174; 63rd
Army, 145, 174; 64th Army, 145, 174
Chinnampo, 134, 147
Cho Byung Chan, 126–27, 215–16
Cho-do, 59, 60, 62, 120, 124, 126, 161,
162, 163, 164, 165, 166, 167, 168
Choryong, 59

Clark, Eugene F., 122
Combat Infantryman's Badge (CIB),
    211–13
Combined Command Reconnaissance
    Activities Far East (CCRAFE), 190,
    198
Combined Command Reconnaissance
    Activities, Korea (CCRAK), xii, 27,
    112, 113, 130, 178, 185, 186, 187,
    188, 189, 190
Cuba, 36
Culp, James, 50

Da Nang, 209
Darlac Province, 201
Dawkins, Pete, 214
de Jarnette, John, 138–40
Demilitarized Zone (DMZ), 188, 191,
    214, 216
Detachment 101, 37, 39
Donkey leaders, 8, 24, 57–60, 107,
    113–14, 127; assassination of D-4, 2,
    47, 48, 61; D-1, 57, 58, 60, 171;
    D-4, 2, 8, 46, 47, 48, 52–53, 56–57,
    59–61, 64, 68, 118, 172, 173, 181;
    D-10, 162–63; D-11, 57, 59, 60;
    D-13, 59; D-15, 59; D-16, 115–16
Donkey units, 2, 54, 55–61, 74,
    125–26, 142, 145, 164, 167, 172–73;
    Donkey-1, 59, 171; Donkey-3, 60;
    Donkey-4, 2, 4, 6, 8, 47–48, 57,
    59–62, 68, 69, 70, 72, 75, 79, 81–82,
    83, 100, 107, 110–11, 116, 118, 128,
    146, 147, 149, 152, 155, 157, 161,
    169, 170, 174, 176, 177, 178, 180,
    181, 182, 185, 194, 203, 213;
    Donkey-10, 57, 162; Donkey-11, 57,
    58; Donkey-15, 58; organization of,
    27, 28, 57–59; origin of name, 56–57
Dye, Tom, 75, 80, 83, 91, 111, 115–16,
    127, 128, 146, 147, 152, 160, 161,
    167–68, 194, 200

Eighth Army Ranger Company, 15
Eighth U.S. Army, Korea (EUSAK),
    3, 16, 17, 18, 38, 55, 56, 107, 111,

130, 168, 184, 185, 187, 188, 189,
    190, 191; command and control of
    partisans, 20, 21–23, 24–25, 26, 133,
    134, 141, 142; role in formation of
    partisan units, 17–21, 184
8086 Army Unit, 22, 26
8177 Army Unit, 190
8078 Army Unit, 190
8240 Army Unit, xi, xii, 12–14, 24, 26,
    27, 28, 30, 39, 40, 44, 46, 52, 54, 61,
    66, 83, 107, 117, 121, 126, 127, 128,
    132, 138, 140, 141, 144, 176, 177,
    178, 186, 187, 188, 189, 195, 197,
    199, 203, 205, 209, 211, 212;
    Guerrilla Division, xi, 13, 14, 30, 66,
    83, 107, 123, 141, 144, 172, 176, 177,
    178, 188, 189, 195, 203, 205, 209,
    211, 212
8242 Army Unit, 27, 178
8213th Ranger Company, 15
8250 ROK Army Unit, 189, 190
Eisenhower, Dwight D., 179
Emerson, Hank, 216
Ethiopian Brigade, 139–40

Far East Command (FEC), xii, 14–15,
    18, 19, 20, 22, 23, 24, 26, 27, 40, 55,
    121, 122, 123, 130, 133, 134, 135,
    141, 142, 168, 175, 177, 178, 184,
    188, 189, 198; Attrition Section, 19,
    22; Far East Command Liaison
    Detachment, Korea [FEC/LD(K)],
    24, 26, 27, 55, 142, 178, 189; Far
    East Command Liaison Group
    (FEC/LG) 22, 24, 26, 27;
    Miscellaneous Division, 15, 17, 19,
    20, 21
Flying Fish Channel, 122
Fort Benning, 32, 33, 34, 35, 154, 203
Fort Bragg, 34, 194, 195, 196, 197,
    198
Fort Gordon, 196
Fort Knox, 34, 35, 68, 71, 195

Givens, William L., 143
Guadalcanal, 13

guerrillas; as different from partisans, 17, 38–39, 55; in Burma, 18, 39, 72, 109, 184; in the Philippines, 13, 15, 17, 18, 20, 39, 109, 183–84; in Vietnam, 201–10; U.S. Army opposition to, 33; use by CIA in Korea, 130–32

Guerrilla Division, xi, 13, 14, 30, 66, 83, 107, 123, 141, 144, 172, 176, 177, 178, 188, 189, 195, 203, 205, 209, 211, 212

guerrilla tactics, 13, 33, 35, 66–68, 72, 185, 201, 202, 203–5, 207–10

Gurkhas, 72

Haeju, 16, 17, 143

Hall, Jim, 214

Han River, 25, 142, 188, 191, 213

Hearn, John, 135

Hilsman, Roger, 39

Hungnam, 135

Hwanghae Peninsula, 19, 20, 23, 26

Hwanghae Province, xii, 1, 16, 17, 145, 174, 175, 185, 187

Hwangju, 133

Hyong-ni, 134

Inchon, 15, 22, 25, 122, 142

Japan, 9, 59, 130, 184, 189, 198

Johnston, Archie B., 144

Joint Activities Commission, Korea (JACK), 130

Kachin tribesmen, 37, 114

Kaesong, 24, 26, 136

Kanghwa-do, 188, 189, 191

Karyoju-ri, 134

Kennedy, John F., 39, 196, 203

Kim Chang Song, 59

Kim Il-Sung, 173, 185

Kim Ung Soo, 59

kimchi, 44, 111, 151, 180

Kimpo International Airport, 213

Kirkland, 20, 21, 27, 141–43, 175–76, 177

Koje-do, 75

Korea, South, 36–37, 56, 59, 149, 173, 175–76, 181, 183, 191, 213, 214

Kuwol-san, 16

Kyodong-do, 188, 189

Lamm, George, 142

Lawrence, T. E., 37

Lee Jung Hok, 59

Leopard Base, xi, 2, 3, 4, 7, 8, 28, 29, 30, 41, 42, 43, 54, 62, 64, 68, 77, 79, 80, 108, 112, 115, 120, 121, 123, 137, 163, 169, 176, 194; American personnel assigned to, 44, 68, 75, 110; area of responsibility, 26, 121, 133; facilities on, 43–45, 52, 198; intelligence operations of, 125–29; name change, 20, 43; NKPA attack on, 179–80; partisans operating from, 22, 26, 46, 47, 57, 59, 61, 146, 164, 175, 177; shipments of rice to, 113; vulnerability of, 49–51

MacArthur, Douglas, 14, 16, 18, 129, 130

Manchuria, 16, 19, 30, 43, 47, 59

Mao Tse-tung, 37, 38, 66, 205

Mapp, Jim, 164–166, 167–170, 200

Maquis, 38

Marion, Francis, 36

Marshall, S.L.A., 154

McGee, John, 15, 17–22, 24, 56, 178, 185, 188, 196, 199, 200

McKean, Leo, 8, 44, 46–52, 61–62, 68, 75, 80, 111, 116, 127, 128, 200

Meeks, Roy, 171

Merrill, Frank, 72

Merrill's Marauders, 15, 72

MiG alley, 124, 164, 165

Military Assistance Command Vietnam (MACV), 206, 207, 208

Miscellaneous Division, 15, 17, 19, 20, 21

Miscellaneous Group, 22, 25

Mosby, John, 36

Mu-do, 143

Muggelberg, Glenn, 191

Nan-do, 20, 142
Ngo Dinh Diem, 203
North Georgia College, 31, 32, 34, 138
North Korean People's Army
    (NKPA) 1, 2, 3, 4, 15, 18, 35, 49, 51,
    55, 56, 66, 83, 84, 86, 88–89, 91–107,
    142, 143, 145, 146, 149–52, 153,
    156–60, 161, 162, 164, 165, 166, 168,
    169–71, 185, 186; attacks on Wollae-
    do, 7–8, 63–65, 81–82; captured by
    partisans, 57, 73–75, 127; casualties
    of, 26, 67, 73, 104, 106, 118, 171;
    81st Army Unit, 145; I Corps, 145;
    IV Corps, 145, 174; numbers of, 14,
    145, 174–75, 180, 186; on
    Changsan-got, 1, 4–6, 147; partisan
    engagements against, 18, 19, 22, 24,
    46, 47, 55, 56, 59–60, 61, 63–64, 69,
    73, 83–108, 151, 156–57, 169–70,
    171–72; partisans mistaken for,
    74–75, 128; security forces, 37, 59,
    134, 137–38, 142, 177; treatment of
    partisan POWs, 113–14; 23rd
    Brigade, 1, 6, 153
North Vietnamese Army (NVA), 209

Office of Strategic Services (OSS) xi,
    xii, 18, 33, 35, 37, 39, 121, 129, 136,
    196, 199, 203, 205; Detachment 101,
    37, 39; Jedburghs, xi, 196
Ongjin Peninsula, 2, 26, 47, 59, 60,
    141, 142, 143
Operation Beehive, 188
Operation Camel, 188
Operation Plan PAPPY, 188
Operation Quicksilver, 190–91
Operation Spitfire, 134–35, 136
Operation Trudy Jackson, 122
Operation Virginia, 134, 136
Operational Plan One, 19, 185

Paengnyong-do, 21, 42, 43, 119–20,
    125, 127–29, 166, 171, 181, 187, 189,
    215; Americans assigned to, 43–44,
    128, 129, 164; as partisan
    headquarters, 19–21, 43, 59, 114,

127–28; landing strip on, 19, 42, 43,
    44, 46, 60, 166; location of, xi, 2, 19,
    42, 43, 63, 142; physical features of,
    19, 43–44; vulnerability of, 49–51,
    142
Pak Choll, 1–8, 54, 61–65, 68–69,
    87–88, 96, 153; as leader of Donkey-
    4, 2, 5, 7–8, 47–48, 54, 55–56, 61,
    64–65, 68–69, 72–75, 76, 79, 83, 85,
    100–102, 105–6, 107, 145, 146, 147,
    152, 153, 158, 169–71, 172–73,
    175–77; relationship with author, 2,
    3–4, 8, 54, 62–63, 64–65, 72, 80, 83,
    106–8, 116, 146, 147, 148, 152–53,
    161, 178, 180–82, 190
Palmi-do, 122
Panmunjom, 136, 146
Partisan Airborne Infantry Regiment
    (PAIR), 177
Partisan Infantry Regiment (PIR), xi,
    144, 177, 188; 1st PIR, xi, 177; 2nd
    PIR, 177, 188; 3rd PIR, 177; 5th
    PIR, 177
partisans, xi, 2, 16–22, 26, 36, 38, 39,
    40–41, 46–47, 53, 55, 57, 60, 64–65,
    66–67, 71, 79, 83, 87, 100, 105, 107,
    113–14, 117, 125, 126, 131–32, 145,
    146, 151–52, 153, 159, 164, 167, 171,
    175, 183–85, 186–88, 189–93, 194,
    215, 216; advisers to, xi, xii, 3, 24,
    46, 54, 59, 83, 114, 142, 144, 171,
    186, 193, 199; command and control
    of, 20, 22, 23, 24, 26–28, 55, 135,
    177–78, 187, 188–89, 193; desertion
    rate of, 137, 142, 176, 191; in
    Albania, 38; in Burma, xii, 15, 18,
    33, 34, 35, 37, 38, 39, 72, 109, 114,
    129, 184, 196; in Denmark, 38; in
    France, xi, xii, 18, 33, 38, 184, 196;
    in Greece, 38; in Norway, 38; in
    Russia, 37–39, 184; in Yugoslavia,
    18, 33, 38, 184; integration into
    ROK Army, 177–78, 181, 183–84,
    189–91; intelligence collection by,
    xi, xii, 13, 19, 27–28, 46, 60, 63, 69,
    72, 121–22, 123, 125–28, 131, 132,

133, 140, 141, 142, 145, 146, 164, 174; legal status of, 17, 54–55, 183–84, 189; logistics for, 18, 46, 51–52, 55, 109–20, 179; morale of, 25, 56, 107, 145–46, 173, 175, 180–82, 184, 186–87, 188–91, 199; North Korean, xi, 8, 20, 36, 38, 39, 42, 53, 178; numbers of, 17, 21, 22, 28, 46, 62, 116–17, 133, 144, 175, 176, 185, 186, 187, 191; safe area on Changsan-got, 3–6, 37, 63–64, 170, 181; tactics of, 2, 6, 25–26, 36–39, 66–69, 72, 74, 83, 87, 100, 105, 113–14, 120, 146, 151–52, 153, 159–60, 164, 170–71, 177, 183, 185, 203, 205, 208; weapons of, 6, 15, 17, 21, 25, 26, 49, 60, 70–71, 84, 105, 110–11, 172, 190–91

Patterson, William, 13

Philippines, 13, 15, 17–18, 33, 35, 37, 39, 109, 172, 184, 196

Plan ABLE, 19

Plan Phase I, 185

Plan Phase IIA, 185, 188

Plan Phase IIB, 185

Pleiku, 201, 209

prisoners of war, 55, 73–75, 84, 167

Psychological Warfare Center, 197

PT boats, 117–20

Pusan, 10, 15, 20, 21, 130, 134, 214; K-1 air base, 20

Pyongyang, 26, 124, 133, 135, 145, 161, 167

Red Beach, 209

refugees, 15, 16–17, 21, 28, 44, 60, 101–2, 118, 121, 133, 138, 175, 184, 188, 189

Republic of Korea, 38, 55, 177, 178, 181, 183–85, 187, 189–91

Republic of Korea Army, 23, 37, 44, 49, 55, 105–6, 122, 126–27, 139, 142, 175, 177, 178, 181, 184, 188, 189, 190, 191, 214, 216; integration of partisans, 177–78, 181, 183–84, 189–91

Republic of Korea Marines, 23, 44

Republic of Korea Navy, 16, 20, 22, 23, 37, 59, 142, 184

Rhade tribesmen, 204

Rhee, Syngman, 16, 173, 178

Royal West African Frontier Force, 72

Saigon, 207–9

Sams, Dr. Crawford, 123

Sariwon, 17, 20, 26, 145

Schinz, Albert W., 165–66, 168

2nd Infantry Division, 113, 203, 213, 215; 2nd Brigade, 203, 213

Seibert, Don, 171, 200

Seoul, 3, 10, 12–13, 16, 24, 27, 28, 30, 43, 44, 46, 54, 74, 75, 83, 105, 106, 110, 112, 115, 123, 124, 125, 126, 127, 128, 138, 140, 152, 160, 163, 172, 176, 179, 181, 195, 212, 213, 214, 215; K-16 air base, 12, 30, 124, 125

Silver Star, xii, 107–8, 212

Singlaub, John, 130

So-Suap, 143

Sokkyo-ri, 147, 148, 149, 150

Sol-som, 20, 142

Song Won Jae, 3, 160

Special Forces, xii, xiii, 18, 40, 155, 177, 186, 194–200, 204, 206, 209, 211, 213; A-teams, 186, 195, 198, 204; 10th Special Forces Group, 197

special operations, 18, 40, 130, 167, 178, 190, 194, 195, 196, 197, 205, 207, 209, 210, 211, 213, 216

Sternberg, Ben, 207

Stilwell, Joseph, 72

Stilwell, Richard G., 130

Sunwi-do, 143, 144

survival training, 34

Tactical Liaison Officer (TLO), 28, 138, 139, 140; line crossers, 13, 121, 133, 138–40

Taedong River, 47

Taegu, 15, 16, 20

Tan Son Nhut, 209

Task Force William Able, 20
10th Special Forces Group, 197
3rd Armored Division, 34, 68
3rd Infantry Division, 10, 11
38th Parallel, 16, 28, 34, 43, 59, 130,
    133, 142, 188
Tito, Josip Broz, 33, 38
Tofte, Hans, 130–31
Tokyo, 9, 10, 11, 14, 15, 22, 26, 27,
    123, 160, 212, 213
Tongduchon, 214
Truman, Harry S, 14
25th Infantry Division, 15, 135

U.S. Air Force, 18, 23, 24, 40, 43, 44,
    105, 119, 124, 125, 127, 128, 129,
    130, 143, 147, 160, 162, 163, 165–66,
    167, 174, 179, 215; Fifth Air Force,
    127, 147, 166, 179; radar station on
    Paengnyong-do, 19, 43, 44, 119, 179
U.S. Army, xii, xiii, 9, 10, 12, 14, 18, 22,
    23, 27, 29, 31, 32, 33, 34, 35, 36, 40,
    41, 43, 44, 53, 54, 71, 75, 107, 109,
    112, 117, 122, 123, 129, 130, 139, 147,
    155, 177, 178, 179, 181, 184, 186, 187,
    188, 189, 191, 192, 193, 194, 195, 196,
    197, 198, 199, 200, 202, 204, 204, 209,
    211, 212, 213, 215, 216; Eighth U.S.
    Army, Korea (EUSAK), 3, 16, 17,
    18, 38, 55, 56, 107, 111, 130, 168, 184,
    185, 187, 188, 189, 190, 191; Eighth
    Army Ranger Company, 15; 8086
    Army Unit, 22, 26; 8177 Army Unit,
    190; 8078 Army Unit, 190; 8240
    Army Unit, xi, xii, 12–14, 24, 26, 27,
    28, 30, 39, 40, 44, 46, 52, 54, 61, 66,
    83, 107, 117, 121, 126, 127, 128, 132,
    138, 140, 141, 144, 176, 177, 178, 186,
    187, 188, 189, 195, 197, 199, 203, 205,
    209, 211, 212; 8242 Army Unit 27,
    178; 8213th Ranger Company, 15;
    82nd Airborne Division, 213; 187th
    Regimental Combat Team, 197; 2nd
    Infantry Division, 113, 203, 213, 215;
    Special Forces, xii, xiii, 18, 40, 155,
    177, 186, 194–200, 204, 206, 209, 211,

213; A-teams, 186, 195, 198, 204;
    10th Special Forces Group, 197; 3rd
    Armored Division, 34, 68; 3rd
    Infantry Division, 10, 11; 25th
    Infantry Division, 15, 135
U.S. Marine Corps, 44, 48, 49, 50, 76,
    80, 84, 87, 92, 94, 104, 128, 139, 166,
    179, 209; 9th Marine Expeditionary
    Brigade, 209
U.S. Navy, 18, 23, 24, 40, 44, 46, 50, 105,
    122, 125, 128, 130, 160, 166, 167, 174
unconventional warfare, xi, xii, xiii, 2,
    14, 15, 17, 18, 21, 22, 28, 32–36,
    39–41, 56, 65, 117, 140, 144, 177,
    179, 186, 187, 189, 190, 192, 193,
    194–200, 202, 203, 204, 205, 209,
    210, 211, 213, 216
United Nations, 6, 11, 15, 16, 17, 69,
    123, 130, 138, 142, 144, 145, 146,
    177, 180, 189–90
United Nations forces, 6, 11, 15, 16,
    17, 19, 20, 56, 59, 64, 69, 123, 138,
    139, 142, 144, 149, 174, 184
United Nations Partisan Forces Korea
    (UNPFK), 177, 184
United Nations Partisan Infantry Korea
    (UNPIK), 177, 189–90, 191, 212

V-Force, 37, 196
Vanderpool, Jay, 13–14, 24, 25, 28, 29,
    30, 39, 54, 66, 67, 74, 109, 123, 124,
    127, 172, 177, 196, 199, 200
Viet Cong (VC), 172, 202–9
Vietnam, 18, 36, 37, 40, 114, 154, 172,
    192, 200, 201–10, 213; Army of the
    Republic of Vietnam (ARVN),
    201–8

Walker, Alexander, 166
Watson, Lex, 176
William Able Base, 20, 43
Willoughby, Charles, 14
Wingate, Orde, 72
Wolfpack, 26, 28, 41, 42, 47, 118,
    141–44, 145, 174, 175, 177, 189, 215;
    Wolfpack-3, 144; Wolfpack-4, 143,

144; Wolfpack-5, 144; Wolfpack-6, 143, 144; Wolfpack-7, 144; Wolfpack-8, 143, 144

Wollae-do, 59, 61, 63, 64, 68, 70, 73, 75, 77, 78, 79, 80, 81–82, 84, 89, 96, 104, 105, 118, 120, 147, 148, 149, 150; as Donkey-4 headquarters, xi, 3, 61, 62; location of, 63; physical characteristics of, 4, 63–64, 84

Wonsan, 123, 134, 142, 185

Yalu River, 2, 11, 16, 22, 26, 47, 59, 120, 121, 131, 135, 164

Yellow Sea, 1, 5, 19, 21, 41, 42, 47, 60, 63, 87, 92, 124, 125, 128, 142, 161, 164, 165, 167, 179, 182, 215; tidal surges in, 25, 47, 143, 169–70

Yonan, 133

Yong-do, 130

Yonghung-do, 122

Yuk-to, 61

About the Authors

BEN S. MALCOM, a native of Monroe, Georgia, was commissioned a second lieutenant in the regular army in June 1950 after being named a Distinguished Military Graduate at North Georgia College. Sent to Korea in 1952, Malcom was selected to work with a top secret unit conducting combat operations with North Korean partisans more than 125 miles behind enemy lines.

Following completion of his combat tour in Korea in late 1952, Malcom served in a variety of command and staff positions before being sent to Vietnam in 1964 for his second overseas combat tour. While in Vietnam, Malcom served first as G-1 adviser to the 23rd Division of the Army of the Republic of Vietnam and later was a staff officer with J-1 for Military Assistance Command, Vietnam, in Saigon.

Malcom subsequently served as a commander of the 4th Battalion, 20th Infantry, with the 6th Infantry Division in Hawaii and the 1st Battalion, 325th Airborne Infantry, of the 82nd Airborne Division at Fort Bragg, North Carolina. He also served as G-3 of the 82nd Airborne Division.

After attending the Air War College, where he also earned a master's degree in political science from Auburn University, Malcom was selected to attend helicopter flight school as a full colonel and later that year earned his wings.

Malcom returned to Korea in late 1972 to command the 2nd Brigade of the 2nd Infantry Division near the DMZ before being assigned in 1973 to the Pentagon, where he served until 1976 as executive to the Deputy Chief of Staff for Personnel.

He retired in 1979 after commanding Fort McPherson and Fort Gillem in Georgia and Fort Buchanan, Puerto Rico.

Among Malcom's military decorations and awards are the Silver Star, the Legion of Merit with three oak-leaf clusters, the Bronze Star, the Combat Infantryman's Badge, the Airborne Badge, and the Aviation Badge.

Following his retirement from the army, Malcom went to work for Rollins, Inc., of Atlanta, where he was executive to the chairman of the board. In 1983 he became president and major stockholder of Timber Specialties, Inc., in Fayetteville, Georgia, and is still working in that capacity.

In addition to his business interests, Malcom has served on the Chief of Staff of the Army's Retiree Council in Washington and since 1980 has been chairman of the Military Retiree Council, representing more than 27,000 retirees from all services for the north Georgia area.

He and his wife, Joyce, live in Fayetteville, Georgia. They have one son, Ben Thomas Malcom.

RON MARTZ writes on military affairs and national security issues for the Atlanta *Journal-Constitution*. A veteran of the U.S. Marine Corps (1965–1968), he is a 1979 graduate in mass communications from the University of South Florida. He is the coauthor with Jack Terrell of *Disposable Patriot: Revelations of a Soldier in America's Secret Wars*, and with Lawrence R. Bailey, Jr., of *Solitary Survivor: The First American POW in Southeast Asia*.

A native of Elizabethtown, Pennsylvania, he now lives in Roswell, Georgia, with his wife, Cindy, and their three children.